# The Immaculate Mistake

# The Immaculate **Mistake**

## How Evangelicals Gave Birth to Donald Trump

Rodney Wallace Kennedy

FOREWORD BY
Randall Balmer

PREFACE BY
William V. Trollinger

CASCADE *Books* · Eugene, Oregon

THE IMMACULATE MISTAKE
How Evangelicals Gave Birth to Donald Trump

Copyright © 2021 Rodney Wallace Kennedy. All rights reserved. Except for brief quotations in critical publications or reviews, no part of this book may be reproduced in any manner without prior written permission from the publisher. Write: Permissions, Wipf and Stock Publishers, 199 W. 8th Ave., Suite 3, Eugene, OR 97401.

Cascade Books
An Imprint of Wipf and Stock Publishers
199 W. 8th Ave., Suite 3
Eugene, OR 97401

www.wipfandstock.com

PAPERBACK ISBN: 978-1-7252-8631-3
HARDCOVER ISBN: 978-1-7252-8632-0
EBOOK ISBN: 978-1-7252-8633-7

*Cataloguing-in-Publication data:*

Names: Kennedy, Rodney Wallace, author. | Balmer, Randall, foreword. | Trollinger, William V., preface.

Title: The immaculate mistake : how evangelicals gave birth to Donald Trump / by Rodney Wallace Kennedy ; foreword by Randall Balmer ; preface by William V. Trollinger.

Description: Eugene, OR: Cascade Books, 2021 | Includes bibliographical references.

Identifiers: ISBN 978-1-7252-8631-3 (paperback) | ISBN 978-1-7252-8632-0 (hardcover) | ISBN 978-1-7252-8633-7 (ebook)

Subjects: LCSH: Trump, Donald, 1946-—Language. | Rhetoric—Political aspects—United States. | Christianity and politics. | Evangelicalism.

Classification: BR516 .K45 2021 (print) | BR516 (ebook)

09/16/21

To the courageous and
Faithful progressive priests, pastors, and professors
(especially rhetoricians, historians, and scientists)
Who every moment seek the truth
And contend with lies—
Some of them, religious

*"You must understand this, that in the last days distressing times will come. For people will be lovers of themselves, lovers of money, boasters, arrogant, abusive, disobedient to their parents, ungrateful, unholy, inhuman, implacable, slanderers, profligates, brutes, haters of good, treacherous, reckless, swollen with conceit, lovers of pleasure rather than lovers of God, holding to the outward form of godliness but denying its power."*

—*2 Timothy 3:1–5*

# Contents

*Foreword by Randall Balmer* | ix
*Preface by William V. Trollinger* | xi
*Acknowledgments* | xv

The Immaculate Mistake: How Evangelicals Gave Birth to Donald Trump | 3

Chapter 1—Billy Sunday: Vaudeville Revivalist | 20

Chapter 2—J. Frank Norris: A Circus of Enemies and a Rhetoric of Perversion | 45

Chapter 3—Jerry Falwell, Sr.: Racism, Revenge, and Television | 60

Chapter 4—Robert Jeffress: High Priest of American Nationalism (Formerly Evangelicalism) | 92

Chapter 5—An Alternative Set of Biblical Tropes or Trump in a Lesser Light | 129

Chapter 6—An Alternative Pair of Kingly Tropes for Trump | 141

Chapter 7—Aristotle to the Rescue: Or, Alternative Rhetorical Tropes for Evangelicals and Trump | 161

*Bibliography* | 195

# Foreword

## By Randall Balmer

The number was staggering to anyone who took seriously the Religious Right's claim to be the guardians of probity and "family values." In the 2016 presidential election, 81 percent of white evangelicals supported Donald Trump, a thrice-married former casino operator, and self-confessed sexual predator. How could this possibly be true? Leaders of this movement, after all, had excoriated Bill Clinton for his tawdry encounters with Monica Lewinsky. How could they turn a blind eye to Trump's multiple extramarital affairs and hush payments to a porn star and a Playboy model?

Since that election, there have been no shortage of pundits who have tried to explain this phenomenon. Some have suggested that the Religious Right's relationship with Trump was purely transactional, while others have discerned a hankering for a kind of hyper-masculinized swagger.

In the interest of full disclosure, I have offered my own conjectures. First, evangelical support for Trump derived from the Religious Right's long-standing, frequently stoked, and somewhat irrational antipathy toward Hillary Clinton. Many expressed this openly. However much they felt uncomfortable with Trump, their hatred for Clinton ran even deeper.

Second, evangelicals for the better part of a century have portrayed themselves as victims in a society they see as rapidly secularizing. Whether that is objectively true or not is highly debatable, but it is certainly *subjectively* true for many evangelicals, and leaders of the Religious Right have consistently employed the vocabulary of victimization for everything from prayer in school to same-sex marriage. The connection with Trump is that there are few individuals in the twenty-first century who speak the language of victimization more fluently than Donald Trump. It's always about him, of course—he's the victim—but evangelicals have long identified with that rhetoric.

Finally, the 2016 election allowed the Religious Right finally to drop the pretense that theirs was a movement devoted to "family values"; it is simply not possible to make that argument while supporting Trump. More to the point, the white evangelical embrace of Trump represented the return of the Religious Right to the charter principle of its formation: racism. Despite the persistence of the abortion myth, the fiction that the Religious Right coalesced in the 1970s to overturn *Roe v. Wade*, the Religious Right was born out of a defense of racial segregation at places like Bob Jones University and other evangelical "segregation academies." The 2016 election saw the movement come full circle in the embrace of an openly racist candidate.

It is especially on this last point that Rodney Kennedy's *The Immaculate Mistake* makes a valuable contribution to the discussion. Rooted in wide reading of literary and historical materials coupled with a deep understanding of evangelicalism, Kennedy offers here a trail of bread crumbs leading us back to such characters as Billy Sunday and J. Frank Norris for an understanding of evangelicals' improbable embrace of Donald Trump.

Although I very much doubt that Kennedy will have the last word in this long-running and continuing conversation, his voice nevertheless deserves to be heard.

# Preface

BY WILLIAM V. TROLLINGER

Thanks to a major grant from the Lilly Foundation, in the 1990s I co-directed the Re-Forming the Center project, which included three conferences (1994–96) at Messiah College (Pennsylvania), five articles, and a book.[1] As I noted in a 2002 article, at the heart of this project was the argument that

> the two-party model of Protestantism in the United States—conservative vs. liberal, fundamentalist vs. modernist, and so on—does not take into account the remarkable complexity and diversity of the Protestant religious experience in America, and in some sense presents a distorted picture of that reality.[2]

While American religion (and, relatedly, politics) have become increasingly polarized in the last two decades, I would still argue that it is much too simplistic to explain American Protestantism on the basis of a two-party model—it seems to me that there are just too many groups and individuals who cannot be shoehorned into this schema. And whether or not I am right in this general argument, I can say that the Rev. Dr. Rodney Kennedy is the quintessential example of a Protestant preacher who cannot be shoehorned into either the conservative or the liberal "party." Instead, Kennedy is the (to quote from his introduction) fundamentalist "misfit who believes Jesus, who he was and is, what he taught and preached."

I first encountered Kennedy in early 2007. It was a very difficult moment in my life, and I was casting about for a church. That spring semester I was teaching a PhD seminar at the University of Dayton on American evangelicalism, and a few of my doctoral students in the class told me and my soon-to-be fiancé Sue about their pastor, Rod Kennedy of First Baptist Church. They were so insistent about his great gifts and his exemplary commitments that, while

---

1. Jacobsen and Trollinger, *Re-Forming the Center*.
2. Trollinger, "Is There a Center?," 380.

we were skeptical (I had grown up Baptist and did not want to return), we concluded that we had to check out the church and its pastor.

Now, First Baptist is a mainline Baptist church. I had been attending mainline churches for twenty-five years (including a Mennonite church that was in many ways much more mainline than Anabaptist). And while it was a relief to be out of the evangelicalism of my youth, especially as white evangelicalism became increasingly wedded to the Christian Right and the Republican Party, I was never quite at home with what sometimes felt like the "Kiwanis at prayer" vibe in mainline Protestantism. So it was a bit of a shock to be in the First Baptist pew and hear, week after week, someone who knew the Bible so well, who was so devoted to it, and who was so determined to preach it. It did not take long for us to be enraptured by his preaching. We joined FBC-Dayton in 2007 and were married there the next year, and we had the great privilege of hearing eight years of Kennedy sermons until he returned to Louisiana in 2015.

To understand Rod Kennedy, one must start with the fact that he grew up in a fundamentalist Southern Baptist family—one in which in he lived under the regimen of memorizing one hundred Bible verses a week—and was ordained as a Southern Baptist minister at a very young age. And while he is now "as far removed from being a fundamentalist as the 'east is to the west,'" (to quote again from this book's introduction)—to the point that he takes it as one of his primary Christian tasks to attack (again and again and again) contemporary fundamentalism on the grounds that it is not at all Christian—he has not (unlike so many ex-fundamentalists I know) renounced his faith or his upbringing. In particular, Kennedy remains passionately devoted to Scripture, not as simply an academic exercise, but as the book that orders his life.

And his sermons. As he likes to say, "No text, no sermon." Having absorbed his sermons at FBC-Dayton for eight years, I can say that his preaching—and first and foremost Rod Kennedy is a preacher—is all about the Bible. No cute stories, no feel-good uplift messages, no paeans to positive thinking. Instead, the Bible. Not biblical literalism (whatever that means), but the Bible. And some of these sermons have been published, and are worth checking out. I had the privilege to co-write the foreword to his 2011 book *Sermons from Mind and Heart*.[3] And I was particularly pleased to be given the opportunity to respond to his sermon, "Are American Christians Persecuted?," for a very creative (and courageous!) 2016 book (*Preaching Conversations with Scholars*) in which he invited scholars to critique the content of his preaching. The sermon I commented on is a terrific example

---

3. Kennedy, *Sermons from Mind and Heart*.

of how Kennedy has directly confronted some of the ludicrous but dangerous (and even more dangerous now) claims put out by the Christian Right. As I note in the book:

> A very large number of evangelicals and a good number of mainline Protestants and Catholics have been persuaded that laws and policies that reflect America's religious pluralism and that are designed to protect religious minorities are actually aimed to restrict the "religious freedom" of Christians . . . In response to this ideologically-driven nonsense Kennedy bluntly and rightly asserts that "spoiled, pampered, soft American Christians growling about their rights" know nothing of what it means to be truly persecuted . . . [And] what gives Kennedy's sermon real power is that, in his reference to John the Baptist and the 16th-century Anabaptists and the twenty-eight nations where Christians are persecuted today, he suggests the possibility that authentic Christianity will never be a "majority" religion, that authentic Christianity exists on the margins and in the shadows. That is to say, to truly follow Jesus is to invite persecution, as the Jesus message is always at odds with the powers-that-be.[4]

Here one gets a good feel of Kennedy's Anabaptist commitments, and—relatedly—his determined opposition to the white nationalism at the heart of the contemporary Christian Right. Rod's project of exposing and opposing politicized evangelicalism is one that is near and dear to me, both in my writing,[5] and in the blog Susan Trollinger and I maintain at rightingamerica.net. Rod is a frequent contributor to our blog, and in posts such as "Jerry Falwell, Jr. Unzipped His Pants for the Camera . . . But It's Not About Sex" and "Finally, An Evangelical Defense of Donald Trump Worth Responding To (It's Still Terrible, but There It Is)"[6] one gets a feel for his determination to save "authentic Christianity" from the Christian Right.

I have spent the last few years urging Kennedy to write this deeply biblical and Christian (and rhetorically astute) critique of the white evangelical devotion to Donald Trump. And it is a deliberately provocative critique—it would not be Kennedy if it were not deliberately provocative—in that he goes after scholars and journalists who are determined to tell the story of Trump and evangelicals as a story of "lost evangelical innocence," or as a story of ignorant but well-meaning evangelicals who have been

---

4. Trollinger, "The Church, Persecuted and Grateful," 93–96. I should note that Susan Trollinger also penned a response to this sermon.

5. See, for example, Trollinger and Trollinger, *Righting America at the Creation Museum*; and Trollinger, "Religious Non-Affiliation."

6. Kennedy, "Jerry Falwell, Jr."; and "Finally, An Evangelical Defense."

duped by Donald Trump. Instead, Kennedy argues, Trump is not only the strong man evangelicals desperately wanted, but evangelicals—particularly their preachers—actually helped birth Trump, and in many ways they are running the show.

One final point. As you read this book it is very important to keep in mind that Kennedy is first and foremost a preacher. In the end, *The Immaculate Mistake* is an extended sermon, both a lament of the ways in which the Christian Right has distorted the Scriptures and the historic faith in order to pledge its allegiance to Donald Trump, and a call to Christians to heed the Gospels and follow Jesus to the margins of American cultural and political life, where the "least of these" reside. Amen.

# Acknowledgments

As usual I need to thank Johnelle for all that she had done to make this book possible. She has read the various chapters, made suggestions that improved the work, and given maximum encouragement when I thought the book was a doomed effort. I am also indebted to a group of scholars who have been my friends, mentors, and challengers: Sue Trollinger, Bill Trollinger, Brad Kallenberg, Tom Lasley, Roy Vice, and in loving memory, the historian Jacob Dorn. I am indebted to rhetorical scholars Andrew M. King, Louisiana State University A & M, and Kenneth Zagacki, North Carolina State University, for reading the manuscript. I would like to thank Rodney Clapp and the fabulous people at Cascade Books for guiding me and for the many outstanding books they publish in Christian theology. Finally I want to thank the American Baptist congregations for the freedom to write and say what I write and say—First Baptist Dayton, Ohio; First Baptist Peoria, Illinois; Upper Merion Baptist, King of Prussia, Pennsylvania; and First Baptist Church, Ottawa, Kansas. I am grateful to have served four of the many congregations that insist on the life of the mind and the heart.

*Obama was born in Hawaii; Kamala Harris in California, but, pray tell me, where was Donald Trump born? It's a fair question because Trump's political career started with his "birtherism" conspiracy. As late as 2017 Trump was still saying that Obama's birth certificate may have been fraudulent. Sure, they have a dossier saying Trump was born in New York, but like Donald says, anyone can suggest that it's fake. As with his taxes and his college transcripts, Donald would sue before he showed his birth certificate because he wasn't even born on earth. He was created in the alternate universe of evangelicalism and sent here in a space vehicle, where he was raised by a New York family with questionable financial dealings. Donald Trump was not born in the USA. He is a hybrid droid of evangelical preaching, tel-evangelists, and reality television. He's rich. He's a celebrity. He's a superstar. He lacks human qualities of empathy, compassion, understanding, curiosity, openness, rapport, caring. No way he was born on this planet. He was conceived in a laboratory that was a hundred years in producing the exact "dream" candidate for evangelicals. From the vaudeville revivals of Billy Sunday, to the raising hell populism of J. Frank Norris, the segregationist Jerry Falwell, Sr. and Bob Jones, to the wacky conspiracy theorist Pat Robertson, to the con artists Oral Roberts, Jimmy Swaggart, Jim Bakker, and a host of others, to the "American nationalism" of Billy Graham and David Barton, to the fawning, slick Rev. Dr. Jeffress and the voyeuristic Jerry Falwell, Jr., and a carnival of fake prophets, charismatics, Pentecostals, and independent network preachers on television, has come Donald Trump—secular apocalyptic preacher. Donald Trump is not from here.*

# The Immaculate Mistake: How Evangelicals Gave Birth to Donald Trump

*"We need to read Trump, not as a politician with policies but as a kind of religious leader with parables."*[1]

*The people around the president are "increasingly the true believers, and it's almost like a religious revival when he shows up at Mar-a-Lago, they jump up and down, they shout, they scream his name."*[2]

Evangelicals were once proud to be an odd bunch. Flannery O'Connor's dictum, "You shall know the truth, and the truth shall make you odd," seemed a perfect fit for evangelicals. There was a deep connection to the conviction that being a Christian put one in tension with and even opposition to the world. Now, the presumption that evangelicals are different from the world is bit of garden variety small change. What's odd now is that those called to be odd, different—other words for holiness—are no longer odd. The evangelicals have succumbed to the temptation of investing faith in the secular politics of the nation. This move, not exactly unusual for Christians of all stripes, doesn't make them dumb or gullible or irrational.

I have spent more than four decades attempting to carry the banner of the evangelical faith, but I no longer have the ability to do so. I am able only to offer the argument that evangelicals are not dupes of Trump, not newcomers to the rough-and-tumble world of Machiavellian politics. Their eyes are wide open and they know exactly what they are doing. This I cannot defend.

Understanding the relationship between American evangelicals and Donald Trump has puzzled pundits, psychologists, historians, sociologists, political scientists, and a host of liberal critics. I am not a historian, a psychologist, or a philosopher. I am a preacher. For more than 2,500 weeks

1. Williams, "Demagogues and demigods."
2. Lippman, "Trump Cuts Loose."

I have written a sermon manuscript meant to be heard rather than read. Identifying the genre of my writing will be a difficult task because I'm not sure if I'm a theologian, a rhetorician, or a half-baked historian. I'm sure there will be sufficient evidence to suggest that I'm none of these in any way. My hybrid writing style is the result of attempting to write scholarly in popular language. These two worlds are not as interchangeable in writing a book as they are in preaching a sermon.

I was lucky enough to be born a southerner, of the tribe of Irishmen who inhabited the hills of north Louisiana, a redneck born of rednecks; as to the faith, a fundamentalist, of the Bible-believing, rapture-preaching, hell, fire, and damnation variety; as to zeal, an evangelist for Jesus, of the "save-the-world" type; as to righteousness, of the strict, moralistic, sober people. A word of explanation about the boast of being born southern. Reynolds Price, a southern novelist, says that southerners came from long, long generations of people who had spoken the English language. "And our language," he claims, "added to it, a great leavening and enriching factor, something that British English never had—a profound involvement with African American language."[3] Like Carlyle Marney once explained, I have been standing, hat-in-hand, for more than sixty years before the two great traditions of white, seminary-trained, Aristotelian preachers and the Black prophetic preaching tradition. My life's work has been an attempted synthesis of these two mighty streams in the history of American preaching. I take it as ironic that the most racist region in the nation has been the most influenced by Black preaching. Since at least 1978, in southern towns riddled with racism, I have been preaching a form of "Black rhetoric," and the congregations, unknowing, have responded in mostly positive ways. If you can forbear to stay on this side-road for a moment longer, I have a personal anecdote that gives warrant to my explanation. When I became the pastor of the First Baptist Church of Bogalusa, Louisiana, a town where racial tensions overflowed in the 1960s, many of the participants in those race contests were sitting in the pews of First Baptist on Sunday mornings. While my theology leaned to the left more than many congregants liked, they supported me. I wasn't sure until one Sunday, in the parking lot (where all knowledge in a Baptist church resides), a district judge, Buddy Crain, who was a deacon in the church, engaged me in conversation that opened my eyes. "One day when they figure out what you are saying, when they move beyond your style, which they like, you are going to need a friend. I want you to know that I will be that friend."

---

3. Quoted in Ketchin, ed., *The Christ-Haunted Landscape*, 85.

Then college happened, in particular Louisiana Baptist College. Old Testament professor James Kautz happened. He told me Adam and Eve were not real people. A light came on in a room I had not known was dark, and I changed sides forever. James Young, New Testament professor, happened and I fell in love with interpretation of the New Testament. There was no going back. Like Stanley Fish, "I stopped worrying and fell in love with interpretation."[4] My vocation as a reader had found a permanent home and I have been reading ever since.

As advance notice, I try to intersect with Flannery O'Connor and the parade of other southern novelists such as Reynolds Price and Alan Gurganus. Southern novelists will make appearances in this work. I am a convert of Reynolds Price, who taught me that "the whole point of learning about the human race presumably is to give it mercy."[5]

There's some of Allan Gurganus in me: "What held me from childhood was the sermon itself as a possibility. As I listened to a thousand dull sermons and several dozen good ones, I began to understand that while I seemed to be a skeptical, detached, twelve-year-old just passing the time in church, the lessons of the gospel spoke to me, changed me and moved me."[6] The sermon is my form and wedged between the covers of this book are the words of a preacher—a preacher trained in the white-seminary tradition, and the Black rhetorical tradition, and in the academic discipline of rhetoric. Call me Aristotle with a Bible.

There's also something of a historian in me. For example, some of the best theology I have read in the last twenty years has been written by historians: Randall Balmer, William Trollinger, David W. Blight, Kevin Kruse, John Fea, Paul Boyer, and Doug Frank. I would put Doug Frank's *A Gentler God* up against an entire army of double-edged predestinarian hyper-Calvinists.

Utilizing sermonic, historical, theological, and rhetorical materials, artifacts, and tropes, I have set for myself the task of tracing the continuity between evangelicals and Donald Trump. Billy Sunday, J. Frank Norris, Jerry Falwell, and Robert Jeffress are my chosen vessels for this journey of discovery. I argue that the revivalist, populist rhetoric of the early twentieth century moves with shape-shifting swiftness, across time and place; its moments seemingly disconnected from each other. They are not. This speech shares a fundamental grammar—a rhetorical logic. People predisposed to this outlier rhetoric are attentive to its sound and attracted to its resentfulness of the establishment.

---

4. Fish, *Is There a Text in This Class?*, 6.
5. Quoted in Ketchin, ed., *The Christ-Haunted Landscape*, 79.
6. Ketchin, ed., *The Christ-Haunted Landscape*, 379.

While I am as far removed from being a fundamentalist as "the east is to the west," I am not void of those influences. When you grow up in a religion, a religion that involves pain to the mind, it goes in deep and is remembered forever. Having been baptized by immersion as a fundamentalist, there's some of that bayou water still in my veins. The disruptive, argumentative, chip on the shoulder of a swaggering fundamentalist remains.

I am not at war with the Christianity that made me Christian, but I am in a war mode with evangelical politics, theology, and rhetoric. Pat Conroy, southern novelist, speaks for me. I prefer "a climate of intemperance, rhetoric, and feverish melodrama."[7] As Flannery O'Conner suggested, "When you can assume that your audience holds the same beliefs you do, you can relax a little and use more normal means of talking to it; when you have to assume that it does not, then you have to make your vision apparent by shock—to the hard of hearing you shout and for the almost blind you draw large and startling figures."[8]

I confess to the temptation of dismissing evangelical rhetoric of the political sort as symptomatic of one or another particularly noxious pathology. There's also my own impatience at what I discern as the absurdity of evangelical political messages confidently delivered by persons who seem to have made no discernible effort to ascertain the contestability, the nuances, the ambiguities, the partial truth and majority lies that are contained in their utterances. The tribe of evangelical preachers seem to share an imagination that Christianity, in its birth, was as certain, as evangelical, as political as they are now. The perorations and tirades of these "court evangelicals" as they gravely and condescendingly inform me that I have taken leave of my senses and that my deepest theological convictions are irrational, that the God I worship is the product of my elitist imagination, and that I need to repent at last of my pagan, demonic, savage credulity leaves me incredulous.

I am not void of the Christian influence that cautions some degree of equanimity should be present, and some Christian forbearance be exercised, but I write with some "white-hot" anger that resembles the rhetoric of the prophets. I am not a prophet, but I prefer their passionate rhetoric to the usual smooth rhetoric of the milder mannered tribe. "Did that make your hair bristle? Good. I can work with that."[9]

In 1991 I wrote that evangelicals created a metaphor, an archetypal metaphor, that defines their reality: Life is war.[10] That's the part of

---

7. Conroy, *The Lords of Discipline*, 305.
8. O'Connor, *Mystery and Manners*, 34.
9. DiAngelo, *White Fragility*, 94.
10. Kennedy, *The Creative Power of Metaphor*, 1.

my training in evangelical faith that has never left me. I attack, defend, counterattack, strategize, wound, seek to destroy arguments, and attempt, like Aristotle, to utilize all the available means of persuasion and all the verbal metaphors of a war footing. I live with the hope that I'm one of the good people, knowing I fight like an evil one.

I have never wished for a different childhood; I enjoyed a blessed childhood of baseball and the Bible. Evangelicals can swear that the Bible is the book for them, that the Bible tells them so, that they own the copyright to all of its truth, but I'm not buying a ticket to that circus. The Bible is the church's book and evangelicals are not its keepers. The Bible was, is, and shall be the book for me.

On March 5, 1967 a group of Southern Baptist preachers and deacons laid hands on me, set me apart to the ordained ministry. They gave me a Bible—a King James Version, Scofield Reference Bible—and told me to preach what God told me to preach. Ever since I learned to read, thanks to a saintly mother with a ninth-grade education, I have been reading the Bible, the same Bible evangelicals now use to give Trump divine approval. With all the appreciation I can muster for my academic training, I don't want to just be another writer pouring my heart out only to other people with PhDs. Frankly I am more influenced by a childhood of absorbing Scripture—the memorize-a-hundred-verses-a-week regimen—than any other book in my library. I think it impossible to understand me without knowing my ongoing commitment to Scripture.

In my southern fundamentalist upbringing, the world of the Bible had everything in it, and it refuses to leave me. I am not a biblical scholar, but I have read like a man on fire my whole life because the genius of biblical scholars touched me with the dazzling complexity of the symbolic language of faith. Reading the Bible offers multiple epiphanies, each new one exploding like fireworks at the Dayton, Ohio Fourth of July celebration. Because of them I agonized with Adam in the garden and danced with David in a white linen ephod before the Lord, with all my might (even though dancing was forbidden in my tribe) and wrestled with God with Jacob, rescued a lamb from a bear, had nightmares about Satan going to and fro across the earth looking to devour, and walked the streets of Jerusalem with Jesus and warmed my hands at the fire of Pilate, and made up a hundred stories from the life of Jesus, and walked, head down, flag dragging in the dirt, with the children of God into captivity and slavery. I came up out of Egypt with Moses and crossed the Red Sea on dry ground and walked on the water with Peter. I have sat entranced in church as the preacher waved his Bible and threw out fighter jets and army tanks and vast armies to oppose Gog and Magog.

I've looked in every crack and crevice of every verse in more than thirty translations, gloried in the street language of the Greek New Testament, fumbled and fumed over the intricacies and sparseness of the Hebrew texts. I've been in Jericho, Jerusalem, Babylon, Bethlehem, and a thousand biblical cities and introduced myself to a million Ethiopians and King Asa in my amazing Bible-reading career, and every morning the words of God are new and fresh and stimulating and surprising. All of this because I listened to my brilliant teachers and soaked up every single thing those magnificent men and women had to give. I cherish and praise them and thank them for finding me when I was a boy and presenting me with the precious gift of the Bible. After all, even Jesus submits to be taught a lesson of holiness by a woman Matthew deliberately casts as a "Canaanite." This is what my approach to the Bible entails: "exercising profound, even godly, humility, opening oneself to learn something previously unimaginable about the fundaments of life with God—and to learn it from 'least of these.'"[11]

The ordainers should have never ordained me. If they had known what they were unleashing on their view of the world, they would have flunked me right then and there. I'm a theological and ecclesial "Misfit." Yes, I know it's an awful metaphor to choose, but it is what it is. That's me, the Misfit who believes Jesus, who he was and is, what he taught and preached. Like another preacher of sorts in O'Connor's portfolio, I see Jesus, not as meek and mild, but as wild and ragged and demanding everything.[12] Yes, I have matriculated at the school of writing taught by Flannery O'Connor. I can never escape the text she used at the opening of one of her novels, "From the days of John the Baptist until now, the kingdom of heaven suffereth violence, and the violent bear it away."[13] I retain that evangelical insistence that belief in Christ is a "matter of life and death," even as I watch evangelicals betray that very commitment in allegiance to Donald Trump. Perhaps evangelicals need to consider a question from "Slow Train Coming"—a question of what convictions they are abandoning.[14]

I don't, however, accuse them of hypocrisy or self-righteousness. Nor do I think them easily duped or lacking in sincerity. They are very serious believers. Like Roderick Hart, in his work *Trump and Us: What He Says and Why People Listen*,[15] I believe that evangelicals are worthy of being considered politically, rhetorically, and theologically. There have been compelling

---

11. Davis, "Critical Traditioning," 177.
12. O'Connor, *Wise Blood*, 16.
13. Matthew 11:12, KJV.
14. Dylan, "Slow Train Coming."
15. Hart, *Trump and Us*.

and intelligent answers to the question of how evangelicals and Trump got together—written by academics, journalists, and cultural commentators. My perspective is that the evangelicals, after decades in the laboratory of another world, a safe world they created to nourish, develop, and maintain their view of the world, managed to give birth to a prodigy of their own making, Donald J. Trump. He bears no physical family resemblance, but don't be fooled by the genes; in gesture, tone, and attitude he is his father's son. He mirrors evangelical preachers, especially in style. He is stamped with that signature sneer of certainty, that look of rightness, that utter disdain for the unwashed heathens. To overlook the dramatic performance of the evangelical preacher is to miss what matters.

When Trump was caught on tape practicing a speech in March 2017, he seemed to be rehearsing the facial expressions he would use. "We see Trump cycle through three practiced expressions: a sneer; an almost-ecstatic, ferocious pieta in which Trump stares upward with an open-mouth grimace; and a sort of triptych in which Trump mimes three glares in rapid succession, bobbing his head and sharpening his stare with each beat."[16] This is the face of an angry evangelical preacher. "The visual rhetoric of Trump's body—'controlling, coercive, and conceited, a combination of traits that embody' evangelical and televangelist preaching."[17] The face, the gestures, the sounds, the voice—in other words, the method, not the message, augments Trump's power. "It consolidates his status as humiliator-in-chief."[18]

Donald Trump is exactly the president evangelicals wanted. Trump is not only attached to the evangelicals; the two have become one body. This is about fear, anger, and resentment. It's about politics and theology, but mostly it's about pragmatic evangelicals who wish to control what John Howard Yoder called "the handles of history." This is about winning, the take-no-prisoners, bare-knuckled, no-holds-barred kind of winning. This is the story of the lines of connection, the merging of styles, the similarities in the rhetoric, the smooth alliance of two entities of wealth and celebrity, and the potential destructive tendencies of this aligning of the stars.

This is not a shotgun wedding, but it is a marriage that has produced a political offspring, and since it involves a deeply moral and righteous people, the evangelicals, it bears the title of *The Immaculate Mistake: How Evangelicals Gave Birth to Donald Trump*. This is an artificial insemination at least a century in producing an offspring: a tough, resentful man; a messiah anointed by the conservative evangelicals, a man whose gospel centers on

---

16. Schaefer, "Whiteness and civilization," 11.
17. Ott and Dickinson, *The Twitter Presidency*, 31.
18. Ott and Dickinson, *The Twitter Presidency*, 36.

getting even, a strongman to stand up to the perfidious liberals. This book is not an attempt to prove a hypothesis or to suggest that an absolute causal relationship has been established. I suggest that the evidence points in the direction of Trump being the offspring of evangelical conservatives, who in becoming more and more secular, have at long last produced a political prodigy who thinks and acts like them, but is not hindered by any religious scruples. Instead of being a collection of dummies, the evangelicals are the organ grinders; Trump is their monkey. The divisive, often offensive, over-the-top, blustery, rhetoric of the preachers provided the seed that issues in the speeches and tweets of Donald Trump.

Evangelical preaching lives in a crystal sea of certainty. There is no suggestion or hint of probability, only the definite "this is the way it is." Flannery O'Connor, in *The Habit of Being*, says, "The mind serves best when it's anchored in the Word of God. There is no danger then of becoming an intellectual without integrity . . ."[19] This would be helpful to evangelicals if they were so anchored, but in reality, they are only anchored in the black leather cover of the Bible—a symbol of literalism unrelated to the actual canon. Billy Graham habitually intoned, "The Bible says." Donald Trump often says, "Believe me." The words "God told me" are prominent in this kind of preaching. This language is a powerful persuader for a people trained to think of the Bible as literal truth and the pastor as the keeper of that literal truth.

Robert S. McElvaine, in *The Great Depression*, says, "In the reckoning of Believers, 'in fact,' is a phrase as weightless as an astronaut in space. Evidence that goes against received Truth thereby proves itself to be false. True believers prefer saying 'the evidence be damned' to being damned by the evidence. There are no hypotheses for people of faith. Blind faith would not be blind if it could see facts."[20] In the minds of evangelicals they are a tribe besieged by an encroaching secular, liberal enemy. They feel trapped, discounted, and demeaned. Perhaps they suffer from forms of post-traumatic shock that come from engaging in at least one hundred years of war with modernists and liberals. Buried within the evangelical conviction that this is a war, there's the psychology of treating the enemy as less than human. For example, participants in Trump rallies project Democrats as pedophiles, as agents of sex slavery, as murderers. Jeff Sharlet, in an extended interview with a Trump supporter at one of these rallies, is told that the Clintons are killers. The term the Trump supporter uses is "Arkan-cide."[21] David Livingston Smith chronicles the pro-

---

19. O'Connor, *The Habit of Being*, 134.
20. McElvaine, *The Great Depression*, xix.
21. Sharlet, "'He's the Chosen One,'" 8.

cesses by which we reduce fellow human beings to being animals, demons, enemies. Nowhere does this tendency manifest itself as in war. The propaganda of warring countries concentrates on depicting the enemy as a bunch of animals, fit only to be killed. "The great chain of being," Smith says, "continues to cast a long shadow over our contemporary worldview. It's also a prerequisite for the notion of dehumanization, for the very notion of subhumanity—of being less than human—depends on it."[22]

Donald Trump is part revivalist Billy Sunday, part antagonist J. Frank Norris, part televangelist Jerry Falwell, Sr., and part prosperity gospel preacher. If Billy Sunday is religious vaudeville; J. Frank Norris, Barnum and Bailey's Circus; and Falwell, Sr., the televangelist; Donald Trump is the secular revivalist/televangelist. He is the culmination of evangelical faith, minus the faith. He combines revival rhetoric with declension messages; he demonizes a large array of enemies with a dogged certainty that would have made Sunday proud. He combines wealth and Christianity. Donald Trump is the most famous secular evangelist in the world. I confess to disliking Trump as much as every hellfire and damnation evangelist that disrupted the dreams of my childhood.

When Trump somehow won the presidency, a group of evangelicals gathered in a New York ballroom were shouting and some were crying. "It was as if God had answered our prayers and the impossible had happened," said Steve Strang of *Charisma* magazine.[23] Strang is the pioneer founder and CEO of Charisma Media and was dubbed by *Time* magazine at one of the twenty-five most influential evangelicals in America. He's been featured on Fox News, CNN, MSNBC, CBN, Dr. Dobson's *Family Talk*, and many other Christian outlets. Strang's recent book is entitled *God, Trump, and the 2020 Election*, and he claimed, "We had a new president: an outsider we believed God had raised up to shake the United States out of its comfortable slide toward globalism."[24] It was reminiscent of Eisenhower seeing his win as a national mandate for a revival: "I think one of the reasons I was elected was to help lead this country spiritually," he said. "We need a spiritual renewal."[25]

Conservative evangelicals celebrated coming in out of the cold, coming home from intellectual exile, political defeat, and decades of injurious accusations of being a bunch of dummies. They now felt not only their usual righteousness, but good. Never discount the power of "feeling good" when it comes to evangelicals. Trump tapped into the insatiable desire of

---

22. Smith, *Less Than Human*, 42.
23. See Boston, "God Wanted Trump."
24. Strang, *God, Trump, and the 2020 Election*, 85–86.
25. Kruse, *One Nation Under God*, 64.

evangelicals to "feel good" rather than shamed by the civic morality of gay rights and immigrant rights and abortion rights. Donovan Schaefer argues that "feeling good" is the product Trump sells his followers. Schaefer offers a visual metaphor that I find illuminative of evangelical leaders: Pepe the Frog, a human-bodied frog character created in 2005 by cartoonist Matt Furie. Pepe, "unflappable when confronted, waves off all embarrassment with a stoner smile and a breezy" catchphrase, "Feels good man." Shaefer says, "Pepe's smug but goofy hangdog routine evolved into the perfect emblem for [evangelicals'] approach to politics—a refusal to be shamed. Pepe's shtick is to deflect every attack with a shrug. His grinning defiance of every effort to shame him became theirs."[26]

The cartoonish Pepe has been incarnated in a real-life scene of Jerry Falwell, Jr., a now discredited evangelical leader, standing on a yacht with what looks like a rum and coke, with his arm around a young woman. His pants and hers are partly pulled down and unzipped. Falwell, Jr. insists that this was good clean vacation fun, but Liberty University trustees were not laughing.

With Trump's victory, the depth of evangelical emotions rivaled that of the Chicago Cubs winning the World Series in 2016 after a 108-year drought. There was a sense that all the shame of the maligned and discredited movement of the early twentieth century had finally been vindicated. Revenge would now be served in the person of Donald Trump, the man whose favorite Bible verse is "an eye for an eye and a tooth for a tooth."

The residual resentment of evangelicals, simmering since the summer of 1925, at the embarrassment of their warrior-hero, William Jennings Bryan, at the Scopes Trial, was now satisfied. This is the story of the rise, fall, and rising again of the fundamentalist-to-evangelical Christian movement. It is the story of how a movement that in the nineteenth century was committed to the social nature of the gospel became a movement steeped in biblical literalism, dispensationalism, and nationalism. The second resurrection in 2016, like a rapture substitute for evangelicals, arrived with the election of Donald Trump. The evangelicals have more lives than the number of Hal Lindsey predictions for the return of Jesus.

Evangelical policy set the tone for the Trump administration. The appointment of conservative judges to the Supreme Court, undoing legal protections for the LGBT community, loosening environmental regulations, making race a central ideology, dividing the country over immigration, stoking the fires of fear, nostalgia, and patriotism, and the list goes on and on. While President Trump doesn't usually attend church, the imprint of his

26. Schaefer, "Whiteness and civilization," 1.

conservative evangelical producers and handlers are large on his administration. Eighty-one percent of evangelicals voted for Trump.

Evangelicals anxiously await even more positive Trump-enabled decisions that might make abortion illegal, put prayer back in school, along with the teaching of Bible courses and scientific creationism, the instituting of strict restrictions on immigration, religious freedom to refuse service to gays, and the elimination of the Johnson Amendment so that churches that now serve as de facto units of the Republican Party will not risk losing tax-exempt status.

Stephen Mansfield argues that Norman Vincent Peale had the most influence on Donald Trump's religious views, suggesting that Trump "for many an hour had listened to Peale as he spoke of the example of Jesus,"[27] but the importance of Peale is mitigated by Trump's own gospel of getting even. Almost anyone that makes a kind, uplifting speech could be said to be influenced by Peale—Robert Schuller and the Crystal Cathedral and Joel Osteen and a downtown Houston congregation are two more recent examples. Peale and the Marble Collegiate Church may be the public face of Trump's religious pedigree, but it had little to do with the darker impulses of the more sinister undercurrents of American conservative evangelicalism that formed Donald Trump. The evangelicals could say of Donald Trump, "Before I formed you in the womb I knew you, and before you were born I consecrated you; I appointed you a prophet to the nations."[28] After all, evangelicals detested Peale's positive thinking as much in Peale's career as they now embrace his positive thinking, prosperity-laced gospel.

The inauguration of President Donald Trump was much more than a passing of the baton of political power. It was the coronation of a religious constituency—conservative evangelicals. In Christian liturgical terms, this was the born-again baptism of a president who had been over a century in coming to life from the womb of fundamentalist-to-evangelical conservatives. Franklin Graham, showing his biblical gymnastics ability, turned a biblical reference to rain as a sign into blessing by saying, "Mr. President, in the Bible, rain is a sign of God's blessing. And it started to rain Mr. President when you came to the platform." When a biblical baptism seems far-fetched, any ordinary earthly facsimile will suffice.

Here was the secular baptism of Donald Trump without the liturgy of baptism. There was water, in the form of rain, suggesting to some a baptism by sprinkling, but no one asked the president and his followers, "Do you

---

27. Mansfield, *Choosing Donald Trump*, 22.

28. Jeremiah 1:5. (Scripture quotations from the New Revised Standard Version unless stated otherwise.)

renounce Satan and all the spiritual forces of wickedness that rebel against God?"[29] Having accepted the gifts of Satan—power, wealth, influence—it would have been hypocritical to say otherwise.

By supporting Trump, evangelicals expressed loyalty to their deepest assumptions. Believing as they do that America is threatened by an array of domestic enemies, they are delighted that a strongman has appeared to stop those enemies. *Liberalism* will here serve as the umbrella term for all the ideological enemies that Trump supporters feel are undermining the America they love and cherish. Stephen Mansfield in *Choosing Donald Trump* says, Trump "has most understood that they [evangelicals] have been unrepresented, that they felt traumatized by the Obama years, that they were terrified at the prospect of any Hillary Clinton years and that they had some fundamental gripes, to put it sarcastically, that weren't being championed—everything from a 'War on Christmas' to the Johnson Amendment to just having the government off the backs, so to speak, of the clergy."[30]

A number of scholars have addressed the relationship between conservative evangelicals and Donald Trump.[31] John Fea, history professor at Messiah College, in *Believe Me: The Evangelical Road to Donald Trump*, offers an incisive analysis of the relationship, and walks a fine line between empathy for his fellow evangelicals and critical appraisal. He believes evangelicals hold legitimate grievances against Democrats. He explains that during the Obama administration evangelicals experienced setbacks at a dizzying pace, particularly with respect to matters of gender and sexuality. Obama's stance on abortion could be taken as a given, but his change of mind on same-sex marriage—if it was indeed a change of mind—was an unwelcome surprise. Fea perceives attacks on religious liberty in the Affordable Care Act's requirements concerning birth control and the Obama Justice Department's enforcement of civil rights for LGBT persons. All these factors motivated evangelicals to believe that they and their movement were under siege. From my perspective this underscores the evangelicals' simmering distaste for a Black man being in their White House.

29. *Book of Common Prayer*, 302.

30. Mansfield, *Choosing Donald Trump*, 15.

31. There are already numerous books on this subject, but they differ significantly from this one in both focus and scope. Consider for example: Alberta, *American Carnage*; Anderson, *White Rage*; Balmer, *Evangelicalism in America*, *Mine Eyes Have Seen the Glory*, and *Thy Kingdom Come*; Barrett-Fox, *God Hates*; Bowler, *Blessed*; Christerson and Flory, *The Rise of Network Christianity*; Fitzgerald, *The Evangelicals*; Greene, *No Depression in Heaven*; Harris, *Fundamentalism and Evangelicals*; Hochschild, *Strangers in Their Own Land*; Howe, *The Immoral Majority*; Jones, *White Too Long*; Kruse, *One Nation Under God*; Maltby, *Christian Fundamentalism and the Culture of Disenchantment*; Posner, *Unholy*; and Worthen, *Apostles of Reason*.

Evangelicals long for a mythical Christian past, and Trump's "Make America Great Again" mantra appeals directly to that troubled nostalgia. Fea argues, "Christians should be very careful when they long for the days when America was apparently 'great.'"[32] Are we appealing to the post-war boom in church attendance, which occurred with Jim Crow in force and when marital rape was legal? And by embracing prominent evangelical leaders, whom Fea labels "court evangelicals," Trump assuages evangelicals' gaping wound—disenfranchisement—by granting them access to power.

Fea repeatedly calls Trump a "strongman," suggesting the threat of authoritarianism. I would press this analogy from a biblical/historical perspective that messianic hopes always include the desire for a "strongman." Evangelicals insist they like Trump because he says what he thinks, that he is "the toughest SOB." As historian William Trollinger says, "It is ridiculous to accept at face value the repeated comment from Trump-supporting evangelicals that they like him 'because he says what he thinks'; no—they like Trump because he says what they think."[33] This is not a tale of lost evangelical innocence. This is what they wanted. Having given birth to him, the evangelicals are the doting grandparents and protective parents of their prodigy.

Randall Balmer traces the evangelical's dark side of racism in "Under Trump, Evangelicals Show their True Racist Colors." Just decades ago, conservative white churches constituted what amounted to cultural Christianity in the South. Before the rise of the Religious Right, they saw little common cause with Northern evangelicals. But while other evangelicals feel tension with the broader culture over religion, southern evangelical alienation is largely about being southern. And being southern is all about race. The nation now speaks with a southern accent and that has to do with race.

Rodney Clapp, in *Johnny Cash and the Great American Contradiction: Christianity and the Battle for the Soul of a Nation*, depicts America as now influenced by the South. Barefoot, ragged, dirty Confederate ghosts are rising out of the fog that covers our land and they are winning this time. As Clapp claims, "All of America now speaks with a southern accent."[34]

Failing to take Trump seriously, the Democrats and their progressive Christian allies were shocked at losing the 2016 election. Like moderate Southern Baptists when they lost control of their denomination, Clinton and her followers were in shock. The strategy of Southern Baptist evangelicals in the 1980s was to bus in thousands of delegates, many from newly incorporated charismatic churches, and elect a president. This strategy was

---

32. Fea, *Believe Me*, 134.
33. Trollinger, email correspondence, 2019.
34. Clapp, *Johnny Cash*, 1.

used again as more mainstream evangelicals included the Pentecostals, charismatics, and Independent Network leaders from the fringe in the rush to support Trump. Together they helped Trump win.

Writing off evangelicals as a bunch of dummies is like ignoring a small fire ant bed that suddenly appears in your backyard. Untreated, the fire ants, working furiously from below, out of sight of the rest of the world, will eventually build a mound that seems to stretch to the heavens, a kind of insect version of the biblical Tower of Babel. Once the fire ants are at full strength, if you poke a stick in the mound, they will send out waves of warrior ants intent only on afflicting as much pain as possible. They spread out in formations, covering the ground around the mound in circular attacks within ten seconds of the alarm. It is not a pretty sight, but fundamentalists are the fire ants of our culture. To ignore them, as was the case from the 1920s to the 1970s, except for some historians, fails to take into account that there was a thriving evangelical world evolving in the woods that was completely different from the world of journalists and scholars. This is now a world where credentials are a negative and being "anointed by God" a necessity. To ignore evangelical justifications is to be unprepared.

If evangelicals are not duped by Donald Trump, if Donald Trump is not a magician, a guru of political insight, then what accounts for the reverent support of evangelicals? Perhaps William Cavanaugh is right when he argues in *Theopolitical Imagination* that the nation-states have always found it quite useful to play different religious loyalties off one another in order to concentrate power. "The state so constituted now replaces the church as the exemplification of universal values." On this reading evangelicals aren't hypocrites; they are faithful disciples of this bastardized "American Christianity" where America has become the church and war has become the liturgy.[35]

Mark Noll in *America's God* claims that America is a synthesis of evangelical Protestantism, republican political ideology, and commonsense moral reasoning. Americans synthesized these antithetical traditions by making their faith in God indistinguishable from their loyalty to a country that insured them that they had the right to choose which god they would or would not believe in.[36] Trump is the grand finale of this synthesis as he offers his congregation a facile salvation without repentance and without sacrifice.

The "Christians" in this strange version of faith, Stanley Hauerwas argues, mean that they "want to live in a world in which they feel safe no

---

35. Cavanaugh, *Theopolitical Imagination*, 6.
36. Noll, *America's God*, 11–13.

matter what the cost of securing their safety imposes on the rest of the world."[37] Hauerwas pushes the argument that "America has conquered Christianity." Perhaps evangelicals have produced only people who are unable to recognize when they are serving powers foreign to the gospel and are now addicted to aiding the rule of those powers. If this is the case, then we are witnessing Christians who have decided to imitate the powers and the principalities for ends they deem necessary and by whatever means necessary. In short, evangelicals are now secularists, and it no longer matters whether God exists or not. They would pretty much keep doing what they are doing if God were shown to be an illusion. That's not that far from Christians living in contradiction of the faith they once held dear. Such a commitment manages to avoid the reality that "God's kingdom cannot be forced into existence using the means of the devil."[38]

The evangelicals are apocalyptic warriors—the literal kind that interprets apocalyptic literature as an appeal to escape rather than a mandate for taking responsibility for the world. This is a war to the death for conservative evangelicals. Liberals and their allies, wed to a scholarly set of niceties, have brought books, a collection of scholarly papers, and a Bible to a gun fight. They should have been reading *The Art of War* alongside theology, history, and philosophy.

The conservative evangelicals have infiltrated the seats of power with unrelenting persistence. They have wormed their way into every crack and crevice of power. Again, Hauerwas: "All you need to know to understand America is that the FBI is made up of Catholics and southerners. This is because Catholics and southerners have to try to show they are more loyal than most Americans, since southerners have a history of disloyalty and Americans fear that Catholics may owe their allegiance to some guy in Rome. That is why the FBI is given the task of examining graduates of Harvard and Yale—that is, high-culture Protestants who, of course, no longer believe in God—to see if they are loyal enough to be operatives for the CIA."[39] We should know that we have a problem when we keep turning out graduates willing to be agents of the modern state.

Now the evangelicals have taken all the hopes and dreams of a worldly, powerful, secular messiah and produced Donald Trump. They are, like Jewish parents in a Broadway play sending their only child to college, crying out, "Everything we got's wrapped up in you, boy. Everything

---

37. Hauerwas, *The State of the University*, 123.
38. Hauerwas, *Working with Words*, 120.
39. Hauerwas, *War and the American Difference*, 34.

we got's wrapped up in you."[40] This is the gamble of the evangelicals. They are betting the church on Donald Trump giving them the keys to political power. Like a casino gambler down to his last stack of chips, they have shoved them all into the center of the table, desperate to win holding at best a pair of Jacks and a Joker. Evangelicals are "all in"—"everything we got's wrapped up in Donald."

For more than a generation, evangelical preachers, parading about like proud peacocks, immersed in wealth, pop theology, and an authority rooted in a claim of being anointed by God have talked and preached and performed in ways that are now all unleashed in Donald Trump, without the religious trappings. Making the case for this assumption about the creation of Donald Trump is the burden of this work. What I argue in this book, historically, biblically, and rhetorically, is that paying attention to the rhetoric of evangelical preachers is a key to understanding Donald Trump. Evangelical preaching, and its most visual component, televangelism, produces style over substance. Style trumps content. With style and sizzle an audience was developed over decades that was predisposed by the preaching they heard to receive the ideology of Donald Trump as "word from God."

Chapters 1 through 3 consider the preachers who are part of Trump's family tree and the historical ideas that produced a nation of evangelicals predisposed to accept the message of Donald Trump: Billy Sunday, vaudeville revival preacher; J. Frank Norris, circus promoter and provocateur of all who stood in his path; and Jerry Falwell, Sr., televangelist and dedicated segregationist.

Chapter 4 presents the current evangelical culmination of the century that produced Sunday, Norris, and Falwell in Robert Jeffress, senior pastor of First Baptist Dallas. By now, Jeffress's regular appearances as a Fox News consultant has made the evangelical defense of Trump almost old news. Instead of rehashing all the evangelical defenses and biblical support of the president, I concentrate on how evangelical themes from Sunday, Norris, and Falwell are encapsulated in Jeffress. A pair of sermonic artifacts are displayed to show the historical and underlying tensions that have been part of our faith and politics since at least 1920. A sermon by Robert Jeffress and a sermon by Jeremiah Wright provide the representative overview of what continues to be the great religious/political divide in our nation.

Chapters 5 through 7 suggest rhetorical and biblical alternatives to the evangelical arguments used in support and defense of President Trump. There are biblical texts with alternative readings that may be applied to President Trump. After all, when it comes to evangelicals, it is always somehow about the Bible. Then there are rhetorical secular tropes that are suggested as alternatives to the biblical ones preferred by Trump evangelicals.

40. Cited in Buttrick, *Homiletic*, 358.

President Trump is the messiah of conservative evangelicals. They gave him birth, they taught him their ways, as nefarious as they often are, and they have supported him with their words, congregations, and lives. The desire for a redeemer, a messiah, who is tough and strong—a strongman stronger than all others—has always tempted those who would wear the crown. In the time of Jesus, there were various candidates who sought the nomination. In the Acts of the Apostles we read, "Gamaliel, a teacher of the law, respected by all the people, stood up and ordered the men to be put outside for a short time. Then he said to them, 'Fellow-Israelites, consider carefully what you propose to do to these men. For some time ago Theudas rose up, claiming to be somebody, and a number of men, about four hundred, joined him; but he was killed, and all who followed him were dispersed and disappeared. After him Judas the Galilean rose up at the time of the census and got people to follow him; he also perished, and all who followed him were scattered."[41] He names Theudas and Judas as two men claiming to be the messiah, as he puts it, "claiming to be somebody," and neither was the messiah.

I can't read these verses without thinking of all the Republicans who stepped up and presented themselves as redeemer, savior, messiah to the party, seeking to win the crown, and carry the rod of God as the New Moses. Early in the nominating process, these candidates displayed their evangelical bona fides. Jeb Bush, Ted Cruz, Marco Rubio, and Mike Huckabee all claimed to be the best choice to carry the banner of evangelicals. Yet, the evangelicals, having been disappointed by the two previous Republican presidents, felt that all these candidates were too much like the Bushes. In this case, it turns out that two Bushes was more than enough. Now, they were looking for a street fighter, a barroom brawler, a candidate that was a pugnacious outsider. That person turned out to be Donald Trump. Evangelicals chose Donald and anointed him as messiah, a particular kind of messiah—the conquering general entering the city on the back of a white stallion, the strongman standing up to those barbaric liberals, and laying waste to his enemies.

These Christians uncritically worship President Trump as a matter of political faith. They uphold him in every self-created crisis. This is not the work of a bunch of dummies. This is not a tale of lost evangelical innocence. This is what they wanted. I repeat myself: having given birth to him, the evangelicals are the organ grinders; Trump is the monkey. To ignore this power is to do so at our own peril.

---

41. Acts 5:35–37.

# Chapter 1—Billy Sunday
## *Vaudeville Revivalist*

Donald Trump belongs to the tribe of revival preachers and fundamentalist-to-evangelical Christians. His story begins early in the twentieth century. The evangelical family tree that gave birth to Donald Trump originates in the defining soil of American revivalism and populism. The expressions of populist rhetoric mingle easily between preachers and politicians. It is hard to tell whether politicians first started sounding like preachers or if preachers started sounding like politicians. What is clear is that both are tributaries of the same mighty river that runs through the heartland of American politics and religion: Populism. As Paul Taggart comments, "For such a commonly used term, it is surprising how little attention populism has received as a concept." He then adds, "It is hard to understand politics in the United States without having some sense of populism."[1]

Notoriously difficult to define, populism has been described as having a "chameleon-like nature,"[2] as a "Zeitgeist,"[3] and a nesting ground for demagoguery. Most studies of populism have focused on politicians, not preachers, but the populist preachers share the same argumentative framework as political populists. Margaret Canovan suggests two themes are dominant in all forms of populism: a trust of "people" and a distrust of the "elite."[4] Ghita Ionescu and Ernest Gellner claim that the language of populism is "elusive and protean. It bobs up everywhere, but in many contradictory shapes."[5] Michael Kazin argues that populism is accessible to all "those who claim to speak for the vast majority of Americans who work hard and love their

---

1. Taggart, *Populism*, 10, 25. Lee, "The Populist Chameleon," 356. Gunderson, "The Calamity Howlers"; Erlich, "Populist Rhetoric Reassessed"; Lee, "The New Populist Campaign"; Burkholder, "Kansas Populism."
2. Lee, "The Populist Chameleon."
3. Mudde, "The Populist Zeitgeist."
4. Canovan, *Populism*, 264.
5. Ionescu and Gellner, eds., *Populism*, 1.

country."[6] In Kazin's view populism is "a language whose speakers conceive of ordinary people as a noble assemblage not bounded narrowly by class, view their elite opponents as self-serving and undemocratic, and seek to mobilize the former against the latter."[7] It is within the parameters of these scholarly depictions of populism that I argue that Billy Sunday, J. Frank Norris, and Jerry Falwell, Sr. are populist preachers.

Populism stands as testament that the nation's future often advances by "coordinates set by the past."[8] This can only be true if history is being read correctly. Evangelicals have coordinates set by a past that has never existed and therefore cannot be a navigating guide for democracy in the present. The populist drive of evangelicals embodies the worst of the xenophobia and jingoistic tradition of a European settler society: racism, sexism, homophobia, inward and backward looking, preoccupied with preserving the old ways of life, defensive, provincial, and at times, conspiratorial. Add to this the populist tendency to pick the wrong enemy and the wrong kind of messiah. For the virtues that populism can bring forth, when it is tethered to the Declaration of Independence, at its worst, and in this case, in its evangelical clothing, there is an uncompromising, nativist, and exceptionalist narrative that violates the most basic pluralist convictions. With this background survey of populism in the evangelical stream, the story of the birth of Donald Trump begins.

Three factors are at play: the prominence of religious commitment on the part of ordinary people; the prominence of populist, charismatic religious leaders; and the vitality of mass democratic movements that reflect the charisma and organizational skills of the popular leaders. Popular religious leaders like Billy Sunday, J. Frank Norris, and Jerry Falwell, Sr. continue a long tradition of democratic religious authority. Rather than treating these characteristics in a chronological order or as the province of history alone, I weld Sunday and Trump into a typology to show that they share a common argumentative frame that has been a persistent force in shaping American political and theological argument.

After suggesting possible lines of connection between Sunday and Trump, I overlay those connections with the framework of populist argumentation. There are parallels, consistencies, and contours of a sustained political structure with roots located in the nation's origins as a republic. In the case of Billy Sunday, the secular trope that informs his work is vaudeville; the rhetoric he uses is that of masculinity. Billy Sunday, incorporating

6. Kazin, *The Populist Persuasion*, 5.
7. Kazin, *The Populist Persuasion*, 1.
8. Browne, "Jefferson's First Declaration of Independence," 416.

populist themes of "the people," "the enemy," and "the system" became a powerful religious and political force in the nation. For example, his preaching likely played a significant role in the adoption of the Eighteenth Amendment (the prohibition of alcohol) in 1919.

Billy Sunday was America's first superstar evangelist—a bigger star than the leading lights of American vaudeville, the major entertainment venue of Sunday's time.[9] Evangelicalism is a form of religious populism that plays into Trump's rhetoric. Billy Sunday is a populist preacher who mimics a vaudeville performer.

Billy Sunday's "people" were the common people, the people of the streets. Alan Jackson, country singer, lifts up the most powerful of populist themes in his song, "Little Man." He contrasts the values of small towns and the "little man" with the corporate titans that corrupt and defeat small towns and the "little man."[10]

In particular there are four traits of Billy Sunday's populist/revivalist ministry that stand out as essential in Trump's campaigns and rhetoric: A nontraditional entertainment style of preaching that offended tradition, his lack of decorum in the use of language, an obsession with large crowds, and a super-macho masculinity. The rhetorical marker of Sunday that finds the strongest replication in Trump is the sense of the heteronormative masculinity. The energy, mood, and experience of a Sunday revival and a Trump rally are an emotional match.

Sunday "thumbed his nose" at what he considered the elite, and they responded to him with scathing criticism. Trump shares with Sunday the obsession with attacking the elite, the establishment, pitting the people against the establishment. Sunday made one adjustment to the usual populist vision of the "people" as a righteous chosen people and classified them as sinners in need of the sawdust trail.

Sunday was an outlier, an exception to the usual garden-variety preacher of his time. He can even be termed an "outlaw" because he operated outside all the norms, expectations, decorum, and propriety of what was deemed appropriate for a preacher. Today, Sunday seems tame, but at the dawn of the twentieth century, his preaching seemed rebellious and controversial—fine for the "sawdust trail," the tent revival, and the temporary wooden cathedrals, but not fit for a high-steeple fancy church with expensive pews.

Billy Sunday was to American religion what outlaw singers were to country music. Among these artists were Willie Nelson, Johnny Cash,

---

9. McLoughlin, *Billy Sunday Was His Real Name*, xvii.
10. Jackson, "Little Man."

Waylon Jennings, and Kris Kristofferson. Their music was labeled "outlaw country" because it rebelled against the standard, status quo restrictions of what was then country music. These country singers were long-haired, loud, and ornery. Their kindred spirits were the freewheeling rock stars of the day, not the suit-and-tied acts favored by the Grand Ole Opry. Billy Sunday was the outlaw preacher, not the robed divinity dons of First Church, Main Street, USA.

When the perception of the law as unjust is widespread, the heroic criminal emerges as a national figure. Among these criminal heroes have been Jesse James, William Bonney, John Dillinger, Bonnie and Clyde, and Charles Arthur (Pretty Boy) Floyd. These outlaw entrepreneurs "market" themselves to an adoring public as something more than outlaws—as strong and powerful men capable of sticking it to the law and doing what has to be done. The public then lives out its own rebellion against the system in the acts and antics of the beloved outlaw.

Billy Sunday approaches this concept of the beloved outlaw, but even more so, Donald Trump is the political equivalent of the beloved outlaws of American history. Donald's history of borrowing billions of dollars from banks, his multiple bankruptcies where he walked away with the cash, his legal troubles and untold lawsuits, his brash, disruptive personality, his ability to transgress all known standards of political decorum and escape unscathed and more popular, demonstrate his "beloved outlaw" status.[11]

Sunday and Trump offer a gendered performance, a Janus-faced masculinity of outlaw and good father in their leadership styles. They are "bad boys" but good fathers. "The result is a Janus-faced masculinity of outsider-yet-insiders, bad-boys-yet-good fathers, standing above the citizenry, mediating and fostering a conservative political order."[12]

The era of Billy Sunday was the zenith of that great American spectacle known as vaudeville. Vaudeville was a performance made up of a series of separate, unrelated acts grouped together on a common bill.[13] S. D. Trav claims that Satan was the first vaudevillian of all time offering the "first act of nonconformity by any sentient being."[14] Maybe St. Paul had some original

---

11. Kooistra, "Criminals As Heroes," 217–39.

12. Eksil and Wood, "Right-wing Populism."

13. Vaudeville has a direct connection to television. It is in the movies and television that vaudeville made it greatest contribution. At the beginning of the twentieth century, most film actors also played on vaudeville. The silent movies incorporated the animated physical comedy of vaudeville. Billy Sunday did the same in his preaching. Even today, *Saturday Night Live* continues the traditions of vaudeville. Televangelists, the direct descendants of Billy Sunday, maintain that same continuity.

14. Trav, *No Applause*.

vaudeville performance in mind when he penned the words, "Entirely out of place is obscene, silly, and vulgar talk."[15]

Sunday was the most politically important preacher of his time. He was outspoken and partisan, and the attention paid to him by the *New York Times* would have made Trump jealous. "Sunday was a media star . . . . as likely to get publicity as the major leagues, Broadway, or the burgeoning new film industry."[16] He was the last star of vaudeville.

A Sunday revival had the trappings of a vigorous workout program, complete with the physical exercise, the shocking performances, the sexual language, and the inappropriate rhetoric. Sunday was a nonconformist, a natural actor, and he put on a show that was part acrobat, part professional speaker, part actor, and full-orbed preacher of heaven or hell.

Billy Sunday hated the saloon; it was his sworn enemy as if it were the devil incarnate. Populism dies without an enemy, and for Sunday, the enemy was the saloon—the powerful enemy of the gullible people. "The saloon is a liar," shouted Sunday. "It promises good cheer and sends sorrow." Sunday unleashed a fury of hyperbole at the saloon: "The saloon is the sum of all villainies. It is worse than war or pestilence. It is the crime of crimes. It is the parent of crimes and the mother of sins. It is the appalling source of misery and crime in the land. And to license such an incarnate fiend of hell is the dirtiest, low-down, damnable business on top of this old earth."[17]

An ardent champion of temperance from his earliest days as an evangelist, Sunday's most famous sermon was "Get on the Water Wagon," which he preached on countless occasions with both histrionic emotion and an impressive array of statistics.[18] Sunday said, "I am the sworn, eternal and uncompromising enemy of the Liquor Traffic. I have been, and will go on, fighting that damnable, dirty, rotten business with all the power at my command."[19]

## The Crowds

Over the course of his career, Sunday probably preached to more than one hundred million people face to face—and, to the great majority, without electronic amplification.[20] Sunday did not preach to a hundred million dif-

15. Ephesians 5:4.
16. Hankins, *Jesus and Gin*, 42.
17. Frank, *Less Than Conquerors*, 187.
18. Frank, *Less Than Conquerors*, 187.
19. Dorsett, *Billy Sunday*, 112–13.
20. Firstenberger, *In Rare Form*, 39, 120–23; Dorsett, *Billy Sunday*, 150–52;

ferent individuals but to many of the same people repeatedly over the course of a campaign. In a comparison that should be noted now, many Trump supporters travel across the nation to attend Trump rallies. One supporter says, "Trump makes us feel free."[21]

Success, of course, meant big numbers. "At the turn of the century, Americans were increasingly falling under the spell of big numbers. The New York newspapers published daily box scores of attendance and conversion figures during Sunday's meetings in that city."[22] Douglas Frank describes the big business preparations for a Sunday revival: Sunday had an array of specialists "dictating (and sometimes stage-managing) the kind of citywide invitation Sunday would accept, supervising the design and construction of the tabernacle, arranging for financial support, recruiting volunteer workers, a total of 50,000 persons for the New York City revival."[23] Success became a secondary god for evangelicals. Big crowds were a sign of God's blessing, a way of saying, "We must be right. Look at all these people." The primordial metaphors have lasting value among evangelicals: More is better; bigger is better. The advent of the megachurch waited in the wings.

With Trump, it's always about the numbers. He frequently boasts of the large crowds at his rallies. In San Antonio, for example, Trump spoke of his crowd: "That place was packed. . . . That was some crowd. And we had twice the number outside. And then you had this crazy Beto [O'Rourke]. Beto had like 400 people in a parking lot, they said his crowd was wonderful."[24]

Whether counting the crowd at a vaudeville performance in Peoria, the number of people in a Sunday revival, or the followers at a Trump rally in Tulsa, it's all about those primordial metaphors: More is better; bigger is better. Big crowds, big ratings, big success.

## The Language

An examination of the language of Billy Sunday reveals a raw, visceral, vaudevillian rhetoric. Richard Weaver argues that "language is sermonic."[25] All speakers are thus preachers. "We have no sooner uttered words than we have given impulse to other people to look at the world, or some small part of it, in our way. The measure of a speaker lies in the ethos of his or her

---

Weisberger, *They Gathered*, 254.
   21. Surma and Fifield, "Meet the MAGA diehards."
   22. Frank, *Less Than Conquerors*, 176.
   23. Frank, *Less Than Conquerors*, 176.
   24. Diamond, Klein, and Tapper, "Trump Brags."
   25. Weaver, *Language Is Sermonic*, 225.

language." As Weaver puts it, "The rhetorician is a preacher. . . . Noble if he tries to direct our passion toward noble ends and base if he uses our passion to confuse and degrade us. Since all utterance influences us in one or the other of these directions, it is important that the direction be the right one, and it is better if the lay preacher is a master of his art."[26]

It's not so much what Sunday said because plenty of previous evangelists had preached the alleged "old-time religion"; it was how he said it and that he said it at all. Sunday's language was not learned in Sunday school. Sunday flouted the rules of style, decorum, and appropriateness and did so, not only sans apology, but with forethought and deliberation. He refused to be cowed by tradition or propriety. His language was designed to shock, to gain attention, to mock eloquence. Sunday's claim that he used ordinary language instead of the fancy words of theologically trained preachers offers the key to his rhetorical and religious populist strategy. Sunday admitted, "I don't know any more about theology than a jackrabbit knows about ping-pong, but I'm on my way to glory."[27] The universal audience Sunday created in his mind was not a gathering of literary critics, theological professors, or the wealthy. His universal audience was of one piece with the earth—earthy, physical, common. His rhetorical aims were clear and bold.[28]

For example, Sunday told a revival crowd, "God almighty never intended that the devil should triumph over the Church. And if you think that anybody is going to frighten me, you don't know me yet."[29] Sunday would have been extolled by the ancient Greeks with their reverence for the frank and fearless truth-speaking known as parrhesias. Such speakers spoke truth to their audiences even in the face of consequences. No doubt Sunday was a fearless preacher. As a faithful practitioner of parrhesias Sunday was willing to "give a complete and exact account of what he [had] in mind. . . . He use[d] the most direct words and forms of expression he [could] find."[30] This frankness may have been Sunday's most powerful calling card. Sunday said, "What do I care if some puff-eyed, dainty little dibbly-dibbly preacher goes tibbly-tibbling around because I use plain Anglo-Saxon words."[31] And he mocked, "When the English language gets in my way, I walk over it."[32]

---

26. Weaver, *Language Is Sermonic*, 225.
27. McLoughlin, *Billy Sunday Was His Real Name*, 128.
28. Perelman and Olbrechts-Tyteca, *The New Rhetoric*.
29. Sunday and Ellis, *The Life and Death*, loc. 106.
30. Skinnell, "What Passes for Truth," 77.
31. Sunday and Ellis, *The Life and Death*, loc. 83.
32. Sunday, Brainyquote.

At times he would take pot shots at biblical scholarship with an exhibition of anti-intellectualism. "When the word of God says one thing and scholarship says another, scholarship can go to hell," Sunday shouted. He encouraged his audiences to have a disdain for theologians as vicious as Trump insisting that his followers despise Democratic leaders: "The Lord is not compelled to use theologians. He can take snakes, sticks or anything else, and use them for the advancement of his cause."[33] Sunday's rhetorical choices of crude language reflects his separation of his preaching from the seminary-trained preaching of the high-steeple churches. "He usually perturbs fastidious folks who think that literary culture and religion are essentially interwoven."[34]

A theological opponent of Sunday, Universalist minister Frederick William Betts, wrote:

> Many of the things said and done bordered upon things prohibited in decent society. The sermon on amusements was preached three times, to mixed audience of men and women, boys and girls. . . . But an experienced newspaper reporter told me that the sermon on amusements was "the rawest thing ever put over in Syracuse." . . . [A friend] says that Mr. Sunday's sermon on the sex question was raw and disgusting. He also heard the famous sermons on amusements and booze. [He] says that all in all they were the ugliest, nastiest, most disgusting addresses he ever listened to from a religious platform or a preacher of religion. He saw people carried out who had fainted under that awful definition of sensuality and depravity.[35]

A liberal Congregationalist minister in Oak Park, Illinois, William E. Barton (1861–1930), likewise attacked Sunday's pulpit manner, "We wish he would stop his profanity. . . . damned stinking something-or-other, 'To hell with' something or somebody. . . . We wish he were a gentleman. . . . He is a harsh, unjust, bad-tempered man . . . a very defective Christian."[36] Rev. Barton sounds like evangelical preachers being upset at the profanity of President Trump. In this case I agree that cursing is an expression of anger and aggression. As Michael Gerson says, "I don't think political discourse is improved by language more appropriate to a bar fight. I do think the presidency is diminished by public scatology and sacrilege. And I really don't give a darn if you think this is old fashioned." The puzzle is that evangelicals

---

33. Sunday and Ellis, *The Life and Death*, loc. 83.
34. Sunday and Ellis, *The Life and Death*, loc. 95.
35. Betts, *Billy Sunday*, 30, 36, 43.
36. Quoted in Betts, *Billy Sunday*, 43.

are offended by language but not by unjust policies against the poor, the children of immigrants, the least of these.

In one sermon, Sunday growled, "Listen, if I heard shrieks and cries coming from a house and I ran in there and I found a great big broad shouldered whiskey soaked Joe weasel, dragging his wife about by the hair, and over here, two children are unconscious from his blows and kicks and another one screaming in terror, do you think I would apologize for being there? No! I'd knock seven kinds of pork out of that old hog."[37] How Donald!—of Islamic State terrorists, "You got to knock the hell out of them. Boom! Boom! Boom!"[38]

Sunday also unleashed scorn against women. In a story, probably apocryphal but indicative of Sunday's attitude, Sunday allegedly started a sermon by asking all the ladies on the front row to cross their legs. "Now that the gates of hell are closed, I can preach the gospel." In other statements of Sunday, we find, "The average girl today no longer looks forward to motherhood as the crowning glory of womanhood. She is turning her home into a gambling shop social beer-and-champagne drinking joint, and her society is made up of poker players, champagne, wine and beer drinkers, grass widowers and jilted jades and slander-mongers . . . She is becoming a matinee-gadder and fudge eater."[39] Sunday even passed out beauty advice: "If some of you women would spend less money on dope and cold cream and get down on your knees and pray, God would make you prettier."[40] Considering Trump's attacks on Gail Collins—"face of a dog"—Carly Fiorina's looks, Megan Kelly's anatomy, Rosie O'Donnell's temperament, Senator Elizabeth Warren's ancestry, and his attack on Ghazala Khan, the mother of a soldier killed in Iraq, of Sunday it can only be said, "How Donald!"

Sunday's burlesque, carnival barker language is precursor to the incivility, crude, profane, bull-in-a-china-shop rhetoric of Donald Trump. Trump has repeatedly called his opponents "stupid," "horrible," and "weak." "Such statements and accusations make him seem like a guy who can and will cut through all the b.s. and do what in your heart you know is right— and necessary," said Michael Kazin, a historian at Georgetown University, echoing the slogan that Barry Goldwater used in his 1964 presidential campaign.[41] As granny would have said in 1950: "Such language!"

---

37. Sunday and Ellis, *The Life and Death,* loc. 7940.
38. Jaffe and Johnson, "Trump Delights."
39. Frank, *Less Than Conquerors,* 186.
40. Sunday and Ellis, *The Life and Death,* loc. 3908.
41. See Healy and Haberman, "95,000 Words."

## Trump as Anti-Carnival Revivalist

In the rhetoric of Donald Trump, we don't find the "light entertainment" of vaudeville, but the populist paranoid style that I characterize as anti-carnival. The ancient carnival, as presented in the theory of Mikhail Bakhtin,[42] was a temporary transgressive celebration that gave permission to make fun of and mock the hierarchy, the establishment. Donald Trump, borrowing elements from the ancient carnival, has invented the anti-carnival. Part of carnival in the Middle Ages was the "Feast of Fools."[43] The central idea of the feast appears to have been a brief social revolution, in which power, dignity, and impunity was briefly conferred on those in a subordinate position. It was a day of revelry, but more, it was a day of rebellion against propriety, decorum, standards of morality.

Bakhtin explains, "Carnival festivities and the comic spectacles and ritual connected with them had an important place in the life of medieval man."[44] The Feast of Fools "was a parody and travesty of the official cult, with masquerades and improper dances."[45]

Donald Trump has made every day a Feast of Fools, the ethical space of anarchy, a space that engenders no fixed orders or institutions, a space where all that is made can be unmade. In the Trump anti-carnival every day is a suspension of order, hierarchy, standards, decorum, and rules. Scholars of presidential rhetoric say that we have never had a president who speaks as President Trump speaks. English professor Robert L. Ivie says of Trump, "The language of excess—hyperbole, incivility, and an appeal to nostalgia that relies on significant erasures—threatens to become the enduring and defining feature of the nation's politics."[46]

Trump's anti-carnival creates a zone in which victimization, resentment, and revenge are inverted civic virtues. It also encourages the return of repressed, prohibited negative and destructive energies. The authoritative voice of the dominant discourse loses its privilege.

Trump's rhetoric aims to make permanent the spirit of the anti-carnival. Trump lends credibility to Michel Foucault's study of rhetoric and power as a war. Foucault investigates the proposition that politics is

---

42. Carnivalesque is a literary mode that subverts and liberates the assumptions of the dominant style or atmosphere through humor and chaos.

43. See Harris, *Sacred Folly*. My interest here is the connection between a feast that violated all norms one day a year and the recent "Feast of Fools" dominating every day in the Trump White House.

44. Bakhtin, *Rabelais*, 5.

45. Bakhtin, *Rabelais*, 74.

46. Ivie, "Trump's Unwitting Prophecy," 707.

the continuation of war by other means. Trump anchors his language in a display of force and violence that he establishes with his sneering looks, his choppy sentences, and his blustery threats. He attempts to maintain a sense of disequilibrium. Every speech is a trial by fire so that his "rallies" might better be dubbed "battles." There is a warlike clash, a struggle between Trump and the forces of evil.[47]

Rhetorical scholar Craig R. Smith says that "Trump seized on the fear and anger aroused by terrorist attacks and illegal immigration. He deployed the populist paranoid style of Hamilton, McCarthy, and Buchanan, but his version had distinct rhetorical markers that included hateful, misogynistic and bellicose bar talk, braggadocio, and branding."[48] These markers apply equally to Sunday. Building on Smith's argument I will trace Trump's use of language.

## Bar Talk

The first characteristic of Trump's "invention" of anti-carnival is his bar talk. Take any guy from a bar, feed store, barber shop, or coffee shop and give him a political pulpit to the nation and you get Trump bar talk. Smith says, "By bar talk, I mean that Trump said things from his political pulpit that one would normally only hear after a few drinks in the privacy of an unlit bar."[49] What concerns me, as much as my disappointment that Trump won, was the feeling that I had been listening to Trump rhetoric my entire life in explosions of loud, angry words from white males in the South; from a disgusting uncle who ruined every family reunion by drinking too much, cussing too much, and insulting everyone; from every redneck convinced that he could do a better job of running the nation than those worthless politicians. It turned out that Trump said out loud on television, at rallies, and in his tweets, the sort of language I heard growing up from the resentful, tired, working men of our poor communities. We would roll our eyes at the boasting, the blasting of the government, and the insistence that our uncles could all do a better job of running this country.

When President Obama gave the most important speech of his campaign for president as a response to the criticism of his pastor using the phrase, "God damn," in a sermon, Obama talked about the anger of African Americans at injustice: "That anger may not get expressed in public, in front of white co-workers or white friends. But it does find voice in

47. Foucault, *"Society Must Be Defended,"* 16.
48. Smith, "Ronald Reagan's Rhetorical Re-Invention," 52.
49. Smith, "Ronald Reagan's Rhetorical Re-Invention," 59.

the barbershop or around the kitchen table."⁵⁰ Obama also said that white anger was not always expressed in polite company or in public. David A. Frank, dean of the Honors College and Professor of Rhetoric at the University of Oregon, suggests that Obama was utilizing the concept of "hush harbor."⁵¹ This private place, at home, at a local bar or barber shop, or the Black church, was a safe place to express rage. Frank borrows the "hush harbor" phrase from Vorris Nunley.⁵²

It turns out that the seven words you can't say on television, you can say at political rallies. In his post-acquittal speech, in addition to vowing to do his favorite thing—"get even"—Trump went off on a rant about several things, including calling the impeachment "evil, corrupt, witch hunt, leakers, liars, disgrace, disaster, dirty cops, bad people." Then he proclaimed it was all "bullshit," to uncomfortable laughter from the crowd.⁵³

During Trump's speech at the House Republicans' annual retreat in Baltimore, he ranted about wind power. He concocted a conversation between a husband and wife wondering why their television was not working. "Darling, the wind isn't blowing," Trump's fictional husband said. "The goddamn windmill stopped."⁵⁴

In a single speech Trump managed to throw out a "hell," an "ass" and a couple of "bullshits" for good measure. During just one rally in Panama City Beach, Florida, he tossed out ten "hells," three "damns" and a "crap."⁵⁵ The audiences cheered and whooped and applauded. "I'd say swearing is part of his appeal," said Melissa Mohr, the author of *Holy Sh\*t: A Brief History of Swearing*, published in 2013. "It helps create the impression that he is saying what he thinks, 'telling it like it is.' We tend to believe people when they swear, because we interpret these words as a sign of strong emotions. In his case, the emotion is often powerful anger, which his supporters seem to love."⁵⁶

Mohr says, "He knows they like him to use words that lie over the edge of the traditional boundary of presidential decorum. His controversial word choices are an aspect of his role as the disrupter he promised his constituents he would be."⁵⁷ In other words, the profanity is scripted

---

50. Obama, "A More Perfect Union."
51. Frank, "The Prophetic Voice."
52. Nunley, "From the Harbor to Da Academic Hood."
53. *The Guardian*, "'It was all bullshit.'"
54. Zauzmer, "Trump uttered."
55. Baker, "The Profanity President."
56. See Baker, "The Profanity President."
57. Quoted in Baker, "The Profanity President."

and accepted even by evangelicals. Trump apologist Jerry Falwell, Jr., told *Politico*, "We all wish [Trump] would be a little more careful with his language, but it's not anything that's a deal breaker, and it's not something we're going to get morally indignant about."[58]

For example, during a televised ceremony celebrating the Boston Marathon bombing heroes, Red Sox baseball star David Ortiz used profanity in his message of support. Here is what Ortiz said: "This is our fucking city and nobody is going to dictate our freedom. Stay strong." Within hours of the Ortiz statement, the FCC Chair Julius Genachowski shared his thoughts via Twitter: "David Ortiz spoke from the heart at today's Red Sox game. I stand with Big Papi and the people of Boston"[59]

According to the FCC, Ortiz secured public decency rather than violating it. A rhetorical synergy was produced between profanity and civility because it was "from the heart." Even President Obama chimed in his support and called it "a proud moment"[60] Thus, language that would normally earn a "bleep" from television didn't cause a blip on the political or evangelical outrage meter.

In the evangelical world, cussing now passes the ethics bar at the lowest end. "I think conservatives for decades have felt bullied by the left, and the default response was to roll over and take it," megachurch pastor Robert Jeffress has commented.[61] And if that comes with a little profanity—well, warriors are forgiven their excesses. It appears that a Trump rally crowd believes that President Trump is cursing from the heart and he knows the tune. They are certainly dancing to it.

Trump's was the profanity presidency,[62] gleefully provoking the political establishment bothered by his norm-shattering ways. "His entire campaign is run like a demagogue's—his language of division, his cult of personality, his manner of categorizing and maligning people with a broad brush," said Jennifer Mercieca, an expert in American political discourse at Texas A&M University. "If you're an illegal immigrant, you're a loser. If you're captured in war, like John McCain, you're a loser. If you have a disability, you're a loser. It's rhetoric like Wallace's—it's not a kind or generous rhetoric."[63] Martha Joynt Kumar, a longtime scholar of presidential communication, said gritty language was part of the show put on by Mr. Trump, the onetime reality

58. Einbinder, "White evangelicals."
59. Jordan, "Profanity from the Heart."
60. Hyber, "Barack Obama Approves."
61. Gallagher, "Evangelicals finally find a reason."
62. Baker, "The Profanity President."
63. Quoted in Healy and Haberman, "95,000 Words."

television entertainer, for his fans. "He knows they like him to use words that lie over the edge of the traditional boundary of presidential decorum," she said. "His controversial word choices are an aspect of his role as the disrupter he promised his constituents he would be."[64]

No American president has championed coarse, cruel, and dangerous language as Trump has. His words have led the charge of an explosion of profanity, sexual innuendo, and racial slurs from State Houses to high school classrooms to the streets.[65] All the while, newspapers have wrestled with how to report on the language and its implications.

There is a danger: Each profanity by the president lessens its subsequent rhetorical efficacy, reducing him to just another guy who cusses too much and loses respect. Trump's profanity adds nothing to his message nor does it elevate our civic sensibilities, but in a perverse reversal his followers love his cussing.[66] When the president departs from his scripted speech, he goes from zinger to zinger to get laughs, and then he takes whatever train is leaving the station that is the Trump mind, and he rides it until it crashes. During his rants, the profanity comes out like rats from the sewers in New York to the delight of his supporters. But again, Trump's use of profanity runs the risk of making his language too familiar and less meaningful. "Trump just gives his profanity away, freely seeding it across the cultural landscape."[67]

## Braggadocio

Closely related to barroom talk is the second characteristic of Trump's rhetoric, bragging. He crows, hoots, exaggerates, lies, and makes stuff up, so he will look good, and his supporters "feel good." He has bragged about knowing about the danger of the coronavirus earlier than anyone: "We're the ones that gave the great response, and we're the ones that kept China out of here. . . . If I didn't do that early call on China—and nobody wanted that to happen. Everybody thought it was just unnecessary to do it."[68]

At the turn of a phrase, he can pull out a plethora of boasts. "No one reads the Bible more than me," says the man who referred to "Two Corinthians" at Liberty University. Believing as did the Apostle Paul that he has more reasons to boast than normal people, Trump takes rhetorical flight: "I have

64. Baker, "The Profanity President."
65. Gottlieb, "All the Swear Words Fit to Print."
66. Mercieca, "Dangerous Demagogues"; and Gunn, "On Political Perversion."
67. Selk, "How Trump Took Swearing Mainstream."
68. Yen, "Trump's inaccurate boasts."

the best words."⁶⁹ "I have the world's greatest memory."⁷⁰ "I think I'm much more humble than you would understand."⁷¹ "I am the most popular person in the history of the Republican Party. I beat Honest Abe."⁷²

Trump often claims to know more about everything than everybody. He regularly claims that "no one" has done more for gays, women, and African Americans than he has. "I know more about drones than anybody. I know about every form of safety that you can have." "I know more about people who get ratings than anyone." "I know more about ISIS than the generals do." "I understand social media. I understand the power of Twitter. I understand the power of Facebook maybe better than almost anybody, based on my results, right?" "[W]ho knows more about lawsuits than I do? I'm the king." "I think nobody knows more about taxes than I do, maybe in the history of the world." "I'm the king of debt. I'm great with debt. Nobody knows debt better than me."⁷³

## Branding

The third rhetorical marker of Trump's language is branding. Here may be the key to Trump's rhetorical genius. Branding, marketing, image-making—he excels in all the arts of self-promotion. Rhetoricians have long recognized the importance of identity to politics. As Trevor Parry-Giles and Michael J. Steudeman rightly point out, US "political campaigns" are as revelatory of "political identity" as "public policy."⁷⁴ In *Political Identity and Social Change*, Jamie Frueh investigates political identity as an amalgamation of various sub-identities such as physicality, beliefs, knowledge, experience, and personality.⁷⁵ Trump supporters accept Trump's brand as confident, patriotic, honest, moral, a strong leader, a freedom fighter, a breath of fresh air, a man who says what he thinks and walks the walk. This is the essence of a successful brand.

Voters were attracted to who he was and how he talked, not what he said. Evangelicals revel in his incivility; he is their raging bull of "Bashan." In the campaign against Hillary, he faced an opponent who was supremely rational, even wonkish, and uninspiring as a speaker. Trump was pure pathos

69. Poniewozik, "Trump Said."
70. Yilek, "Trump Defends 9/11 Claims."
71. Cillizza, "Donald Trump's Interview."
72. Benen, "Trump on his popularity."
73. See Britzky, "Everything Trump Says."
74. Parry-Giles and Steudeman, "Crafting Character, Moving History."
75. Frueh, *Political Identity and Social Change*.

over Clintonian logos. Trump lacked Clinton's virtues: her policy sharpness, her attention to detail, her polymathic hunger for information, her delight in the details. The differences between them were palpable. It was form over content. He's P. T. Barnum, a plethora of southern demagogues, a reality television celebrity, a con artist, and a consummate salesman all wrapped in one orange package—a Halloween color. Rev. Robert Jeffress, with cloying approval, said that Mr. Trump told him how he practiced the nicknames that he gave people because Trump brands people like a cowboy branding new calves with a hot branding iron. And the branding sticks. Trump bragged to Jimmy Kimmel on December 17, 2015 that Jeb Bush's distinguished name was no match for Trump's ability to brand—"'I defined him,' Trump crowed. Trump has a knack for branding; he has a particular ability to polarize people by branding his and their shared enemies."[76] Even the media defers to Trump's nicknames and keeps them circulating. Bad nicknames refuse to die when promoted by the media.

Trump knows how to create an overall image with numerous affects. "What Trump lacks [is] mediation, and circulation. His creation of an in-group that is implicitly and explicitly white, Christian, native-born, and overwhelmingly male, his denigration of an out-group comprised of people of color and women who vote for Democrats and coddle violent immigrants, and his manufactured outrage on a series of perceived crises construct an image of a man of "the people," a champion. . . . And the sole arbiter of justice."[77]

The red cap is the topping on the brand, speaking volumes about Trump. Anna M. Young, chairperson of communication and theater at Pacific Lutheran University, observes, "The ball cap (made in Chiinnnaaaa) . . . has a kind of Ashton Kutcher-esque, ironic trucker hat feel, like the wearer can afford to spend $30 on a something that looks like it came from the corner gas station in order to appear as if he is connecting with the people."[78] Trump's speech is the speech of his followers. His mind is their mind. Trump and his supporters are like a good piece of linoleum—the same from wall to wall. A New York billionaire comes across as a man of the soil, a rural farmer, a long-distance truck driver, a mechanic in the garage, an average American. It's as if he knows the barnyards of a dairy farm and the executive offices of a Wall Street investment firm. Trump could have played Eddie Albert's role in *Green Acres*.

76. Mercieca, *Demagogue for President*, 8.
77. Young, "Rhetorics of Fear," 34.
78. Young, "Rhetorics of Fear," 29.

For Trump supporters, his aggressive and politically incorrect rhetoric was his best argument for why he should be president. His roughness and vulgarity gave him the appearance of what the ancient Greeks called a parrhesias—"the one who speaks the truth." Earlier I argued that Billy Sunday was a true parrhesias; Donald Trump is a fake one.

Trump has perverted paralepsis and occultation into deception, dishonesty, and lying. "His constant disavowals, his reliance on paralepsis and occultation, his transgressions, his denial of consensus reality, are all underwritten by a perverse form of enjoyment that frees his supporters from legal, rhetorical, and psychic strictures."[79] In other words, he is quite up-front about his deception, lying, cheating, and dishonest rhetoric. He calls his claims "truthful hyperbole," a phrase invented by the ghostwriter of Trump's *Art of the Deal*, Tony Schwartz. "I wrote *The Art of the Deal*," Schwartz confesses. "Donald Trump read it."[80] In a *New Yorker* interview Schwartz claims he invented the "artful euphemism" in order to put an acceptable face on Trump's loose relationship with the truth. Schwartz explained that "truthful hyperbole means 'it's a lie, but who cares?'"[81] As rhetoric scholar Ryan Skinnell puts it, "Trump lies because lying works, plain and simple."[82] Call him a con artist, call him a demagogue, call him a truth teller, but call him "Mr. President" even though he ripped the "ship of state" from the traditional dock and set it on the wild seas to enrage the public's escalating and oscillating disillusionment with public institutions.

Evangelicals have stopped singing the old Gospel hymn, "Haven of Rest," and embarked on the wide seas and the "tempest" that is Trump sweeping over the "wild, stormy deep." He makes hatred and rage acceptable expressions for his supporters. Bonnie J. Dow says Trump "communicated most effectively through hyperbole, untruthful and often incoherent claims and threats against his opposition, using such strategies to whip huge crowds into a frenzy"[83]

Void of rhetorical filters, Trump lacks circumspection, truth-shading skills, and has no ability to shut up even when he needs to be silent. When Trump told his supporters at his Tulsa, Oklahoma rally, "When you do [COVID-19] testing to that extent, you're going to find more people, you're going to find more cases. So, I said to my people, 'Slow the testing down, please.'"[84]

---

79. Kelly, "Donald Trump and the Rhetoric of *Ressentiment*."
80. Schwartz, "I wrote the Art of the Deal."
81. Hancock, "Donald Trump's Ghostwriter Tells All."
82. Skinnell, ed., *Faking the News*, 77.
83. Dow, "Taking Trump Seriously," 136.
84. Quinn, "Trump Draws Criticism."

The next day his spin doctors, staff, and other supporters told the media that the president was joking. White House trade advisor Peter Navarro: "That was a light moment for him at a rally." Treasury Secretary Steve Mnuchin said the president must have been joking. White House press secretary Kayleigh McEnany, said, "It was a comment he made in jest." Trump turned that defense upside down by then saying, "I don't joke."[85]

## The Manly Man

I have identified the "manly man" trope as Sunday's archetypal metaphor. In word and action, Sunday portrayed his image of a real man. "The Old Testament in particular, Sunday believed, 'exalts and emphasizes and shows what real, true manhood is.'"[86] No wonder today's evangelicals scurried through their Bibles looking for Trump analogies among the great men. The manly man theme excites them so they conjured up Cyrus, Nehemiah, Nebuchadnezzar, David, Samson, and Solomon. They see Trump as a real man. His supporters regard Trump as "strong." His battles with adversaries reveal him as "tough." He is a real man. Somehow his bragging, insults, defiance, rule-skirting, and shredding of familiar standards of how a president should act—in this more sympathetic light—looks like charisma. It gives him the aura of "a winner." His backers regard him as *a real man*—possessed of a virility that flows not in spite of his excesses but because of them. In these minds, Trump represents a certain ideal of male power in exaggerated form.[87]

Sunday made fun of those who wanted to be a "little man" when one could be a "big man." Of David, Sunday proclaimed, "He didn't want [Solomon] to be an old woman or a sissy sort of fellow, but a man with knotted muscles on his arms, a big heart in his body and plenty of matter in his head."[88] Trump denigrated John McCain for being a prisoner of war, mocked a disabled reporter, and had an ad making fun of Joe Biden's stuttering. He doesn't like losers; he like real men! "How Donald!"

Heteronormative white masculinity has major affinities with evangelical notions of the male that are rooted in literal readings of the Bible that make men superior to women. Over against the heteronormative image there has been the development in the study of the Bible that shows it to "emanate from a culture whose ethical presuppositions and dispositions were inferior to

85. Choi, "Trump trade adviser"; and Gittleson, "Trump says 'I don't kid.'"
86. Frank, *Less Than Conquerors*, 189.
87. Harris, "Is Donald Trump a Manly Man?"
88. Sunday, "Shew Thyself a Man," from *Hot from the Preacher's Mound*.

the best of our own, a culture that was xenophobic, patriarchal, classist, and bloodthirsty."[89] None of this would have occurred to Billy Sunday as he exuded this masculine image. He insisted that the world was looking for strong men, real men, men it can admire. Old Testament men were idealized, their sins overlooked. "David was one of the greatest and best men who ever lived, a man after God's own heart, which means that he just suited the Lord."[90] David's penchant for deception and violence are left out.

Sunday acted out his vision of the manly man in his method of preaching. His physical exertions during a sermon surpassed that of a video exercise today. Sunday gyrated, stood on the pulpit, ran from one end of the platform to the other, and dove across the stage, pretending to slide into home plate. Pastor Kyle Childress recalls being told by an old-time rural preacher, "If you're not hoarse and standing knee-deep in sweat when you've finished preaching, then you haven't preached."[91] Sometimes Sunday smashed chairs to emphasize his points.

He portrayed an image of the all-American man: plain-spoken, unabashed, athletic, patriotic, professional, and hyper-masculine, delivering a form of old-time religion with entertainment, toughness, and passion. Sunday thundered, "" I don't expect any of those ossified, petrified, dyed-in-the-wool, stamped-on-the-cork Presbyterians or Episcopalians to shout 'Amen,' but it would do you good and loosen you up. It won't hurt you a bit. You are hidebound."[92] "Lord save us from off-handed, flabby-cheeked, brittle-boned, weak-kneed, thin-skinned, pliable, plastic, spineless, effeminate, ossified three-karat Christianity."[93]

Sunday's macho attitude parallels the southern ideal of the "good old boy." He exuded an aura of bold assertion and someone with a chip on his shoulder. His admiration for all things physical was a huge attraction to the men and women who thronged to watch his manly performances. Watching Sunday preach could be favorably compared to watching a fifteen-round heavyweight fight between Sunday and Satan, with Sunday winning with a TKO. Sunday would have loved Charlie Daniels' tale of a boy named "Johnny" who challenged the devil to a fiddling contest for a fiddle of gold.

One of his best-known sermons, "Shew Thyself a Man," is a celebration of manhood. The biblical text for "Shew Thyself a Man" reads "Be

---

89. Davis, "Critical Traditioning," 165.
90. Sunday and Ellis, *The Life and Death*, loc. 4037.
91. Childress, "Worship and Becoming the Body of Christ," 1.
92. Sunday and Ellis, *The Life and Death*, loc. 867.
93. Sunday, AZ Quote.

thou strong, and shew thyself a man."[94] Sunday begins with the statement: "No one can read the Bible in a thoughtful way without being impressed with the fact that it makes much of manhood."[95] "Real manhood is a great thing in the world."[96] He lifts up the "colossal manhood of Abraham,"[97] the "rugged manhood"[98] of Caleb, and David.

"God loves to watch a real man go out and grow."[99] David "wanted [Solomon] to aim high, as a king's son should, knowing that if his aim was high his endeavor would not be wasted. He wanted his son to raise his chin high enough to look the sun in the face, and so he said, 'Solomon, be a man!'"[100]

## The Manly Man Rhetorical Trope in Evangelical History and Now

Billy Sunday's emphasis on being a man connects across the century to the current manly man themes of evangelicals and President Trump. Evangelicals have a male-based religion. Current battles within denominations are as much about maleness in 2020 as they were in 1920. Randall Balmer says that Billy Sunday "cajoled the men in his audiences to 'hit the sawdust trail' and give their lives to Jesus. 'Many think a Christian has to be a sort of dishrag proposition, a wishy-washy, sissified sort of galoot that lets everyone make a doormat out of him.'"[101] Balmer notes the muscular Christianity movement in the early twentieth century along with the appearance of Charles Sheldon's novel *In His Steps*, portraying Jesus as a successful businessman. Manly man plus successful business executive has produced a president in Donald Trump.

The arguments for the supremacy of males originate in how evangelicals read the Bible. They have a small collection of texts intended to prove the priority of the male over the female. They worry that the church and the nation is being feminized. Many evangelicals do not believe that other Christians take the Bible seriously as a guide to faith and life. In this case, "seriously" is another term for "literalism."

94. 1 Kings 2:2, KJV.
95. Sunday and Ellis, *The Life and Death*, loc. 83.
96. Sunday and Ellis, *The Life and Death*, loc. 83.
97. Sunday and Ellis, *The Life and Death*, loc. 2462.
98. Sunday and Ellis, *The Life and Death*, loc. 1520.
99. Sunday and Ellis, *The Life and Death*, loc. 3908.
100. Sunday and Ellis, *The Life and Death*, loc. 6591.
101. Balmer, *Evangelicalism in America*, loc. 2297.

Evangelicals have been attracted to Donald Trump's gender-performative approach because it mirrors evangelical worship of the male, even though Trump's model for a "real man" is as far removed from Jesus as can be imagined. Rhetorical scholar Jennifer Mercieca says, "Trump appealed to frustration, sexism, and fragile masculinity by reifying women (treating people as objects) and successfully turned gender into a wedge issue to activate his followers."[102]

Like Billy Sunday extolling the virtues of Old Testament male heroes, evangelicals selected biblical allusions/illusions to depict Donald Trump as God's man, the manly man. Trump encouraged the comparisons because he had monarchial pretensions, indicating on any number of occasions his desire to be president for life. As Foucault noted, in relations between right and power, the default setting in Western societies is "essentially centered around royal power."[103] "Right is the right of the royal command,"[104] the signing of an executive order. Evangelicals lean in the direction of theocratic ideas of a godly king and would, in my view, gladly assist Trump in constituting monarchical, authoritarian, administrative, and yes, ultimate power. Again, Foucault's words sound more like an alarm: "I believe that the king was the central character in the entire Western juridical edifice. The general system . . . was all about the kings: the king, his rights, his power,"[105] and his desires. There may have never been a democratically elected president more convinced that everything, absolutely everything is about him. Trump grumbled at restrictions on his power from the judicial and legislative branches, seeming to believe that his power was invested as a living body of sovereignty, and that his power was "perfectly in keeping with a basic right."[106] The system of right is completely centered on the king. This is a man who wishes to be king with all the privileges and powers of oppression, domination, superiority, and subjugations "appertaining thereunto."

Trump has lived his life as a sort of Sun King—"He has believed himself to be above the law, never permitting himself to be held accountable for his actions."[107] He announced his candidacy for president with all the paraphernalia and pretensions of royalty. "Donald Trump and his wife Melania slowly descended from the upper reaches of the fifty-eight-story Trump Tower

---

102. Poniewozik, *Audience of One*, 266.
103. Foucault, *"Society Must Be Defended,"* 25.
104. Foucault, *"Society Must Be Defended,"* 25.
105. Foucault, *"Society Must Be Defended,"* 25.
106. Foucault, *"Society Must Be Defended,"* 26.
107. Mercieca, "Afterword," 177.

toward the stage below."[108] He used his rhetoric in unethical ways to help him get what he wanted. He lives oblivious to the words of the great French preacher who opened the funeral service of the Sun King with the immortal words: "Only God is great." Louis's coffin bore silent witness to the temporal nature of earthly greatness. It is a story evangelicals know well, but are ignoring because of the promise of the man who glibly says, "He who has the gold makes the rules," even if, in Trump's case, it is fool's gold.

Billy Sunday's emphasis on being a man connects across the century to the current manly man themes of evangelicals and President Trump. Evangelicals have a male-based religion. "God is a masculine God," the firebrand John R. Rice insisted to a male audience in 1947. "God bless women, but he never intended any preacher to be run by woman."[109] "Many think a Christian has to be a sort of dishrag proposition, a wishy washy, sissified, sort of galoot that lets everybody make a doormat out of him," Sunday intoned. "Let me tell you that the manliest man is the man who will acknowledge Jesus Christ."[110] A later evangelical lamented, "We no longer have a warrior culture."[111]

The typology of strong, masculine religious leaders have survived, prospered, produced offspring, and come to a new demonization in the Age of Trump. They are afraid that immigrants threaten the white, heteronormative values of their nation, and never lose sight of the fact that they claim America as their own. An attack on their beliefs, they believe, is an attack on America.

The movie *Fight Club* (directed by David Fincher) has resonated with evangelicals.[112] Billy Sunday's manly man returns in "various evangelical men's ministries across the country"[113] who have adopted the name "Fight Club" and draw images, slogans, and inspiration from the film. Having previously attempted to bring back muscular Christianity in the 1990s with Promise Keepers, the newest male movement incorporates the old tropes of masculinity. Not only do evangelicals honor and biblically support the ideology of gender superiority for males, but they imitate cultural expressions of the warrior man. Here again we have the evangelical imitation of the secular culture as we have already demonstrated with Sunday and

---

108. Mercieca, *Demagogue for President*, loc. 161.
109. Balmer, *Evangelicalism in America*, loc. 1837.
110. Quoted in Frank, *Less Than Conquerors*, 193.
111. Eldredge, *Wild at Heart*, 175.
112. Hays and Werse, "Evangelicals and the Film *Fight Club*."
113. Hays and Werse, "Evangelicals and the Film *Fight Club*."

vaudeville. The church is "constantly tempted to imitate the false politics of the world for its own life."[114]

This is a response to evangelical feelings about the growing feminization of the church. Standards of manhood, based on a strict reading of the Bible, had to be protected. These passages define men as those whom God has created specifically to rule, to lead, and to provide. This ideology fits the "strict father" metaphor outlined by George Lakoff in *The Political Mind*.[115] Images of power, physicality, control, and fierceness dominate this worldview.

There's an underlying fear that the church will die unless the men conform to standards of masculinity that are derived (supposedly) straight from literal biblical truth. If an evangelical church in the Southern Baptist Convention ordains a woman to the ministry, or a gay person, that church must be expelled.

*Fight Club* opens with a look at the idea of the "man fail." The narrator is the paradigm of the "man fail" as he seeks comfort in support groups that involve meditation, shares feelings, and a group for men where the members hold one another while they weep. The point of this scene is to insist this is not true masculinity. The narrator is passive and enslaved to a feminine nesting instinct and his IKEA purchases. He admits: "We used to read pornography. Now it was the Horchow Collection."[116]

The movie then leads the narrator into a club where real men engage in real fights. Both evangelicals and *Fight Club* define masculinity in terms of physicality. John Eldredge, an evangelical best-selling author, extols the value of boys being physical: "Little boys yearn to know they are powerful, they are dangerous, [and] they are someone to be reckoned with. . . . Aggression is part of the masculine design; we are hardwired for it."[117]

Underlying this obsession with masculinity is the gnawing fear of the feminine. According to this view, men have been policed into sensitivity, empathy, rapport, understanding, expressing feelings—not being real men. The devil term in this metaphorical construct is *political correctness*. The simplicity of the dualism speaks volumes to evangelicals: The Bible, good; political correctness, evil. This model of masculinity makes fun of good manners, propriety, decorum, rules, respect, and tradition. It rips

114. Hauerwas, *In Good Company*, 9.

115. Lakoff, *The Political Mind*, 77. "The strict father is the leader of the family, and is to be obeyed. The family needs a strict father because there is evil in the world from which he has to protect them—and Mommy can't do it" (77). This is the image Trump presents.

116. Hays and Werse, "Evangelicals and the Film *Fight Club*."

117. Eldredge, *Wild at Heart*, 10–11.

aside the curtain that often hides the difficulty of communication between men and women. Communication scholar Deborah Tannen has revealed that boys and girls grow up in different worlds of words. Thus, boys are reared with languages of independence, being up-one, don't tell me what to do, reporting, bragging, competition. Girls grow up with languages of cooperation, rapport, and intimacy. Of all the feminine rhetorical attributes, rapport best describes what bedevils evangelicals and progressives. Rapport means a close and harmonious relationship in which the people or groups concerned understand each other's feelings or ideas and communicate well. Evangelicals and others are raised in different worlds of words, parallel universes of reality.

As the film develops, the narrator becomes a real man. He moves from being in support groups, meditating, sharing feelings, and so on to duking it out in bouts of fistfighting. He graduates from shopping at IKEA for interior décor to fighting in a ring against another man.

Such an emphasis has deep roots in evangelical faith. During the nineteenth century there was a movement known as "muscular Christianity," which emphasized "manly men."[118] As if Donald Trump were channeling the evangelical manly man literature, like a graduate student reviewing the literature, much of what he says contradicts decorum. He is offensive and bigoted. His unrestrained rhetoric and his demolition of presidential norms reinforced his masculine image. His projection of a persona to his supporters as an outsider and a strict father confirmed their belief that he would disrupt and destroy. That he even dares say what he says becomes disruptive. Supporters applaud his willingness to flout the rules and remain unapologetic, marvel at his dismissal of propriety, and cheer his gall. Trump rings the bell on all three of the gendered ideological tropes: identity as a strong man, privilege as a white male, and belonging as a white man ordained of God to be in charge.

## Conclusion

The comparisons between Billy Sunday and Donald Trump are suggestive of a populist argumentative trope that can be traced across centuries. Sunday is a vaudeville, revivalist populist; Trump is an anti-carnival populist in the tradition of the worst specimens of American populists. They are rhetorical signs to the reality that revivalism and populism always retain a certain amount of power in American politics and religion. Both are obsessed with crowds as a sign of success. Both have a fixation on the manly man trope.

118. Lee and Sinitiere, *Holy Mavericks*, 19.

There is one primary reason I believe Billy Sunday stands first in line in the genealogy of Donald Trump—Sunday was seen as the hero who could rescue the nation. Douglas Frank put it best: "Those who loved Billy Sunday best were the millions of evangelical Americans who made him their champion and who counted on him to change the course of history. On this one man's shoulders, in the eyes of many, suddenly fell the formidable task of bringing America back to God and ending a period of disorientation and confusion for God's people. This man would stop the drift toward moral anarchy; he would convince America that it was flirting with God's judgment, and he would point to the way of salvation."[119] Thus, we have Sunday (vaudeville and manliness) and Trump (anti-carnival and manliness).

---

119. Frank, *Less Than Conquerors*, 180.

# Chapter 2—J. Frank Norris
## A Circus of Enemies and a Rhetoric of Perversion

J. Frank Norris, fundamentalist Baptist pastor, was a fierce Texan with an insatiable appetite for a fight and an attraction for making enemies. Norris was "Donald Trump" before there was Donald Trump. Borrowing what Jennifer Mercieca has isolated as Trump's tropological calling tweet—"How Donald"—I apply it to J. Frank Norris. As Sam Hill remarks in a blurb for *God's Rascal*, "The fact that Norris's role ranged from cantankerous to confrontational to criminal makes this investigation into his life and times simply fascinating."[1] The story of J. Frank Norris reads like that of no other preacher. He seems more of a character for inclusion in *Preachers and Misfits, Prophets and Thieves*, by G. Lee Ramsey Jr. But J. Frank Norris is not fiction, he's real and so is his exaggerated personality. One might suppose that Norris is the incarnation of hyperbole. Just when the reader of a Norris biography thinks he can't do or say something more obnoxious, he says it and does it. The same holds true for Donald Trump.

My original inclination for this choice seems whimsical. J. Frank Norris shot and killed a Catholic layperson in his office and was tried and acquitted of murder charges. Donald Trump famously said that he could shoot a man on Fifth Avenue and not lose voters. This unusual beginning became the entrance into a dark and foreboding world of enemies, resentment, revenge, and a "mean-spirited" repertoire cohering into a patterned archive.

Kevin Bauder and Robert Delnay write, "[Fundamentalism] features fools, predators, toadies, hypocrites, power grabbers, and character assassins as well as humble servants, insightful leaders, and heroic warriors."[2] Norris, without doubt or question, belonged to the former group. Hankins says, "Norris is a case study of the worst aspects of fundamentalism."[3]

---

1. Hankins, *God's Rascal*.
2. Bauder and Delnay, *One in Hope and Doctrine*, 14.
3. Taylor, "Goodbye Mr. Chipps."

He would have kept a clinic full of therapists engaged in deducing the maladies of his personality. Hankins reflects on Norris: "I'm convinced he had at least a personality disorder if not outright mental illness."[4] Recall that a number of mental health experts violated professional propriety to diagnose Trump as a handbook example of "narcissistic personality disorder, characterized by grandiosity, an exaggerated sense of self-importance, and a lack of empathy."[5]

When it comes to characters like Norris and Trump, I think that it is more about persona than prose, thus making it imperative to consider ethos, the Aristotelian mode of proof that keeps company with logos and pathos. In the cases of Norris and Trump, form "trumps" content. Controversy begets celebrity and becomes an insatiable appetite for more enemies. Finally, I argue that Norris and Trump developed a hyperbolic sense of masculinity in being outsider-renegades.

Yet having a rhetorical handbook for Norris's tropological tricks doesn't help us know how his mean-spirited, controversial, attack mentality merges into a patterned evaluation. Hankins says that the stereotype of the militant fundamentalist applies to Norris. "He was a rascal. He twisted the truth, sometimes in ways that were outright lies, in order to attack his perceived enemies."[6] Some of the stories are as incredible as the prophet Elisha dispatching she-bears to maul young boys who teased him for being a bald-headed preacher.[7]

While Norris was considered a great preacher, it was his persona that produced the controversy. He was as much a publicity man as a preacher. One critic commented, "He's Barnum with a Bible."[8] Hankins, in an interview says, "With Norris it's always difficult to tell how much he was driven by theological principle and how much by ego. He loved to fight, and he hated the SBC leaders—George Truett, J. M. Dawson, Louie Newton (that's Louie, not Huey the Black Panther), and others. His antics, his fighting spirit, his mean-spiritedness, and his holding of grudges drew large audiences to hear him preach."[9]

Once Norris advertised a sermon title: "Should a prominent Ft. Worth banker buy high priced silk hose for another man's wife?"[10] At church, Nor-

---

4. Taylor, "Goodbye Mr. Chipps."
5. See Gunn, "On Political Perversion," 163.
6. Taylor, "Goodbye Mr. Chipps."
7. 2 Kings 2:24.
8. Nichols, "J. Frank Norris."
9. Taylor, "Goodbye Mr. Chipps."
10. Wax, "Lessons."

ris introduced the sermon: "Ladies and gentlemen, instead of one banker being guilty of buying a silk hose for another man's wife, three have made confessions, and the guilty banker in question has thrown himself on my hands, and asked for the sake of his family, that I withhold his name. I cannot and I will not lift my hand against a man I believe is sincerely penitent and this matter is a closed incident."[11] Did Norris concoct this story for the publicity? Being unable to verify the story, I can't be sure, but he certainly showed the disposition to make up stories to his personal benefit and this story sounds fake. "How Donald!" John Fea argues that "believe me" is Trump's most significant rhetorical signifier. "In a Trump administration our Christian heritage will be cherished, protected, defended—like you've never seen before! Believe me!"[12] Trump says it when he's not telling the truth, in my opinion.

Over the years, Norris consistently refused to listen to his friends' rebukes. Whenever his sensationalistic preaching was challenged, he appealed to his number of converts. When pastor friends warned that his ministry was losing credibility, he no longer believed they were credible critics. He walled himself off from criticism, surrounding himself only with friends who were fans, which sped up his descent into extremism. "How Donald!"

Norris thought everything was about him and did everything he could to make everything about him. A friend listened as [Norris] talked about receiving "hundreds of telegrams from all over the country."[13] His telephone, he said, had not stopped ringing, adding "I think the congregation showed it was still with me and believed in me."[14] It was, in his thinking, all about him. Though his stated goal was to promote the ministry, the effort, like almost everything Norris did, was about him. In a similar vein, President Trump interrupted his own coronavirus press briefing to move from talking about people dying to bragging about being number one on Facebook.

Norris often went out of his way to start the fight. He was always looking for a fight, in a fight, or recovering from a fight. Norris's legal problems were gargantuan: charged with perjury, arson, and murder. He was on trial three times and found innocent three times. The only legal issue that ever stuck was a libel judgment for which he had to pay a modest sum. "How Donald!"

Trump has been in more lawsuits than he can count (more than 3,500) and was impeached twice. Before his election he settled a lawsuit against

---

11. Schepis, *J. Frank Norris*, 63.
12. Fea, *Believe Me*, 14.
13. Wax, "Lessons."
14. Wax, "Lessons."

Trump University for $25 million. When Trump was impeached, the jury, the Republican-controlled Senate, found him innocent as easily as the judge who presided over Norris's trial for arson. The judge in the arson trial publicly claimed, before the trial, that Norris was innocent. Asked if he would order a retrial in case of a conviction, the judge responded, "That matter will not come up. There will not be a conviction."[15] Compare this to remarks made by Senate Majority Leader Mitch McConnell, R-KY, prior to the impeachment process against President Trump: "I'm not an impartial juror. This is a political process. There's not anything judicial about it."[16] Later McConnell predicted, "We will have a largely partisan outcome."[17]

Norris, like Trump, was ruthless with his opponents. Name-calling was a favorite tactic for both. Trump frequently plays amateur psychologist and offers analysis. He labeled Ben Carson, later a member of his cabinet, as "pathological."[18] He claimed Speaker of the House Nancy Pelosi was a very sick woman with mental problems.[19] He referred to Ted Cruz as a "basket case."[20] Trump's labels and nicknames, no matter how vile and reprehensible, stick like Velcro, and the press dutifully reports them and continues to use them.

When faced with critics and protesters, Norris and Trump are identical twins. At a revival in Rochester, New York, Norris was interrupted by protesters. Norris addressed the hecklers himself: "You fellows, let me show you something—something you never saw in your life—a thing I have used in the West." Norris pulled up his sleeve slightly, implying there was a gun beneath it. Norris then asked, "I want to know if there are twenty young men in this audience over 21 and under 30, free, single and white, who are not afraid, and you are willing to stand for God, home and native land—stand up." After about fifty young men stood, Norris instructed them, "I want about a dozen of you who are standing to go up in the gallery to see that these Communists behave themselves. . . . I'm not going to permit this bunch of Communistic Divinity students to come down here and disturb the meeting."[21] "How Donald!" Norris assumed that the agitators were students at the liberal Rochester Divinity School. It is a mystery that Norris never picked a fight with the social gospel father, Walter Rauschenbusch.

15. Hankins, *God's Rascal,* 17.
16. Barrett and Zaslav, "Mitch McConnell."
17. Barrett and Zaslav, "Mitch McConnell."
18. Gass, "With Carson on the Defense."
19. Nelson, "Trump Calls Nancy."
20. Scott, "Trump threatens to sue."
21. Hankins, *God's Rascal,* 145.

The startling parallels between Norris and Donald Trump revolve around the image of being a real fighter. Trump said in his inaugural address, "I will fight for you with every breath in my body."[22] Jerry Falwell, Jr. blasted Republican leaders and suggested that conservatives and Christians should stop electing "nice guys." "They might make great Christian leaders, but the US needs street fighters like @realDonaldTrump at every level of government b/c the liberal fascists Dems are playing for keeps & many Repub leaders are a bunch of wimps!" Falwell wrote on Twitter.[23]

Trump sprinkles his speeches with his "Get Even Gospel." "Don't let people take advantage. Get even. And you know, if nothing else, others will see that and they're going to say, 'You know, I'm going to let Jim Smith or Sarah Malone, I'm going to let them alone because they're tough customers,'" he said.[24] Virgin Group founder Richard Branson said that years ago Donald Trump spent the entirety of a two-hour lunch vowing to "spend the rest of his life destroying five people" who had declined to help him.[25]

## Norris and Legal Problems

Perjury, arson, and murder may serve as rhetorical markers or material metaphors for the entire life of Norris. His unwillingness to tell the truth about people, his tendency to burn down all who opposed him, and his murderous sense of vengeance all combined to define his life. The charges may or may not have been factually true, but perjury, arson, and murder are tropological markers of his ministry of cantankerous, confrontational, in-your-face controversy.

Perjury means to lie under oath in a courtroom. The preponderance of evidence suggests that Norris lied, created false evidence, and made up stories to inflict injury on his enemies. Perjury, as a trope, is a form of injury, with the weapon being the tongue, and the ammunition being rumor, innuendo, gossip, lies, and exaggerations. In Zora Neale Hurston's first novel, *Jonah's Gourd Vine*, there's a preacher named John Pearson. He is a powerful preacher. His preaching scatters fire among the congregation. But there's a worm that eats away at this Jonah's gourd vine of a man. He is dishonest and rotten to the core. His suffering wife, Lucy, chides him that no matter how slick he is, God can still grease him. "God don't eat okra," she says. Then she tells him that all the fancy preaching in the world will not wash away his

22. Ivie, "Trump's Unwitting Prophecy," 712.
23. Yilek, "Jerry Falwell Jr."
24. Schapiro, "Spokesman Defends."
25. Mikkelson, "Did Richard Branson."

sinfulness. "You can't clean yo'self wid you tongue lak uh cat."[26] There seems to have been something of John Pearson in Norris.

No one questioned Norris's preaching ability, but his willingness to play loose with the truth was a puzzle. W. A. Criswell says of Norris: "He could do anything with a crowd. He could have them weeping, he could have them laughing, he could have them do anything, and when you listened to him you just were moved by him. He was a gifted man. . . . But, oh, underneath Frank Norris there were personal attitudes that were diabolical. They were vicious."[27] For example, Norris had a serious conflict with a federal judge named James C. Wilson. Hankins points out, "Norris used the dispute with Judge Wilson to launch into a diatribe against the power of federal judges that was not unlike the criticisms leveled by the modern Religious Right against the United States Supreme Court."[28]

Norris was also tried for arson, in relation to the fire at First Baptist and his home in January 1914. "Whether or not he was guilty of setting the fires, and it is almost impossible to tell by studying the extant evidence, he had beaten the system by going outside acceptable procedures and coming out on top. This style would mark him for the rest of his life. He would be unpredictable simply because most Baptist preachers were predictable. Norris, bored of playing by the rules of the successful local church pastor, made a momentous decision to become a preacher of sensationalism. Hankins says, "He would now play against those who made the rules."[29] "He would align himself with whomever he pleased whenever he pleased. He had committed himself to outsider status, and he would be a populist preacher."[30] He would burn all his bridges to the Southern Baptist Convention and never look back. He would attack professors at the institutions he attended: Baylor University and Southern Baptist Theological Seminary. Donald Trump fought with his own party's leaders like Norris taking on his fellow Southern Baptists. Trump didn't create the fragmentation of the Republican Party that started with the Tea Party in 2010, but he certainly accelerated it. Candidates for the Republican nominee divided into two camps early in the campaign: outsider renegades and establishment members of the party. Reagan, in contrast, had embraced California GOP chairman Dr. Gaylord Parkinson's "Eleventh Commandment: Thou shall not speak ill of other Republicans."[31]

26. Hurston, *Jonah's Gourd Vine*, 129.
27. Hankins, *God's Rascal*, 132.
28. Hankins, *God's Rascal*, 48.
29. Hankins, *God's Rascal*, 18.
30. Hankins, *God's Rascal*, 18.
31. Boyarsky, *The Rise of Ronald Reagan*, 145.

Donald Trump demolished the Eleventh Commandment as much as he played havoc with the actual Ten Commandments. Trump poured gasoline on the fire of fragmentation by starting the name-calling war. Personal, nasty, childish—all of the above. Jeb Bush called Trump the "chaos candidate."[32] He called Trump a "jerk."[33] Trump claimed Cruz's father had something to do with the assassination of President Kennedy. Rick Perry claimed that Trump was a "toxic mix of demagoguery, mean-spiritedness, and nonsense."[34] Trump lashed out, "Perry doesn't understand what the word *demagoguery* means."[35] Trump, for his part, unloaded his negative branding expertise with nicknames: "Little Marco"; "Low Energy Bush"; "Lyin Texas Ted."[36]

## Enemies

The trope of populism that best defines the life of J. Frank Norris is "enemy." Norris thrived on enemies of any kind. "Norris in effect created his own enemies by portraying himself as the defender of orthodoxy and everyone who opposed him personally as an enemy to the faith."[37] Read any study of Norris and note how the warlike rhetoric required to describe his obsession with enemies jumps off the page: "pitted himself," "belligerent threats," "violent and extreme language," "go head to head," "conjure up images of nameless heretics," "single out," "defense lines drawn," "cut them to pieces."

Michael J. Lee, in "The Populist Chameleon," outlines the four major tropes in populist movements: the people, the enemy, the system, and apocalyptic confrontation. "The people's collective fantasy is a narrative of unseating an enemy that has an unyielding commitment to hoarding power and to destruction of 'traditional values.'"[38] The enemy stands in opposition to everything that is important to the people. The enemy is responsible for corrupting a once fair and democratic political and economic system. The corrupted system provides the battleground for the war against good and evil. "Worse still, the structures designed to uphold justice have become too remote, corrupt, or beholden to 'special interests' to yield redress. The

---

32. Team Fix, "5th Republican Debate, Annotated."
33. Quoted in Smith, "Ronald Reagan's rhetorical re-invention."
34. Skinnell, *Faking the News*, 77.
35. Skinnell, *Faking the News*, 77.
36. Hennigan, "All of Donald Trump's Nicknames."
37. Hankins, *God's Rascal*, 25.
38. Lee, "The Populist Chameleon," 359.

system has been corrupted by political chicanery."[39] The people and their enemy are constituted as a symbiotic partnership. At times the people are only identifiable in terms of their enemy.

Evangelicals have been fighting enemies, real and imaginary, for a hundred years, and by now the enemies can be named "Legion."[40] Like the FBI's "Top Ten Most Wanted," evangelicals have a list of "Top Ten Biggest Enemies and Counting." Norris once preached a sermon entitled, "Ten Biggest Sinners in Fort Worth, Names Given." The place was packed for the sermon, and Norris named names and some of the "biggest sinners" were in attendance.

In the 1920s, Norris counted as subversives all Catholics and immigrants. "The result was an extreme form of American nativism that has been a recurring theme in American cultural history."[41] With his nativist ideas in full view, Norris worked hard to help defeat Al Smith in the 1928 presidential election.

Norris, on edge at all times, as if living in a battle zone, was like King Asa, who awakened one morning to discover he was surrounded by "one million Ethiopians."[42] "If Norris opposed someone, he would 'cut them to pieces.'"[43] *The Christian Century* proclaimed Norris "probably the most belligerent fundamentalist now abroad in the land."[44]

After Norris was acquitted in the murder trial, he returned to his pulpit, not in the least deterred by the killing. His church added 2,000 new members that year. In spite of his legal troubles, charges, and trials, people were attracted to him. Here is the "outlaw" leadership model in full bloom.

## Anti-Catholic, Anti-Immigrant, Anti-Whiskey

Norris lumped Catholics, immigrants, and whiskey into one powerful and seemingly invulnerable enemy. As noted, the anti-Catholicism of Norris showed most vividly in his relentless campaign to defeat the Democrat nominee for president in 1928—Al Smith, a Roman Catholic.

---

39. Lee, "The Populist Chameleon," 361.

40. Mark 5:9. "Legion" can serve as metaphor for evangelical convictions about liberals and Democrats.

41. Hankins, *God's Rascal*, 45.

42. 2 Chronicles 14:9: "Zerah the Ethiopian came out against them with an army of a million men and three hundred chariots, and came as far as Mareshah."

43. Hankins, *God's Rascal*, 26.

44. Noted in Hankins, *God's Rascal*, 26.

Even while claiming that "many of my warmest personal friends are Catholic," Norris said no Catholic should be elected to office. "It knows allegiance only to the Pope. They would behead every Protestant preacher and disembowel every Protestant mother. They would burn to ashes every Protestant Church and dynamite every Protestant school. They would destroy our public schools and annihilate every one of our institutions."[45] By 1924, Norris was saying that Roman Catholics could not be real Americans or real white people.[46]

Norris, barely pausing to catch his breath, moved from attacking Catholics to expressing American nativism and Anglo-Saxon superiority. This coupling of Christianity with the nation led to the insistence that this was a war that threatened the existence of the United States. Charles Taylor, in *A Secular Age*, disavows Christendom, which I argue includes much of evangelicalism. I am convinced that much of the evangelical anger is directed at this secular culture and in response to it they have produced a corrupted, secular version of the faith. John Howard Yoder, for example, identified neo-neo-neo-Constantinianism as the "preoccupation of the church to be allied even with post-religious secularism as long as this is popular."[47] Perhaps what we miss in all the variegated attempts to define populism is the word *popular*. Evangelicals still long to be a civilizational order and becoming secular seems to them a small price to pay. The anti-immigrant and nativist stances would be bequeathed to Trump.

In *Unleashing the Bible*, Stanley Hauerwas argues, "It is not surprising that when fundamentalists confronted the developments of higher criticism, they assumed advocates of the latter were not only attacking the Bible but also the United States' identity as a Protestant nation."[48] The values of America were considered the values of evangelicals. As George Marsden observes, "These values, as well as a traditional and biblical Christianity, had to be saved from the delusion of the critics."[49] As a fundamentalist, Norris was part of what George Marsden labeled as "militantly, anti-modernist Protestant evangelicalism,"[50] and Norris was more militant than the rest.

J. Frank Norris set himself against the rest of the churchly world and he did so deliberately with malice and foresight. He was willing to use every detestable, despicable strategy in the rhetorical toolbox of populists,

---

45. Hankins, *God's Rascal*, 51–52.
46. Hankins, *God's Rascal*, 51–52.
47. Yoder, *The Original Revolution*, 144–45.
48. Hauerwas, *Unleashing the Scripture*, 32.
49. Marsden, *Fundamentalism and American Culture*, 220–21.
50. Marsden, *Fundamentalism and American Culture*, 4.

demagogues, and what Plato deemed "evil rhetors."[51] Smith concludes: "Trump is a populist in the paranoid tradition of such aberrations as Joseph McCarthy and Patrick Buchanan [I add Billy Sunday, J. Frank Norris, and Jerry Falwell].... He is a renegade who turned his talent as a con artist into a political juggernaut."[52]

Norris, as senior pastor of two prototypes of the megachurch, at the same time in Detroit and Forth Worth, willingly turned church into circus. In a preview of the church growth movement, Norris seemed intent on proving that you can get people to come to church to see a show whether or not God exists. Such strategies are popular, even successful, but they are nothing more than secularism in church robes. American historian Barry Hankins, in a brilliant study of Norris, says, "He had beaten the system by going outside acceptable procedures and coming out on top."[53] He was the only show in town if you liked the populist style.

Norris, like Trump, "created his own enemies by portraying himself as the defender of orthodoxy and everyone who opposed him as an enemy of the faith."[54] Norris believed his southern culture was threatened by modernism. Norris fabricated so many enemies the impression is given that he made up new enemies on ordinary days when he was bored with the routines of being a Baptist pastor.

Preachers come and go. The issues and the enemies persist. Enemies are passed along to new generations of preachers like the Hatfields and McCoys. New preachers are born and taught to hate the enemies, preachers who will make the same rhetorical choices Norris made when he decided to be a sensationalist. The preachers of his ilk are ubiquitous. Resurgence is the middle name of evangelical faith. They think they can keep repeating the same old arguments long enough, until they will win. As historian Robert McElvaine put it, "Take the method (as they see it, there is only one) and try it. If it fails, deny its failure, and try is again and again . . . and again . . . But, above all, keep trying the same thing."[55]

---

51. Plato, *Gorgias*.
52. Smith, "Ronald Reagan's Re-invention," 147.
53. Hankins, *God's Rascal*, 18.
54. Hankins, *God's Rascal*, 25.
55. McElvaine, *The Great Depression*, 417.

## Rhetorical Implications: The Rhetoric of Perversion

The evaluation of Norris and Trump suggests a rhetorical perversion. In broad terms, perversion suggests departure from accepted norms, and certainly Norris and Trump can be said to have perverted the assumed norms of religion and politics. Neither preacher nor politician played by the rules. Rhetorically, J. Frank Norris employed "the rhetoric of perversion." Perversion, as used here, is not a psychological description. It is not related to calling Norris a "psycho."

Joshua Gunn, in the Introduction to his *Political Perversion*, argues that there are "perniciously perverse rhetorics." Gunn asserts that our political discourse is a kind of "hypermediated chaos" that "innervates conspicuous eruptions of perversity in popular conversations." When crude language is added to this mixture we get a bewildered world that is "both nutty and predictable at the same time." The word Gunn uses to describe this process is *perversion*. "Perversion defines compulsive and excessive character." It "signifies everything from harmless fun to injurious meanness." Perversion, in this sense, culminates as playfulness gone wrong. This has an important relation to my study in that rhetorical perversion "accrues and coheres through repeated statements that are both verbal (speeches, tweets, tone) and visual (looks, body comportment, gesture. Perversion is a label for a habituated manner of relating to others discernible in gestures sustained over time and retrospectively perceived."[56] "Throughout his career, Norris would delight in going one on one with powerful people, especially when it meant his own notoriety would be enhanced."[57]

Trump is the full-grown expression of the rhetorical perversion of Norris. Joshua Gunn asks, "So, what does it mean to say someone is structurally perverse?"[58] Trump seems to know that many of the things he says and does are offensive, but he says and does them anyway. The pervert seems to know what he or she does or says is wrong, but does or says it anyway: "I know well, but all the same . . ."[59] Or as Dow puts it, "Trump's unrestrained discourse and his disturbing lack of traditional presidential qualities were precisely what enabled him to project a persona for his supporters as an outsider to politics, as someone who would not operate as usual. It's not so much what he said, it's that he would say it at all.

---

56. Gunn, "On Political Perversion," 23.
57. Hankins, *God's Rascal*, 11.
58. Gunn, "On Political Perversion," 170.
59. Mannoni, "I Know Well," 71.

Because someone who would flout the rules of decorum so consistently and remain unapologetic about it was someone who would not be cowed by Washington's ways, who would not let propriety keep him from getting things done."[60] As Gunn puts it, "The pervert refuses to accept the normative rules to which everyone else seems to submit like so many suckers, since s/he has an individual system of rules."[61]

Speaking "Norris" or "Trump" is like learning a new language. The perversity is that Norris and Trump murdered the rhetorical principle of ethos—character, ethical judgment. They replaced it with a rhetorical style that features disavowal, mistrust, and contradiction. This suggests a structural perversity that people respond to because they have heard it before (one hundred years of evangelical preaching). The audience is conditioned to enjoy it (a Trump rally is a church gathering), and looks forward to hearing it again. Norris and later Trump shared their jouissance, resentment, and ressentiment with audiences conditioned to believe it. Trump followers are like a country singer crooning an insatiable appetite for more Trump.

Evangelicals have raised generations of Americans who believe what their preachers tell them. They believe everything the government does is horrible, the country is full of enemies determined to destroy America, all politicians are corrupt, Washington is evil. What Randall Balmer labels as "the rhetoric of declension," couched in apocalyptic language of the second coming of Jesus, has been mixed with political and cultural fears. The cultivation of fear, the constant building up of a sense of being afraid, like planting a field of cotton every spring, is a central identifying mark for modern evangelicals, according to John Fea in *Believe Me*. If generations of outlier, outlaw, angry, resentful preachers fill people's minds with this kind of thought, then Donald Trump is not a surprise.

Actor Michael Caine has observed that Superman is the way America sees itself, but Batman is the way the world sees America.[62] I tweak this notion by suggesting that evangelicals perceive Trump as Superman and they perceive the state of the nation as Batman. In the Batman movie, evangelicals see liberals as the Joker. Liberals are essentially anarchist. Evangelicals point to the riots in American cities as evidence for their conclusions. It is a familiar story: An Edenic community is threatened by an extraordinary evil democratic institutions are impotent against; a selfless hero with superhuman powers, renouncing temptations and aided by fate, emerges to carry out this redemptive task; despite tests of faith, his vigilante methods and

---

60. Dow, "Taking Trump Seriously," 138.
61. Gunn, "On Political Perversion," 170.
62. Treat, "How America Learned to Stop."

virtuous violence secures a decisive victory, thus restoring the community to its paradisiacal condition. Trump, in this movie analogy, is more nearly Batman than Superman. Yet this monomyth of the American superhero, a morality tale of secular supersaviors who wield redemptive violence in outlaw crusades against evil, tacitly flirts with antidemocratic values and fascistic zealotry.[63] Today's charismatic hero, ancient leader-myths warn, risks the hubris of becoming tomorrow's tyrannical demagogue. This dance with the dark side of democratic virtue is central to the superhero *mythos*, born of Depression-era anxieties and fascistic fascinations precipitating World War II. America's superheroic choice is clear: benevolent messiah or avenging vigilante, hope or fear . . . Biden or Trump?

In Trump we had a reality television character as president of a dependent electorate, rendered passive by a spectator democracy. Evangelicals pontificate about abortion, gay rights, immigrants, Others, but they are actually spectators. They are watching democracy dismantled for the sheer jouissance of watching the drama unfold. This is a spectator democracy. For all their bluster and horrific rhetoric of declension and wrath, they are passive citizens who believe they are victims of reverse racism. As Slavoj Žižek suggests, our perverse society of enjoyment trades "being the change we want to see in the world" for a *jouissance* in the status quo "freedom of passivity."[64] Evangelicals make a deal with the devil, surrendering personal freedom and collective responsibility for a self-righteous blamelessness. "In return for interpassivity, [they] enjoy deferred guilt and misdirected culpability for their role in social problems and solutions (like racism, poverty, war, torture, and social justice protests at convention hotels)."[65]

"Always waiting for some Batman to save you," Catwoman offered in *Batman Returns*. She was talking to evangelicals, terrorized subjects forced to decide between becoming outlaws or victims for the necessary fictions they live. For now, they have chosen to stick with Donald Trump, their anointed Superman even as they see the nation as a dark Gotham of despair, violence, and hopelessness.

What makes our political predicament perverse is that many people know that the ends do not justify the means, but they do it anyway. People flocked to hear Norris preach and perform his perverse rhetoric; voters elected a perverse rhetorician as president. The perverse rhetoric of Norris and Trump dismantles the meaning of ethos as a critical concept.[66] To say that

63. Jewett and Lawrence, *The Myth of the American Superhero*.
64. Treat, "How America Learned," 105.
65. Treat, "How America Learned," 105.
66. Gunn, "On Political Perversion," 181.

this pair of rhetors may be defined as perverse is to say that "the technique of disavowal is dominant in their discourse and that there is a profound failure to take responsibility for the speech."[67]

Turning their backs on history, evangelicals are unhinged from foundational beliefs and ethics. The postmodern dismissal of truth and mistrust of authority (as if all authority is authoritarianism) has secularized the evangelicals. Gunn argues that we have a photo op displaying the symbolic evaporation of political authority—South Carolina representative Joe Wilson calling President Obama a liar in the middle of a live, nationally televised address. This "marked the explicit boiling over of a heretofore simmering perversion endemic to our politics."[68]

J. Frank Norris and Donald Trump—in style, temperament, ethos—are a matched pair. The attractors for both speakers have more to do with who they were and how they presented themselves than what they actually said. What is more important—the show or the sermon? Norris and Trump represent the perversion of "entertainment" and politics. Before Trump and reality television there were "the artful deceptions of P. T. Barnum, who also ran for office."[69] Before the circus, there was vaudeville. Evangelicals have been imitating the secular culture in methodology since the advent of the revival. Their imitating the message of the secular culture is their new perversion. At times the show is the sermon and the political rally.

Evangelical preachers flood the airwaves with condemnations of feminists, socialists, persons of color, gays, immigrants, liberal politicians. Political ads relentlessly bombard us with the negatives: the other guy is a bum, the other guy should be in jail, the other guy is a pervert. All that enemy-producing, hell-raising preaching, all that apocalyptic rhetoric of declension eventually produced a president who is absolutely anti-government along with a crude and rude army of Christian warriors.

Slavoj Žižek argues that democratic cultures seem to be moving toward a "kind of generalized perversion, a collective identity in which a people are losing faith in a shared authority or law."[70] This is not a suggestion that individuals are becoming clinical perverts, "but rather, that collectively our speech and behavior evinces a perverse structure through a series of disavowals; the government is broken; Congress is dysfunctional; don't trust the science; historians are hiding the true story of America; exogenous

---

67. Gunn, "On Political Perversion, 181.
68. Gunn, "On Political Perversion," 178–79.
69. Gunn, "On Political Perversion, 177.
70. Gunn, "On Political Perversion," 178.

Others are taking our jobs and we are only left with, I've had it."[71] Here is the rejection of an order that one would restore, the evangelical longing for a nonexistent garden of Eden.

Perhaps we should insist that Trump is nothing more than his persona, that the persona and the person are the same—a rhetorical pervert—and there is nothing more to Trump than his disavowals and his destruction, demolition rhetoric and spectacle—and as aids in his creation, we are part of the spectacle as well.

---

71. Gunn, "On Political Perversion," 178.

# Chapter 3—Jerry Falwell, Sr.

## Racism, Revenge, and Television

Jerry Falwell, Sr. represents the return of fundamentalism from the fringe of American culture and politics. The period of time from Sunday, Norris, and the Scopes Trial may be dubbed "the dark ages" for evangelicals or the "wilderness sojourn"—as they survived from the fringe of American Christianity and culture. Jerry Falwell, Sr. signaled the reentry of evangelicalism into the culture's orbit, and he brought with him a culture war. The primary visual trope of Falwell, Sr. is television and the age of televangelism. While outside the parameters of this discussion, the influence of television, especially religious television, is part and parcel of the current state of evangelical faith. The primary rhetorics of Falwell, Sr. are ressentiment and racism. Extra attention will be paid to Falwell's rhetoric of racism because racism is the defining trope of evangelicals.

Trained by the preachers who trained J. Frank Norris, Falwell seems as if he stepped right out of 1925 for his starring role as evangelical leader of the 1970s. Evangelicals, led by Falwell, aligned against civil rights. Howard Fineman, in his *Newsweek* tribute to Jerry Falwell, wrote: "Born with an instinct for showmanship and business, he became a pioneer in the use of broadcast television to expand a ministry."[1] While Billy Sunday's revivals were a version of vaudeville, Jerry Falwell was the advent of televangelism. I argue that evangelicals married television and the couple gave birth to a son, and they named him the "anointed one of God," Donald Trump.

### The Gospel of Getting Even

From the Scopes Trial to the election of Donald Trump as president, fundamentalists and evangelicals (from the 1950s onward) have been stoking the fires of resentment. I draw a straight line between J. Frank Norris and Jerry Falwell to Donald Trump when it comes to the gospel of getting even. J.

---

1. Fineman, "Jerry Falwell's Political Impact."

Frank Norris and Jerry Falwell were two of the most vengeful of the preachers in the family tree of Donald Trump.

## Jerry Falwell Attacks John Killinger

The gospel of "getting even," promoted with such glee by Jerry Falwell and Donald Trump, came full circle when Trump spoke at Liberty University and told the Christian study body that getting even was the gospel. There in the school that Falwell founded, Trump planted the flag of "Get Even" and a university vice president defended it.[2]

Michael Cohen, Trump's lawyer and now a convicted felon, defended Trump's "get even" remarks. He blamed the biased liberal media for ignoring a successful speech and nitpicking about the "get even" remarks. Cohen told ABC News, "I conferred with Johnnie Moore at Liberty University and questioned whether Jesus would 'get even.' The answer is 'he would and he did.' Johnny explained that the Bible is filled with stories of God getting even with his enemies, Jesus got even with the Pharisees, and Christians believe that Jesus even got even with Satan by rising from the dead. God is portrayed as giving grace, but he is also portrayed as one tough character—just as Trump stated."[3] Somewhere Rowan Williams is saying, "Bad religion is about not trusting God," seeing God as "a presence that is at best critical or hostile, always to be outmaneuvered where possible."[4]

## A Case Study in Personal Revenge

When Falwell made an enemy, he would go to any length to exact revenge. One case study encapsulates Falwell's insistence on exploring the width, length, depth, and height of revenge: John Killinger. Killinger served as senior pastor at First Presbyterian Church in Lynchburg, Virginia, Falwell's city. Killinger, more than anyone else, represents the deep animosity and sense of revenge in personal ways that energized Falwell.

Killinger wrote a book about the experience of opposing the Rev. Falwell—*The Other Preacher in Lynchburg*. A major theme of the book is the means Jerry Falwell went to in order to get back at and exact revenge on Dr. Killinger for daring to oppose him. Killinger recalls that he was called "friend of Satan," "emissary of the devil," "Judas in the pulpit," and

---

2. Schapiro, "Spokesman Defends."
3. Falcone, "Donald Trump's Holy War?"
4. Williams, *Tokens of Trust*, 7–8.

numerous other epithets deemed appropriate for anyone who dared to call the great evangelist into question."[5]

Falwell had reasons to dislike John Killinger. In January 1981 Killinger preached a sermon called "Would Jesus Have Appeared on the *Old Time Gospel Hour*?" While Killinger says he wasn't attacking Falwell and that the sermon was meant only for his congregation, no doubt he knew this sermon would have attracted Falwell's attention. In the sermon, Killinger answered the question: "Yes, Jesus would have probably appeared on the *Old Time Gospel Hour*." In fact, Killinger said, Jesus might have said: "You appear to be very righteous, before your television audience. But inside, you are rapacious, unconverted wolves, seeking only a greater share of the evangelical TV market, without really caring for the sheep you devour."[6]

The next Sunday, in his sermon, Falwell did reply: "I don't want to hurt Dr. Killinger, but we don't need him in this town."[7] Falwell, using ad hominem attacks, made his revenge deeply personal. In the weeks that followed Killinger said that his telephone was tapped, he and his family received threatening phone calls, his oldest son's tires were slashed, and a number of revenge-type actions were taken against him and his family.

Killinger continued the "duel of the preachers," "the shoot-out at Lynchburg," with a sermon on March 15, 1981, "Would Jesus Belong to the Moral Majority?" Killinger took direct aim at the Moral Majority: "The tragedy for the church, when it becomes identified with morality, it that it unwittingly broadcasts the opposite of Jesus' message that God receives sinners." To confuse the church with morality is "to establish a new Phariseeism, to enthrone the enemies of Jesus at the center of what we are about."[8] In the sermon, Killinger answered the question of Jesus joining the Moral Majority with a prophetic "No." While Killinger condemned the Moral Majority, he didn't personally attack the character of Falwell. He avoided ad hominem arguments, unlike Falwell.[9]

There were two other persons from First Presbyterian Church that were "thorns in the side" of Falwell: James J. H. Price and William Goodman, professors at Lynchburg College. In a sermon on January 31, 1982, in remarks to his congregation at Thomas Road Baptist Church, Falwell mentioned that Price and Goodman had organized a program at Lynchburg College with an outside speaker addressing "the evils of Jerry Falwell and religious moralists."

---

5. Killinger, *The Other Preacher*, 1.
6. Killinger, *The Other Preacher*, 32.
7. Killinger, *The Other Preacher*, 34.
8. Killinger, *The Other Preacher*, 38.
9. Killinger, *The Other Preacher*, 39.

Falwell then said, "They're mad because the book was a financial fiasco."[10] He made fun of only eighty people showing up for the lecture. For evangelicals, the size of the crowd always denotes success, power, and authority. Similarly, Jennifer Mercieca points out, "Popularity (crowds, opinion polls, ratings, votes) is the only sign of value to Trump."[11]

Falwell, attacking Dr. Price and Dr. Goodman, was really expanding his attack on Killinger. "You know, there's so many wonderful people at First Presbyterian Church who really love God. I happen to know them. Many of them have come to me and apologized to me for their pastor and associate pastor and for their behavior. They really have. We have many of them support us financially in a heavy way. . . . Don't ever think that the people at First Pres share the sentiments of their pastor and their associate pastor. Some . . . really love the Lord and would never waste a penny or a moment of time to criticize another servant of God."[12] And then he added a rhetorical trick: "You know I feel that if you're out winning souls to Christ, building churches, doing the work of the kingdom, we just don't have time to rip at other preachers. That's why you've never heard me in twenty-five and a half years here criticize a preacher of the gospel. And I'm not going to start doing that now."[13]

Here is a primary rhetorical weapon of the resentful. In speech designed to demolish Killinger, Falwell's tirade can be reduced to "I'm not saying it, I'm just saying it."[14] Falwell then criticized Killinger, attempted to pit him against his own congregation, suggesting that members of First Presbyterian were apologizing for Killinger, without a shred of evidence, and even that members of Killinger's church were writing big checks to Falwell. Then he insisted that he never criticized another preacher. Within one paragraph, Falwell made false claims, used a cheap rhetorical trope, and assailed the character of another preacher.

When Killinger moved to Los Angeles to be the pastor of the First Congregational Church, he was invited to be the guest on a nationally syndicated show that had just moved from radio to television. The next day, Jerry Falwell, via telephone, was the guest on the same show. Falwell said there was "absolutely no truth" in any of the allegations Killinger made. He then made up an alternative script, filled with innuendo and idle speculation. "Dr. Killinger left First Presbyterian Church under pressure," Falwell intoned,

10. Killinger, *The Other Preacher*, 128.
11. Mercieca, "A field guide."
12. Killinger, *The Other Preacher*, 128.
13. Killinger, *The Other Preacher*, 128.
14. Mercieca, "A field guide."

"and the people were quite happy when he left. He wrote a very harsh letter to the press when he left, and to the people."[15] Falwell then intimated that Killinger was very bitter. "It's like he had an emotional breakdown. I hope that's not the case." Once again, he employs paralipsis: "I'm not saying he had an emotional breakdown, but it's like he had one." Falwell concludes with a rather pious diatribe: "I'm sorry John's filled with bitterness, and I'm afraid it will affect the success of his ministry there. He failed in Lynchburg and he's setting himself up for a failure here with that kind of bitterness and dishonesty."[16] The fallacious attack of a person's character has long been a staple in evangelical preachers like Falwell and is proudly carried on now by Robert Jeffress and Franklin Graham.

Falwell, unwilling to let go of his need for revenge, followed Killinger to California the way President Trump followed John McCain and Representative John David Dingell, Jr. to the grave. Trump went so far as to imply that Dingell was in hell: "Maybe he's looking up. Maybe, but let's assume he's looking down."[17] President Trump refused to attend the funeral of Representative John Lewis, publicly stating it was because Lewis didn't attend Trump's inauguration. Revenge is the gospel for Trump. Evangelicals back his play.

When Killinger became a professor at Samford University in Birmingham, Alabama, after teaching at the Baptist university for three and one-half years, he went to Oxford for a one-semester leave to finish a book he was writing. While Killinger was in England, Dr. Falwell was a guest speaker at Samford. During a question-and-answer session after Falwell's speech, he was asked about Dr. Killinger's opposition to his ministry during his years in Lynchburg. Falwell's immediate answer was that he didn't understand how a Christian university like Samford could have a man like that on its faculty.[18]

Killinger returned to Samford to discover that the dean had ordered his name and classes deleted from the divinity school computers. He was not given an office in the new building where the seminary was relocating but was assigned an office in the undergraduate department of religion. There seemed no limit to Falwell's insatiable desire to exact revenge on his perceived enemies.

If this was an isolated incident, perhaps it could be viewed as an anomaly, as a exceptional confrontation between two preachers. When,

---

15. Killinger, *The Other Preacher*, 167.
16. Killinger, *The Other Preacher*, 169.
17. Kelly and Malloy, "Trump implies."
18. Killinger, *The Other Preacher*, 185.

however, Jim Bakker accused Falwell of stealing the PTL Club from him, Falwell responded by saying that Bakker "either has a terrible memory, or is very dishonest, or he is emotionally ill."[19] Again, Falwell attacked another minister by suggesting mental illness. Falwell possessed the spirit of Queen Jezebel, who said to Elijah, God's preacher: "So may the gods do to me, and more also, if I do not make your life like the life of one of them by this time tomorrow."[20]

## Rhetorical Trope for Falwell: Ressentiment

Nothing fuels evangelicals and Donald Trump like resentment and its attendant tropes. Communication scholar Casey Ryan Kelly calls this the "rhetoric of ressentiment."[21] Ressentiment is more than revenge. It is a psychological state arising from suppressed feelings of envy and hatred that cannot be acted upon, frequently resulting in some form of self-abasement. Relatedly, evangelicals have, in the words of Randall Balmer, forsaken Christian ethics: "The Religious Right's wholesale embrace of the Republican Party and of Donald J. Trump, both as candidate and as president, has necessitated a rewriting of evangelical ethics."[22]

Getting even is the primary commandment in the Trump gospel. He claims that he likes the verse in the Bible about "an eye for an eye," except that Trump is not a believer in conditional retaliation. He believes in unlimited retaliation, the most ancient and barbaric way humans have ever responded to offenses. Getting even is an exponential experience for Trump. He doesn't believe in an eye for an eye. The enemy has to be hit harder than that. "One of the things you should do in terms of success: If somebody hits you, you've got to hit 'em back five times harder than they ever thought possible. You've got to get even. Get even."[23]

Trump says, "The point is, one of the things I say later is . . . get even. When somebody screws you, you screw them back in spades. And I really mean it. I really mean it. You've gotta hit people hard. And it's not so much for that person. It's [that] other people watch."[24] Trump willingly and deliberately went where no president had ever gone before. He threatened to put Hillary Clinton and her lawyers in prison if he won the election.

19. *LA Times* Archives, "Bakker Shows No Remorse."
20. 1 Kings 19:2.
21. Kelly, "Donald J. Trump and the Rhetoric of *Ressentiment*."
22. Balmer, "Under Trump, America's Religious Right."
23. Corn, "Donald Trump Is Completely Obsessed."
24. Corn, "Donald Trump Is Completely Obsessed."

He tried to smear Judge Gonzalo Curiel, the American-born federal judge hearing a fraud case against Trump University, as a "Mexican" unqualified to preside over this litigation.[25] In 2011, he addressed the National Achievers Congress in Sydney, Australia, to explain how he had achieved his success. He noted there were a couple of lessons not taught in business school that successful people must know. At the top of the list was this piece of advice: "Get even with people. If they screw you, screw them back 10 times as hard. I really believe it."[26]

For Trump, acts of revenge are an essential way for a person to demonstrate he or she is tough. "This isn't your typical business speech. Get even. What this is a real business speech. You know in all fairness to Wharton, I love 'em, but they teach you some stuff that's a lot of bullshit. When you're in business, you get even with people that screw you. And you screw them 15 times harder. And the reason is, the reason is, the reason is, not only, not only, because of the person that you're after, but other people watch what's happening. I really believe in trashing your enemies."[27] Here the Get Even President is also the Profanity President. Trump's "get even" gospel of screw them five, ten, or fifteen times mocks the math of Jesus: "Do not forgive seven times, but, I tell you, forgive seventy times seven times."[28]

Trump's lack of civility, decorum, and decency, along with his belligerent rhetoric, clashes with the higher standards that had nourished evangelicals for centuries. Having wallowed for a time in the sewer of Trump's revenge motif, in the interest of equal time, the words of Jesus deserve a hearing as well. This is an essential part of the argument of this book. Evangelicals, the self-proclaimed people of Jesus, have embraced a man who is the opposite of Jesus and his teachings about revenge, enemies, repentance, and forgiveness. I am arguing that it is the evangelical lust for revenge, even ressentiment, that has driven them to forsake the gospel of their tradition for the unconditional revenge-seeking, retribution-distributing, ressentiment-jouissance mocking president. Trump humiliates, punishes, destroys, and evangelicals murmur, "Amen."

While the resentment is "deep and wide," there's a companion emotion mixed in the evangelical cocktail of affect: feelings easily hurt. The genius of Trump's rhetoric is his ability to sustain the affective charge of animus without forfeiting the moral high ground of victimhood to his

---

25. Corn, "Donald Trump Is Completely Obsessed."
26. Corn, "Donald Trump Is Completely Obsessed."
27. Corn, "Donald Trump Is Completely Obsessed."
28. Matthew 18:22, KJV: "Jesus saith unto him, I say not unto thee, Until seven times: but, Until seventy times seven."

audience's "oppressors"—Democrats, the press, criminals, immigrants, foreign adversaries, welfare recipients, the #MeToo movement, "globalists," and racial Others.[29]

## Resentment

Aristotle found resentment to be an ungovernable emotion—an undeniably negative civic feeling.[30] A cultural assumption underlies the problem with evangelical resentment. These communities have been preoccupied with the harsh struggle to find acceptance, so resentful of perceived mistreatment, that they have been distracted from the work of the church. This resentment has a material focus: The Bible. James McClendon argues that the resentment nested in struggles over the Bible. "In this struggle, Modernists accused fundamentalists of idolatry, and Fundamentalists accused Modernists of unbelief."[31] The resentment left evangelicals prey to ideologies more rooted in Constantinian than Christian principles.

When it comes to evangelicals, "as it was in the beginning, so it is now." Norris finally settled on communism as the enemy du jour. William Bell Riley feared that modernism was assaulting America. William V. Trollinger, in *God's Empire*, in reviewing Riley's work, *The Menace of Modernism,* says that the book is "saturated with Riley's sense of alarm about an American culture in grave danger."[32] The danger of living by the selection of enemies is that something can go awry with the selection process, as when Norris picked Catholics and immigrants as the enemies and engaged in a vicious nativism. The same tragedy afflicted William Bell Riley's 1930's leap into anti-Semitism. When life is war, when enemies populate the landscape, it is a wonder that more evangelicals did not pick the wrong enemies or invent enemies that only lived in the mind.

The enemy is necessary to provide fuel for the flames of resentment. When one enemy loses traction, a larger enemy is selected. When an enemy doesn't translate into political support, a different enemy is selected. In his inaugural address President Trump insisted that foreign terrorists were our sworn enemy. He spoke in the image of war, the language of demolition, with a dark demeanor. He declared the press "the enemy of the American people." Then the Democrats were the enemy. From the beginning of his campaign, immigrants were the enemy. Three plus years later, Trump

29. Schaefer, "Whiteness and civilization."
30. Engels, *The Politics of Resentment*.
31. McClendon, *Ethics*, 25.
32. Trollinger, *God's Empire*, 35.

expanded his enemy to include millions of Americans who were now designated the enemies of the nation simply for opposing him. Now, the people are the enemy of the people.

In a 2020 Fourth of July speech, Trump left no bitter stone unturned: "our nation is witnessing a merciless campaign to wipe out our history, defame our heroes, erase our values, and indoctrinate our children. Angry mobs are trying to tear down statues of our Founders, deface our most sacred memorials, and unleash a wave of violent crime in our cities."[33] These words could have been taken from any of the writings of Falwell, David Barton, or Robert Jeffress. This is evangelical disdain in secular form—the current state of evangelical faith—belief in belief, belief in America, a rampant Gnosticism.

Robert E. Terrill has argued that Trump unburdens his supporters of all social obligations that might otherwise constrain the pursuit of their self-interest.[34] Chief among these obligations are empathy, equality, and other democratic virtues that demand that citizens acknowledge the burdensome legacy of racism that continues to preclude a truly democratic public culture. Such values trample on the Christian virtue of hospitality, but hospitality makes a space for diversity that evangelicals resent as much as anything in the world. These are the fires of resentment, but they only tell part of the story.

## Ressentiment

Anger, rage, malice, and revenge are not sufficient to account for the intensity of Falwell's attacks on Killinger and the culture at large, or for Trump's relentless attacks on almost everyone. Martin Marty said Jerry Falwell and the Moral Majority felt dispossessed by change and felt they had lost control and power, but mostly they felt "left out of everyone else's liberation."[35] There are multiple strands of affects hanging from the evangelical "Christmas" tree. Most of these are affects that burn out quickly like a "pine knot" used as starter wood for a fire. The affect that better describes the emotional content of evangelicals is the French word *ressentiment*. The dictionary definition says ressentiment is a psychological state arising from suppressed feelings of envy and hatred that cannot be acted upon, frequently resulting in some form of self-abasement. Casey Ryan Kelly defines ressentiment as a "condition in which a subject is addled by rage and envy yet

33. Trump, "Remarks by President Trump at South Dakota's."
34. Terrill, "Post-Racial and Post-Ethical Discourse," 504.
35. Coffin, *The Courage to Love*, 5.

remains impotent, subjugated and unable to act on or adequately express frustration."[36] Evangelicals fit the description: self-serving morality, feelings of powerlessness, and ruminations of past injuries. Whereas resentment can be characterized as bitter indignation that one has been treated unfairly, ressentiment is a "self-poisoning of the mind" in which a subject is consumed by emotions and affects such as "revenge, hatred, malice, envy, the impulse to detract, and spite."[37] Søren Kierkegaard suggested that "just as air in a sealed space becomes poisonous, so the imprisonment of reflection develops a culpable ressentiment."[38] Ressentiment functions as an emotional "Energizer bunny" to regenerate the affective charge of revenge.

Evangelicals from 1920 to 2020 have continually reexperienced a memory of the past, an injury, a psychic wound. They sustained ressentiment without forfeiting the moral high ground of being mistreated, unappreciated, and victimized by an array of enemies. They locked in on ruminations of past injuries that made any reconciliation with liberals and the culture unredeemable.[39] Evidence of the omnipresence of the ressentiment can be heard in the words of Ken Ham at the dedication ceremony for his Creation Museum. Ham spoke of repairing the damage done to Christianity by Clarence Darrow, and the humiliation of it all. "It was the first time the Bible was ridiculed in the media in America," Ham intoned to his audience. "We are going to undo all of that here at the Creation Museum. We are going to answer the questions Bryan wasn't prepared to and show that belief in every word of the Bible can be defended by modern science."[40]

Nursing past slights and injuries becomes almost as crucial to evangelical angst as enemies. Trump's campaign slogan "Make America Great Again" presumes an injury that requires restoration to an imaginary, indeterminate time in which evangelicals were putatively whole—"the toast of the town," so to speak. The problem is that such a time never existed and the rhetoric of ressentiment is melancholic in its continually revisiting past injuries but never successfully mourning them. Evangelicals are locked in the stage of grief known as anger, as they compulsively reexperience the past as if it were happening now. Trump invites them to indulge in this fantasy, but as Barbara A. Biesecker argues, melancholia stages "the loss of an impossible object, ideal, or relation that the subject never had." The melancholy of revisiting past injuries offers a sad picture of a group of men sitting in a bar,

36. Kelly, "Donald J. Trump and the Rhetoric of *Ressentiment*," 2.
37. Scheler, *Ressentiment*, 25.
38. Kierkegaard, *The Present Age*, 20–21.
39. Brown, *States of Injury*.
40. Stephens and Giberson, *The Anointed*, 26.

nursing Bud Lites and revisiting past defeats, one after another, but with no adequate method for mourning them. They are frozen in time and unable to move forward as they compulsively revisit past injuries as if they were happening in the present. Trump takes his audience "back to the future" to ruminate on past injuries and idealize an indeterminate time when they were revered as God's holy people rather than reviled. The con that Trump pulls is that, for all this melancholy, the loss of paradise is a paradise that has never existed. Trump's "Again" is a lie, a conduit to an America that evangelicals never controlled and is merely a constitutive fantasy of the nation's "greatness." Instead of gratification, success, or reconciliation with the past, evangelicals only get more trauma.

This has to be a tough pill to swallow because it is trauma over an object never lost. It's like an evangelical is sitting in the waiting room of the emergency department of the local hospital, weeping over a loved one that is not even a patient. Or evangelicals seem like a character from a country song as she waits at the train for a lover who is never coming. A sense of loss pervades the spirit of country music as it does evangelicalism, hanging over their heads like moss on the trees at a country cemetery.

The underlying deep well of ressentiment in the evangelical memory dates at least from the Scopes Monkey Trial. Clarence Darrow eviscerated William Jennings Bryan on the witness stand. H. L. Mencken painted fundamentalists as backward, ignorant, and gullible hillbillies—images that persist to the present. Harry Emerson Fosdick, in a later sermon, "Shall the Fundamentalists Win?," reduced them to a tribe of narrow-minded, irrational, religious fanatics. The liberals and the press have been piling on this caricature from that moment forward. While the caricature was and remains unfair and doesn't present a fair picture of fundamentalists or evangelicals, it remains the dominant picture.

William Trollinger, in a telling critique, argues that the fundamentalists "deeply resented the modernists, not simply because they held heretical ideas or even because they threatened America," but because they "arrogantly designated themselves the 'solitary progressives of the hour,' the men 'who really think.'"[41] This intellectual chip on the shoulder cut deep. William Bell Riley observed that conservative ministers had "about as good a chance to be heard in a Turkish harem as to be invited to speak within the precincts of a modern State university."[42] This feeling of being slighted, left out, being considered unintelligent, may not have been the heart of the fundamentalist movement, but it definitely raised the temperature of resentment.

41. Trollinger, *God's Empire*, 35.
42. Trollinger, *God's Empire*, 35.

Trump also tapped into an audience of angry yet noble sufferers—the forgotten, the downtrodden, the discarded, and the subjugated. He declared with fiery incredulity: "Every day I wake up determined to deliver for the people I have met all across this nation that have been neglected, ignored, and abandoned. I have visited the laid-off factory workers, and the communities crushed by our horrible and unfair trade deals. These are the forgotten men and women of our country. People who work hard but no longer have a voice. I am your voice!"[43]

As Johnson, Ott and Dickinson, and Terrill have illustrated, Trump's demagoguery targets white Americans who feel victimized by their impending displacement as the nation's demographic majority. Trump's imagined audience is angry. They are angry because they suffer. They suffer because they are powerless. They are powerless because they are virtuous.[44] The country, they are told, has been unfairly taken from them. Part of Trump's rhetorical genius is that he has tapped into an electorate already accustomed to perverse norms. It is not simply that Trump intones resentment and rage but that he invites his audience to see themselves as powerless and incapable of adequately expressing their own frustrations. Trump steps forward to offer himself as the one who will "fight this Philistine."[45]

Trump's indulgence in cruelty, revenge, and victimhood are in sync with the melodramatic norms of evangelical revivalism, the vitriolic rhetoric of fundamentalism, and the sizzle of reality television. As Ott argues, Trump's manner of address, particularly his appeals to white rage, are well-suited to mediums that engender impulsivity, simplicity, narcissism, and incivility.[46]

A Trump rally serves as the recharging station for the ressentiment of his supporters. President Trump's post-election rallies are spectacular, emotionally charged events. Large arenas and jubilant crowds recreate the atmosphere of a rock concert, a wrestling match, music festival, or freewheeling megachurch service. Enthusiastic supporters don all manner of Trump-themed merchandise and clothing items, including the "Make America Great Again" red trucker-style hats. Observing one Trump rally makes any rhetorician nervous with memories of Plato's critique of rhetoric as merely a speaker's knack for creating pleasing appearances, capitalizing on mercurial emotions, and playing the demagogue armed with neither knowledge nor concern for truth.

43. Trump, "Full Text."
44. Ott, "The Age of Twitter," 63.
45. 1 Samuel 17:32.
46. Ott, "The Age of Twitter," 63.

Trump transforms the rally into nearly inexhaustible rhetorical resources. With the rally conducted as a secular church service, Trump and his supporters gleefully participate in enjoying one another enjoying cruelty by mocking, insulting, and degrading others. The oddity of evangelicals enjoying cruelty gives pause even to a fellow believer, yet there appears to be a deep well of the joy of cruelty. Three transgender persons were recently physically attacked in Los Angeles. People stood by, watched, and make videos, but no one offered to help. Los Angeles city councilman, Mitch Farrell: "When I saw the video, like anyone who has seen it who believes in human decency, to see this level of violence celebrated gleefully, so much so that the perpetrator himself posted on social media, is like a sucker punch to all of us who believe in civilized behavior."[47]

Trump supporters have even devised litanies to enhance the cruelty: "Lock her up!" "Send her back!" Prior to the 2020 Tulsa rally Jeff Sharlet wrote, "Trump's rallies—a bizarre mishmash of numerology, tweetology, and white supremacy—are the rituals by which he stamps his name on the American dream. As he prepares to resume them for the first time in months, his followers are ready to receive."[48] A Trump rally is a full-scale assault on the progressive expansions of public morality by an all-out debasement of civic virtue.

One of the defining moments of every Trump rally is his vicious attack on the media. Creating the look of a war crimes trial, the media is ensconced in a metal cage on the arena floor. Trump, now a prosecuting attorney, turns his full-orbed scorn directly at the press. Nothing is more bizarre than Trump's relationship with the press, a veritable love/hate show. He claims that the press will never give him his fair due. They are a relentless enemy that victimizes him and his followers. They're "very bad people" and "scum" and "liars." "Look at them!" he cries, pointing. His thousands turn to the cage to scream hatred, curses, and threats. A popular T-shirt at rallies: "Rope. Tree. Journalist. Some assembly required." The lynching concept feels more real than metaphorical at this point. Trump eggs on the crowd. "Does *anybody* think the media is honest?" "No!" they cry. "Does anybody think they're totally corrupt and dishonest?" "Yes!" they cry.[49] The drama reaches a moment of decision. The crowd seems poised to attack the metal cage, drag the journalists into the arena, and hang them all. The words of Ta-Nehisi Coates seem eerily connected: "The salt-of-the-earth Americans whom we lionize in our culture and politics

---

47. Farell, "L. A. Officials."
48. Sharlet, "'He's the Chosen One.'"
49. Sharlet, "'He's the Chosen One.'"

are not so different from those same Americans who grin back at us in lynching photos."[50] It doesn't take much imagination to hear Trump addressing a crowd gathering to watch a lynching as Sunday afternoon gospel singing, picnic, and the hanging of a man.

The staging of Trump's pain, to use Claire Sisco King's words, constitutes a "restaging traumatic loss so that catastrophe may be refigured as redemption, renewal, and rebirth."[51] In other words, Trump reconfigures suffering and victimhood as exemplars of virtuous leadership and the performance of which entitles him and his supporters to something more grandiose than their present circumstances. Trump went so far as to claim that he is treated worse than President Lincoln: "Although they do say Abraham Lincoln was treated really badly. I must say that's the one. If you can believe it, Abraham Lincoln was treated supposedly very badly. But nobody's been treated badly like me."[52] Speaking at the White House to attendees at Turning Point USA's Young Black Leadership Summit, Trump concluded his official remarks with a series of off-the-cuff and out-of-place statements that are characteristic of his political free verse. Most strikingly, he told the group, "We all get attacked . . . Who gets attacked more than me? . . . I can do the greatest thing for our country, and on the networks, it will play bad."[53]

Simply put, Trump claims, "[p]eople that treat us badly, we treat them much worse than they could ever imagine. That's the way it has to be. That's the way it has to be."[54] At his rallies, Trump typically meanders through a list of enemies—old and new—and chains out fantasies of retribution. But the revenge he calls for need not serve a particular end. Marina Levina says, "What makes Trump cruel is the affective joy with which he performs his policies, speeches, and tweets."[55] *USA Today* describes Trump's cruelty as "basically a 71-year-old kid cackling in delight as he melts ants under his magnifying glass."[56] That weird excitement is exactly the joy of cruelty. "Trump offers his audience an emotional-moral framework in which feelings and affects such as anger, rage, malice, and revenge are never at rest and no one act of vengeance can dissipate the nation's desire for more."[57]

---

50. Coates, "The First White President."
51. King, "It Cuts Both Ways," 6.
52. Kelly, "Donald J. Trump and the Rhetoric of *Ressentiment*," 9.
53. Bennett, "White House Black Leadership."
54. Trump, "Remarks by President Trump at the Conservative."
55. Levina, "Whiteness and the Joys of Cruelty," 77.
56. Levina, "Whiteness and the Joys of Cruelty," 77.
57. Kelly, "Donald J. Trump and the Rhetoric of *Ressentiment*," 3.

In the view of Trump and his supporters they are entitled to ressentiment; it is simply morally correct: cruelty is for its own sake. In addition, the liberal enemies are perceived as deserving cruelty as surely as slaves were deemed worthy of punishment. Affectively, Trump paints a picture of liberals as bodies to which cruelty should stick. This is Sara Ahmed's concept of "stickiness,"[58] in which she says that affects are determined by their attachments. Ahmed uses "stickiness" to explain how affects are felt by the body in concrete and material ways. During the last years, for example, a sense of shame has "stuck" to the bodies and minds of evangelicals. They have felt shamed by the civil public morality that accepted abortion as the law of the land and legalized gay marriage. "What all affect theories share is a commitment to looking at subjects not as self-ruled calculating machines, but as bodies mobilized by the unruly matrix of dense affects working their way through us."[59] Lawrence Grossberg writes that affect "encompasses a variety of ways in which we 'feel' the world in our experience."[60]

Even though "we live in an increasingly saturated shame panopticon,"[61] Donald Trump has marshalled rhetorical strategies that free his followers from the pedagogy of liberal shame. They are able to repudiate shame altogether and ignore the moral demands of the new public morality. Trump turned "political correctness" into a sweeping masterwork of shame, attacked it as if it were demonic, and released his followers from its grip. In other words, shame no longer possessed its "stickiness." Like dried-out glue, it no longer adhered to bodies and minds.

A Trump rally crowd, feeling good and feeling free, knows that their cruelty will stick to various Others—immigrants, Muslims, radical Democrats, congresswomen of color.

Marina Levina, writing about experiencing cruelty as a Jewish child in Russia, says that she was beaten by fellow students as teachers watched. She would sit in class with blood running down her face. She hid the wounds from her parents, for there was nothing they could have done to stop this. In a moving passage she relates, "Even now, 30 years later, my body still bears scars, which as Sara Ahmed astutely writes, 'reminds us that recovering from injustice cannot be about covering over the injuries, which are affects of that injustice, signs of an unjust contact between our bodies and others.'" She then adds, "But as I think back to my childhood tormentors, I do not think of them as sad, or disempowered, or ugly. . . .

---

58. Ahmed, *The Cultural Politics of Emotion*, 202.
59. Schaefer, "Whiteness and civilization," 2.
60. Grossberg, *Under the Cover of Chaos*, 11.
61. Grossberg, *Under the Cover of Chaos*, 11.

I know that being cruel brought them joy—the glint in the eyes, the straightening of the posture, the smirk—the joy of the oppressor is what makes cruelty so effective as a tool of oppression."[62]

Evangelicals are convinced that they are being Christian; they are also convinced that Democrats are not being Christian. Evangelicals are supporting a man sent by God, "God's man in the White House,"[63] to rough up the liberals, save America, and give them the life they so richly deserve for being God's persecuted minority. In short, they have completely accepted Trump's rhetorical trick of turning the vices of revenge, anger, and resentment into virtues. Writing for *The Atlantic*, Adam Serwer reflects upon photographs of lynch mobs: "Their names have mostly been lost to time. But these grinning men were someone's brother, son, husband, father. They were human beings, people who took immense pleasure in the utter cruelty of torturing others to death—and were so proud of doing so that they posed for photographs with their handiwork, jostling to ensure they caught the eye of the lens, so that the world would know they'd been there. Their cruelty made them feel good, it made them feel proud, it made them feel happy. And it made them feel closer to one another."[64] The crowd enjoys the lynching with one another. Their shared laughter at the suffering of others is an adhesive that binds them to one another, and to Trump.[65] There's a descriptive word for this affect: *jouissance*. Somewhere "on the wide spectrum between adolescent teasing and the smiling white men in the lynching photographs are the Trump supporters whose community is built by rejoicing in the anguish of those they see as unlike them, who have found in their shared cruelty an answer to the loneliness and atomization of modern life. Trump shares this jouissance with his followers at his rallies."[66]

Hannah Arendt, in her important work on totalitarianism, spoke of the post-World War II authors and intellectuals for whom "violence, power, cruelty, were the supreme capacities of men who have definitely lost their place in the universe. . . . They were satisfied with blind partisanship in anything that respectable society had banned . . . and they elevated cruelty to a major virtue because it contradicted society's humanitarian and liberal hypocrisy."[67] Evangelicals should smile here because this is their portrait Arendt has taken. In fact, a Trump rally is a cruelty revival. Like the "good

62. Levina, "Whiteness and the Joy of Cruelty," 75–76.
63. Beverley, *God's Man in the White House*.
64. Serwer, "The Cruelty Is the Point."
65. Serwer, "The Cruelty Is the Point."
66. Serwer, "The Cruelty Is the Point."
67. Arendt, *The Origins of Totalitarianism*, 330–31.

guy" destroying the "evil guy" in professional wrestling, Trump destroys his enemies and his crowds are weirdly excited about it.

This is who they really are and this is who they were before Trump mobilized them. Trump is Pat Robertson without the religious veneer. He is Jerry Falwell without the veneer of morality. He is a "pure-dee" secular evangelist. He is a preacher with a perverted rhetoric, and a gospel of ressentiment. There's no floppy calf-leather Bible in his hand, but all the other attributes of evangelist/revivalist/televangelist are evident as Trump sneers, stares, pokes at the air, mocks, insults, and speaks with absolute certainty as if he were speaking the word of God.

Even as they dreamed of giving Trump a second term, evangelicals were acutely aware that *Roe vs. Wade* was still the law of the land, that gay marriage was legal, that the nation was not "returning to God." The Supreme Court has not passed down new rulings opening the classrooms of America's schools to Jesus prayers, or the teaching of intelligent design. Imagining what would energize evangelicals if all their dreams came true leaves one pulling ideas out of the air.

The present ressentiment of evangelicals reveals the inability to craft democratic institutions through exclusionary moral codes, unchanging universals, and a stubborn resistance to the gifts God has given through scholarship, science, and a secular culture. In short, evangelicals failed to account for the onslaught of secularism. The glee with which they have greeted the decline of mainline denominations is simply the "canary" in the deep shaft mine of culture. The same secularity comes for evangelicals as well.

Jerry Falwell, with assists from a plethora of preachers, started the nation down the slippery slide of ressentiment; Trump has turned it into a veritable theme park of slippery slides. His lust for ressentiment, his joy in cruelty, is their joy. Evangelicals seem to have been confused about the slippery slide; it wasn't loose morals; it was secularism that was the slide.

Friedrich Nietzsche said that ressentiment reverses the virtues of good and evil. When evangelicals are unwilling to live up to the moral development of racial and sexual equality, for example, ressentiment allows them a reactive and inverted sense of virtue. For those afflicted by this strange inversion, Nietzsche argues, "the wretched alone are the good; the suffering, deprived, sick, ugly alone are pious, alone are blessed by God, blessedness is for them alone—and you the powerful and noble are on the contrary the evil, the cruel, the lustful, the insatiable, the godless of all eternity."[68] It is an odd revelation when a Nietzsche appellation looks like a portrait of smiling evangelicals in the Oval Office laying hands on Trump.

---

68. Nietzsche, *On the Genealogy of Morals*, 17.

Ressentiment arises because evangelicals believe they are deprived of "religious liberty," and therefore they are "feeling unfree" to act out their hateful and discriminating rhetoric. They tend to see injurious intentions in all kinds of perfectly innocent actions and remarks of others. A baker is incensed when he is fined for not baking a wedding cake for a gay couple. Preachers, even though no one would ever ask them, pretend that they will be thrown in prison for refusing to conduct a gay wedding. "Great touchiness is indeed frequently a symptom of a vengeful character."[69] Evangelicals then experience frustration because they are denied the growing pleasure afforded by invective.[70]

Wendy Brown suggests that such ruminations forge identities that make the past necessarily unredeemable.[71] There's no identity possible between white evangelicals and the actual victims of history. Their cries of oppression and mistreatment ring hollow, as mere echoes of the actual cries from Exodus: "The Israelites groaned under their slavery, and cried out. Out of the slavery their cry for help rose up to God. God heard their groaning, and God remembered his covenant with Abraham, Isaac, and Jacob. God looked upon the Israelites, and God took notice of them."[72] Evangelical efforts to position white men as victims eliminates the fleshly distinction between the injustices beaten into the bodies of Others over the centuries. White men are simply allowed to maintain hegemony with impunity and demonstrate just how much injustice they can perpetuate without moral agony.[73] When asked to show the scars from the whips, the rope burns in the necks, and the blood from the batterings, white people have only "feelings" to show. The claim of punishments they have never experienced lacks the ring of truth.

President Trump and his followers continue to advance invective, insults, negation, detraction, deception, and division in selling his agenda to the nation. Maureen Dowd of the *New York Times* asked Trump during the 2016 campaign why he was ratcheting up his racist bile. Trump thought about it and answered honestly: "I guess because of the fact that I immediately went to No. 1, and I said, 'Why don't I just keep the same thing going?'"[74]

---

69. Scheler, *Ressentiment*, 27.
70. Scheler, *Ressentiment*, 29
71. Brown, *States of Injury*.
72. Exodus 2:23–25.
73. Kimmel, *Angry White Men*, 114.
74. Dowd, "Joe's Fearsome Weapon."

Denise M. Bostdorff argues that while Trump does not offer coherent arguments he does provide an intelligible emotional framework for his supporters that is both attuned to these shifts in the affective environment as well as the ways his audience is to remain in a state of perpetual anger.[75] Evangelicals now have to account for their support of an affect—ressentiment—that represents their faith as its most demeaning caricature: self-serving, emotionally overwrought, and unconcerned with truth or ethics.

Ironically, evangelicals are acting out in order to stem the flow of public morality. Kelly argues, "As ressentiment nests itself into public life its effect is to interrupt, if not reverse, the continued evolution of public morality. Ressentiment does so by inverting the civic good so as to privilege negative emotions such as jealousy and envy that tear at the fabric of moral systems designed to protect against the selfish maximization of self-interest."[76]

Jerry Falwell epitomized ressentiment. "By turns gracious and crude, Falwell was a maddening combination of worthy, lofty ambition—and mean-spirited, uncaring ignorance. His viciousness was well-documented: he said the anti-Christ was a Jew—and was probably alive now. He said 9/11 was the fault of the sin of gays and lesbians. He was always the guy from across the tracks. Democrats were ungodly. The list went on and on and on. He craved acceptance, which he never quite got outside of the world he created for himself and his flock."[77]

It has long been an axiom among certain Christian writers and thinkers that while evangelical faith endangers the democracy and the other churches in the immediate sense, the larger threat is to evangelicals themselves, the shared country, and even the whole world. There is an impulse to blanch at this sort of grandiosity. When Stanley Hauerwas claims that the church is highly compromised and that God is killing the church or James Baldwin claims that we "have brought humanity to the edge of oblivion: because they think they are white," the instinct is to cry exaggeration.[78] But there really is no other way to read the presidency of Donald Trump. The first white evangelical president in American history is also the most dangerous president—and he is made more dangerous still by the fact that those charged with analyzing him cannot control him or hold him accountable because they are invested in his invitation to ressentiment. These are not stupid people, but angry, dangerous people as

---

75. Bostdorff, "Obama, Trump, and Reflections," 698–700.
76. Kelly, "Donald J. Trump and the Rhetoric of *Ressentiment*," 2.
77. Fineman, "Jerry Falwell's Political Impact."
78. See Hauerwas, *In Good Company*, 39; and Baldwin, "On being white."

they trample up and down the country seeking those they may devour and make converts twice the children of hell.

## Jerry Falwell, Sr.: Racism in Evangelicalism

The other defining rhetoric of evangelicals, and, again, in particular Jerry Falwell, Sr., is a commitment to racism. For evangelicals, racism remains a founding principle. While evangelicals swear they are not racists, the denials can't stand up to historical or contemporary investigation. Coates says "Certainly not every Trump voter is a white supremacist, just as not every white person in the Jim Crow South was a white supremacist. But every Trump voter felt it acceptable to hand the fate of the country over to one."[79]

For example, Falwell started Lynchburg Christian Academy in 1967, when his town's public schools integrated. Because *Brown vs. The Board of Education* did not apply to private schools, institutions like Falwell's could practice segregation while still receiving federal tax benefits. But all of this changed with the series of Supreme Court decisions in the late 1960s and early 1970s that forced public schools to integrate and declared racially discriminatory private schools ineligible for tax-exempt status.

These students are shaped by Christian school curricula that purport to teach "traditional values." Randall Balmer, a historian of religion at Dartmouth College and author of *The Making of Evangelicalism*, said many popular textbooks used in Christian schools teach American history in ways that privilege white culture. For example, the books often downplay the displacement of Native Americans or minimize slavery by noting its "positive effects," such as introducing slaves to Christianity.

On his evangelistic program *The Old Time Gospel Hour* in the mid-1960s, Falwell regularly featured segregationist politicians such as Lester Maddox and George Wallace. About Martin Luther King, Jr., he said: "I do question the sincerity and nonviolent intentions of some civil rights leaders such as Dr. Martin Luther King Jr., Mr. James Farmer, and others, who are known to have left-wing associations."[80] In speaking of the *Brown v. Board of Education* ruling, he said, in 1958: "If Chief Justice Warren and his associates had known God's word and had desired to do the Lord's will, I am quite confident that the 1954 decision would never have been made. The facilities should be separate. When God has drawn a line of distinction, we should not attempt to cross that line."[81]

79. Coates, "The First White President."
80. Washington, ed., *A Testament of Hope*, xiv–xv.
81. Blumenthall, "Agent of Intolerance."

Falwell's sermons show "a pattern of racism, anti-Semitism and general intolerance."[82] Dr. James J. H. Price, a religion professor at Lynchburg College, says, "Falwell tells us he is leading a moral crusade, yet he lies. He misrepresents some of the basic tenets of Christianity."[83] What Jerry Falwell used his political capital for was to protest the rescission of tax-exempt status at Bob Jones University and other "segregation academies." In a meeting in Lynchburg about the opening of Falwell's school, Falwell was asked by a local minister, "Will you admit Negroes?" Falwell finally answered, "No." His reason was the certain expedients were necessary for a strategy of successful preaching of the gospel in Lynchburg.[84]

Falwell, in a March 1965 sermon, "Ministers and Marches," evaded the subject of segregation, but took direct aim at civil rights leaders, especially pastors: "Does the Church have any command from God to involve itself in marches such as many ministers are doing today in the name of civil rights reforms? No."[85] In another sermon, Falwell, Sr. made an inexplicable analogy: "There are almost as many alcoholics as there are negroes."[86] Perhaps unwittingly, Falwell tied together two major evangelical tropes: fighting alcohol and civil rights. Falwell also charged Martin Luther King, Jr. and James Farmer with having "left-wing associations and questioned their sincerity and non-violent intentions."[87] In other words, the issue was still race.

Randall Balmer traces the evangelical's dark side of racism in "Under Trump, Evangelicals Show their True Racist Colors." Balmer, researching the origins of evangelical political involvement, notes that the usual explanation is that the issue of abortion was the start of the movement. Balmer argues, "That argument collapses, however, on historical examination."[88] "The religious right was never about the advancement of biblical values. The modern, politically conservative evangelical movement we know is a movement rooted in the perpetuation of racial segregation, and its affiliation with the hard-right fringes of the conservative movement in the late 1970s produced a mutant form of evangelicalism inconsistent with the best traditions of evangelicalism itself. . . . The 2016 election, coupled with the religious right's

---

82. Clifford, "His Critics Speak Out."
83. Clifford, "His Critics Speak Out."
84. Killinger, *The Other Preacher*, 72.
85. Goodman and Price, *Jerry Falwell*, 119.
86. Goodman and Price, *Jerry Falwell*, 121.
87. Goodman and Price, *Jerry Falwell*, 121.
88. Balmer, "Under Trump, Evangelicals Show Their True Colors."

anemic response to racism and white supremacy, suggests that this once proud and noble tradition is morally bankrupt."[89]

For evangelicals still clinging to racist ideas, Trump is an obvious choice: His racially and ethnically charged rhetoric has included assaults on everyone from Latinos to Muslims. Likewise, Trump, along with Senator Ted Cruz (Texas) and other Republicans, has condemned and even ridiculed those agitating for racial justice. The billionaire criticized Senator Bernie Sanders (Vermont) for allowing Black Lives Matter protesters to commandeer one of his campaign events, and suggested that a Black Lives Matter protester at one of his own rallies should be "roughed up." Trump mocked Senator Romney for marching with the protesters over the killing of George Floyd and saying, "Black lives matter."[90] Although lacking almost any trace of detectable faith, Trump has tapped into latent evangelical racism.

Donald Trump's political career began in advocacy of birtherism. Of course, birtherism merely repeats the old trope that Black people are not fit to be citizens of the nation they built. They were not even considered equal at the starting gate, only three-fifths of a person. Trump's ideology is white supremacy, in all its devastating, sanctimonious power. In Donald Trump, evangelicals see one of their own. Dr. Jeffress says, "He is my friend." Falwell, Jr. says, "He's our dream president."

Racism for Donald Trump represents not a symbolic or metaphorical idea, but is the very core of his power and influence. "It is often said that Trump has no real ideology, which is not true—his ideology is white supremacy, in all its truculent and sanctimonious power."[91] Trump's commitment to racism, which he denies, is exceeded only by the depth of evangelical commitment to Trump. The con game being played is that Trump is merely the backlash against contempt of working-class white people. No one in on the con can see that Trump's presidency depends upon an entire whiteness. Racism remains at the heart of the nation's political life as it remains at the center of evangelical faith.

For example, when David Duke ran for governor of Louisiana, he received more than 40 percent of the vote, and he was a former leader of the KKK and a Holocaust denier. A telling quote from a David Duke supporter during the campaign: "What you don't know is that we don't care. What we do care about is the way every city in this country is being reduced to ghettos because of the black race here in this country.... We know about his past, we know about Louisiana's future, we know he doesn't care for Negroes, we

---

89. Balmer, "Under Trump, Evangelicals Show Their True Colors."
90. See Bradner, "Trump"; and Croucher, "Donald Trump Mocks."
91. Coates, "The First White President."

know he doesn't get along with the Legislature and, just maybe, we like it!"[92] Evangelicals now express these same sentiments in support of Trump.

"Trump moved racism from the euphemistic and plausibly deniable to the overt and freely claimed,"[93] writes Coates. The patina of decency built up in the years since the passage of the Civil Rights Act proved easily scrapped away by an overt invocation of bigotry. Evangelicalism was about racism and remains racist. Trump simply pushes the limits of seeing just how much a demagogue can get away with.

## Gnostics Midwife of Racism, Church as Incubator

Jerry Falwell, Sr. and evangelical racism have ancient roots. How we became a culture willing to accept examples of blatant racism is a tortured narrative. The sheer attempt to write a history of racism would take more than a lifetime. Here are a series of historical snapshots intended to show the deep connections of evangelicals to a particularly noxious strand of Christianity. The lived system of race and white supremacy in the United States stretches back to second-century Gnosticism, European colonization of the land swiftly followed by genocidal attacks on indigenous people and enslavement of African peoples—periods in which white ideologies around race were clear and transparent—to the Jim Crow era, which ensured that racial inequalities still remain embedded in social, political, economic, and cultural institutions of today; to the civil rights era, which won landmark legislation, Supreme Court victories, and real advances in Black representation in political life.[94]

J. Kameron Carter, in *Race: A Theological Account*, argues that Christianity served as the incubator or inventor of racism. He asserts that racism is a metaphorical construct, a creation of a new reality designed to give "whiteness" power and permission to subjugate persons of color. "The war that is going on beneath order and peace, the war that undermines our society and divides it in a binary mode is, basically, a race war . . . [one in which the ] social body is articulated around two races."[95]

Christian theology and its variants created the racialized world in which we live. "Modernity's racial imagination has its genesis in the

---

92. Jamieson, *Dirty Politics*, 91.
93. Coates, "The First White President."
94. Lawson, "Introduction," xv–xxxviii.
95. Carter, *Race*, 4.

theological problem of Christianity's quest to sever itself from its Jewish roots."[96] Two related steps made this our racial reality. "First, Jews were cast as a race group in contrast to[97] Western Christians . . . who were also subtly and simultaneously cast as a race group. . . . In this way, Western culture began to articulate itself as Christian culture (and vice versa) . . . through the medium of racial imagination."[98] Second, once Western Christians had racialized Jews in this way, they then deemed Jews inferior to the peoples, cultures, and Christians of the West. "Hence, the *racial imagination* (the first step) proved as well to be a *racist imagination* of white supremacy (the second step)." Third, this racialized and racist worldview infused the Western and Christian social imagination. It shaped the way people see the world. It gave birth to notions of *whiteness* and *blackness*.[99] "Within the gulf enacted between Christianity and the Jews, the racial, which proves to be racist, imagination was forged."[100] Carter calls this the "theological problem of *whiteness*." Christian theology shaped and became enmeshed in colonialism and empire, nationalism and racial ideologies, and white supremacy and global hegemony. In other words, racial imagination is rooted in theology. The result is that Christianity became *white*.

While the church served as incubator for racism, more particularly, it was the ancient heresy known as Gnosticism that was midwife for the birth of our racial imagination with its insistence on cutting off Christianity from its Jewish embeddedness. Carter says, "Christology, that area within the theological curriculum that investigates the person and work of Jesus Christ, was problematically deployed to found the modern racial imagination. For at the genealogical taproot of modern racial reasoning is the process by which Christ was abstracted from Jesus, and thus from his Jewish body, thereby severing Christianity from its Jewish roots . . . In making Christ non-Jewish in this moment, he was made a figure of the Occident. He became white, even if Jesus as a historical figure remained Jewish or racially a figure of the Orient."[101]

By and large, this mistrust of the flesh and the insatiable desire to "spiritualize" everything accounts for Gnosticism being the default setting for evangelicals. This may be called "the current theological problem of whiteness." Gnosticism is at the root of our racial identifications.

96. Carter, *Race*, 4.
97. Carter, *Race*, 4.
98. Carter, *Race*, 4.
99. Carter, *Race*, 4.
100. Carter, *Race*, 4.
101. Carter, *Race*, 7.

The gnostics opposed the fleshly, material, bodily incarnation of Jesus. They went about the business of spiritualizing the entire faith. But any account of Christianity remains deficient that is not "explicated in relation to Israel and the ongoing existence and witness of the Jewish people."[102] The existence of the Jews is that of "embodied being." "The biological being of this people comes first."[103] The church cannot be less material, physical, bodily. It is, after all, gathered from out of the nations.

The gnostic attack on the Jewishness of Jesus produced the "strange fruit" of a white Jesus.[104] Whiteness came to function as a substitute for the Christian doctrine of creation. Jewish flesh in this moment underwent a religious conversion: it was converted into racial flesh, positioned within a hierarchy of racial-anthropological essences, and lodged within a now racialized chain of being. Jesus was made a figure of the Occident; he became white, even if as a historical figure he remained Jewish or racially a figure of the Orient. Armed with a "white Jesus," white people were free to control and dominate the world. "This is the modern problem of imagining the human being in racial terms, and within these terms positioning whiteness as supreme."[105] The claims made by evangelicals that they are not racist don't take into account the theological conviction that being white is somehow better.

An ancient metaphor infects our understanding of whiteness: the great chain of being. Historically, typologies of humans "modestly placed Caucasians at the pinnacle of humanity and relegated Native Americans and sub-Saharan Africans to the bottom, only a hair's breadth away from the apes[106] (an idea that underpinned Thomas Jefferson's infamous claim that male apes preferred African women as mates to members of their own species).[107] Voltaire claimed that "in the hot countries apes subjugated girls."[108]

In snapshot number one, the Christians grinning back at us, as if they were at a "lynching party" in twentieth-century Mississippi, are gnostics. Racism began here and has been institutionalized within the strictures of the church ever since. Gnosticism, once embedded in Christianity, has refused to die.

---

102. Carter, *Race*, 30.
103. Carter, *Race*, 31.
104. Carter, *Race*, 7.
105. Carter, *Race*, 7.
106. Smith, *Less Than Human*, 41.
107. Jefferson, *Notes on the State of Virginia*.
108. Cited in Bernasconi and Lott, *The Idea of Race*, 6.

# Racism as Adolescent: Colonialism and Nationalism

Whiteness turned out to be nonamiable. The irony is that gnostics despised all bodies, but created a racist system that would abuse, oppress, and destroy Black bodies for the next eighteen centuries. Gnostics seem not to have noticed the affect that passed between their denial of the body, and the pain endured by Black bodies. Affectively, Black bodies were now regarded as bodies to which cruelty could stick. Only Black bodies would actually know what racism feels like. As Jose Munoz puts it, "melancholia is a mechanism that helps us (re)construct identity and take our dead to the various battles we must wage in their names."[109]

Etienne Balibar argues, "For my own part, I think the specific articulation of racism is within nationalism . . . The fundamental problem therefore [has been] to produce the people. More exactly, it [has been] to make the people produce itself as a national community."[110] Thus, the attachment of like terms: racism, colonialism, nationalism.

European conquests of the world, in the name of God, firmly established the hegemony of "white Christians." Willie James Jennings, in *The Christian Imagination*, argues that Christianity in the Western world has a diseased social imagination. Jennings shows how the Christian social imagination is wedded to racialized, individualistic, privatized, and rootless identities. We find ourselves in this place because of historical events.

Jennings, recounting the first auction for the sale of Africans in Portugal, argues that the most important part of the event on August 8, 1444 was the ritual. "This ritual was deeply Christian. Prince Henry, following his deepest Christian instincts, ordered a tithe be given to God through the church. Two black boys were given, one to the principal church in Lagos and another to the Franciscan convent on Cape Saint Vincent. The prince also claimed that his motivation was 'the salvation of the soul of the heathen.'"[111] Slavery as salvation—only a perverted Christian mind could make such a claim.

The royal chronicler Zurara narrates the ritual of slave capture and auction. Surprisingly he sets the scene in a penitent prayer:

> O, Thou heavenly Father—who with thy powerful hand, without alternation of thy divine essence, governest all the infinite company of thy Holy City, and controllest all the revolutions of higher worlds, divided into nine spheres, making the duration of

---

109. Quoted in Biesecker, "The Rhetorical Production of the Melancholic," 149.
110. Cited in Carter, *Race*, 39.
111. Jennings, *The Christian Imagination*, 16.

ages long or short according to as it pleaseth Thee—I pray Thee that my tears may not wrong my conscience; for it is not their religion but their humanity that maketh mine to weep in pity for their sufferings. And if the brute animals, with their bestial feelings, by a natural instinct understand the suffering of their own kind, what wouldst Thou have my human nature do on seeing before my eyes that miserable company, and remembering that they too are of the generation of the sons of Adam?[112]

After this moment of introspection, Zurara deploys a rhetorical strategy of containment, holding slave suffering inside a Christian story that will be recycled by countless theologians and intellectuals of every colonialist nation. The event will be enacted as an order of salvation—African captivity leads to African salvation and to Black bodies that show the disciplining power of the faith.

The irony here, according to Jennings, is that Zurara has depicted a suffering Christ image, a passion narrative. The slaves trace out the frame of Jesus' own march to suffering, separation, and death. "Both Jesus and the slaves suffer outside the city."[113] Rome and Portugal engage in a demonstration of their power over bodies. "Like Jesus, these people of distant lands are brought to a place where a crucifying identity, slave identity, will be forever fastened like a cross to their bodies: 'They brought Jesus to the place called Golgatha, which means 'Place of a Skull,' and they offered him drugged wine, but he did not take it. Then they fastened him to the cross.'"[114] The church has never escaped from fastening a cross to Black bodies.

Outside the city of Lisbon, Portugal, in 1442, the church established the hegemony of "white Christians." The cost of this grasping of white power: the slaves are bound to death by being killed. The power of whites over Black bodies is painfully enacted as the slaves are divided into equal lots, "just as all that was left was the dividing of the Savior's garments."[115] In a scene that will haunt human memories for centuries, mothers were beaten as they tried to cling to their children who were being torn from them. Images of children being taken from the parents of people without power or status haunt our time as well. Power—white, male, Christian power in full display of all its cruelty and enacted with no pity. "The holy use of Jesus' body—the one who

---

112. Jennings, *The Christian Imagination*, 17.
113. Jennings, *The Christian Imagination*, 20.
114. Jennings, *The Christian Imagination*, 20. Mark 15:22–24a, NEB.
115. Jennings, *The Christian Imagination*, 22.

became a slave to die as a sinner for humankind—parallels the separation of slaves into lots for Portuguese servitude."[116]

The evangelical lust for political power is still rooted in the ancient hegemony of Protestant Anglo-Saxon whiteness. Our second snapshot shows church and state hierarchies grinning back at us from the decks of ships that carried racism and slavery to the four corners of the earth, and Prince Henry sitting on horseback at the port of Lagos watching the ritual of cruelty and doing so as part of Christian liturgy. Somewhere Smokey Robinson sings, "If you look closer, it's easy to trace the tracks of my tears."

## "One More Rung on the Ladder Is All We Ask"

Our third snapshot of this panoramic journey, our visual portrait of turning points in the making of the diseased social imagination, the "bloody heirloom" of racism, puts us in the eighteenth century as the Unites States struggles with slavery. The tightly intertwined stories of the white working class and Black Americans go back to the prehistory of the United States—and the use of one as a cudgel to silence the claims of the other goes back nearly as far. Like the Black working class, the white working class originated in bondage—the former in the lifelong bondage of slavery, the latter in the temporary bondage of indenture. In the early seventeenth century, these two classes were remarkably, though not totally, free of racist enmity. But by the eighteenth century, the country's master class had begun etching race into law while phasing out indentured servitude in favor of a more enduring labor solution. From these and other changes of law and economy, a bargain emerged: The descendants of indenture would enjoy the full benefits of whiteness, the most definitional benefit being that they would never sink to the level of the slave.

Here we witness a Jacob and Esau deal with Jacob played by the white upper class and Esau by the poor working-class whites. "When the boys grew up, Esau was a skillful hunter, a man of the field, while Jacob was a quiet man, living in tents."[117] The white men "of the field" got the worst of the bargain.

The white aristocratic power constructed a rung on the ladder for "white workers." This rung was a mere one step above the rung that was reserved for African Americans. The bargain would protect white workers from slavery, but it would also allow them, at least in the social imagination, to "sup with" the rich whites. Now, in the fictional creation, in

116. Jennings, *The Christian Imagination*, 21.
117. Genesis 27:25.

biblical language, "on the morning of the fifth day, there was whiteness and blackness. And white people saw that it was good, and they separated the whites from the Blacks."

This imagined equality of all whites did nothing to change the economic vicissitude of working-class whites. They derived less from the bargain than Esau when he sold his birthright to Jacob. The bargain did not protect from near-slave wages or backbreaking labor and always there lurked a fear of having benefits revoked. This early white working class "expressed soaring desires to be rid of the age-old inequalities of Europe and of any hint of slavery," according to David R. Roediger, a professor of American studies at the University of Kansas. "They also expressed the rather more pedestrian goal of simply not being mistaken for slaves, or 'negers' or 'negurs.'"[118] In return for identity as "white" as opposed to "Negro," in return for the "privilege" of appearing as if they were the equal of rich whites, in return for the sense of belonging to the "upper class," working whites surrendered the possibility of actually becoming part of the American dream. For them wealth would remain aspirational, out of reach. They were now conceived as being "better than" Negroes. That affect is the only effect of this nasty bargain.

## Reconstructing the Nation on the Backs of Blacks

Our fourth snapshot of this panoramic journey opens on the Reconstruction era from 1867 to 1877. There was a moment in the tortured history of racism that offered an opportunity to move beyond the Gnosticism, colonialism, nationalism, and whiteness that produced such an evil social imagination. The period, known as Reconstruction, a time when southerners were pressed down into the deep well of defeat to grapple with, for them, the unbelievable defeat and the desertion of God from their cause. The newly freed slaves were given undeniable and long-denied rights. Amendments to the Constitution were ratified to grant civil rights to former slaves. Whiteness, threatened, had to do business with what was the first opportunity to undo the "bloody heirloom" in the reconstitution of the Union, and might then have seriously damaged the persistent existence of racism.

Tragically, the opportunity would be wasted by a sweeping exercise of political pragmatism. Historian David W. Blight, in *Race and Reunion*, tells us that Reconstruction wasn't really the central subject after the Civil War. What actually mattered the most and still does was race. He considers the moral judgment of the nation on the Civil War to be a pivotal moral moment. Blight says, "Americans have had to work through the meaning

118. Quoted in Coates, "The First White President."

of their Civil War in its rightful place—in the politics of memory. And as long as we have a politics of race in America, we will have a politics of Civil War memory."[119]

Blight's model for understanding the memories of the Civil War posits three contending visions of reconciliationists, white supremacists, and emancipationists. This snapshot deserves its place in our survey of racism because, as Blight puts it, "The sectional reunion after so horrible a civil war was a political triumph of the nineteenth century, but it could not have been achieved without the re-subjugation of many of those people whom the war had freed from centuries of bondage."[120] I believe Blight is exactly right when he insists that this is the "tragedy lingering on the margins and infesting the heart of American history from Appomattox to World War I."[121] I would extend his argument from Appomattox to the election of Donald Trump on the grounds of the same racism and I would move it from the fringe to the center of American history.

The reconciliationist vision partnered with the white supremacist vision to thwart the emancipationist vision until the 1960s. Then, the emancipationist vision, left for dead in the dust of racism, was disinterred from the shallow grave and flourished in the ministry and work of Martin Luther King, Jr., and many others, but the scourge of racism refused to die. It merely went underground for a time of incubation and now has returned with fury.

As the segregation policies of Jim Crow embedded their oppression practices into the southern soul, not only did African Americans have to survive loss of rights but also had to fear loss of life. The Ku Klux Klan became the illegal army of Jim Crow after the Civil War and after Reconstruction, lynch mobs joined the party.

## "Southern Trees Bear Strange Fruit"

Our fifth snapshot combines the horror of racism with the crime of lynching. James Cone, in *The Cross and the Lynching Tree*, notes that the Emmett Till lynching was the spark that lit the fire of resistance in Negro masses. Will the death of George Floyd be the Emmett Till of the twenty-first century in the USA? Floyd's death and those of many other innocent African Americans killed by white policemen, shines a glaring white-hot light on the Jericho wall of racism that has been so carefully constructed and so ingeniously made invisible. Now, all America could see, that the wall hasn't

119. Blight, *Race and Reunion*, 4.
120. Blight, *Race and Reunion*, 3.
121. Blight, *Race and Reunion*, 3.

fallen yet because people keep repairing the places were the wall has been broken. In every generation, there are those who invest in "repairing the breaches" and "raising up the ruins" of racism. This invisible wall operates as a defense shield for whites.

Emmett Till's death knocked a hole in the wall. Cone asserts, "the Till lynching was a shocking reminder of the enduring power of white supremacy." Then he adds, "The Till lynching would provide the spark that lit the fire of resistance in the Negro masses, inspiring them, as King said, 'to rock the nation,' and to demand their 'freedom now.' This was the beginning of the civil rights movement in Mississippi . . ."[122] Rosa Parks knocked a hole in the wall. Martin Luther King, Jr. led his people through the breaches in the wall. John Lewis recalled that Till's death "galvanized the country."[123] Lewis said that the young people at the sit-ins were "sitting in for Emmett Till."[124]

Trump's followers are attempting to repair the breaches in the wall like Hard Shell Baptists shouting Isaiah 58:2—"Your ancient ruins shall be rebuilt; you shall raise up the foundations of many generations; you shall be called the repairer of the breach, the restorer of streets to live in." Instead of restoring primitive Christianity, these evangelicals are attempting to maintain the wall of separation between whites and persons of color.

The viciousness of Jim Crow was now on full display in the nation. The awakening of the civil rights movement would now unleash the power of the emancipationist vision against that of the entrenched white supremacist vision. There was genuine hope that at long last the wall would come tumbling down.

That hope would, as always, continue to be tortured by the incessant presence of ongoing racism. While Cone offers a respectful criticism of Reinhold Niebuhr's failure to connect the cross and the lynching tree, in a sense, he is condemning white theologians of all stripes of failure to make the connection. As Cone states matter-of-factly, "white theologians do not normally turn to Black experience to learn about theology."[125] As noted earlier, white people do not take kindly to Black preachers pronouncing prophetic judgment on America.

By placing the lynching tree as analogy for the cross, Cone dramatically shows that racism crucifies Jesus again. The unknown pastor of Hebrews writes: "For it is impossible to restore again to repentance those who have once been enlightened, and have tasted the heavenly gift, and have shared

---

122. Cone, *The Cross and the Lynching Tree*, loc. 2107.
123. Cone, *The Cross and the Lynching Tree*, loc. 2108.
124. Cone, *The Cross and the Lynching Tree*, loc. 2118.
125. Cone, *The Cross and the Lynching Tree*, loc. 1642.

in the Holy Spirit, and have tasted the goodness of the word of God and the powers of the age to come, and then have fallen away, since on their own they are crucifying again the Son of God and are holding him up to contempt."[126] Perhaps Republicans having eschewed repentance by presidential decree (Trump—"I see no need to repent") will not be bothered by the sharpness of the warning from the unknown pastor of Hebrews.

Our selective pictorial of the viciousness of racism represents a collage that brings us to the election of 2016 where evangelicals supported a presidency of overt bigotry, because evangelicalism is racist at its core. Randall Balmer gets at the heart of evangelical support of Donald Trump by forcefully connecting evangelicals to their more transparent racist roots. The statistics tell one story: 81 percent of white evangelicals voted for Donald Trump. The deafening silence from leaders of the religious right in the wake of the neo-Nazi violence in Charlottesville, Virginia, points to an even larger one, which places racism at the very heart of the movement. Evangelicals line up in numbers rivalling the taxi queue at Atlanta International Airport to defend President Trump from the charge of racism. By implication this also means they are defending themselves. The racist legacy of Jerry Falwell, Sr. and his Moral Majority is currently in resurgent mode.

---

126. Hebrews 6:4–8.

# Chapter 4—**Robert Jeffress**
## *High Priest of American Nationalism (Formerly Evangelicalism)*

The Rev. Dr. Robert Jeffress is the senior pastor of the First Baptist Church, Dallas, Texas. His importance here relates to his standing in the historical tradition of J. Frank Norris, Jerry Falwell, and three generations of anguished evangelicals. First Baptist Church Dallas had an earlier well-known pastor, Dr. W. A. Criswell, who was part of the resurgent fundamentalism that captured control of the Southern Baptist Convention in the 1980s. Jeffress matters also because he is, as John Fea dubs him, "a court evangelical." Or as Michael J. Mooney labels him, "Trump's Apostle."[1] Jeffress does interviews on Fox News so frequently that the material in my book needs updating every day. By the time this book appears in print, Jeffress will have said something so hyperbolic and more obnoxious than when I first wrote it.

Jeffress's megachurch, in downtown Dallas, has more than 13,000 members and has long been a flagship church in the Southern Baptist Convention. Jeffress, however, has another position: he is the unpaid minister of defense for President Donald Trump. Like Moses representing the people of Israel before God, Jeffress represents Trump in the alternate universe of evangelicalism. When the president says or does something that appears to contradict traditional evangelical understandings of Christian faith, up pops "Jeffress-on-the-spot" with an interpretation that takes away the insult, the mocking, or the moral mishap. He explains it in evangelical language that smooths over all inconsistencies and contradictions.

With a smooth, machine gun-like delivery, Jeffress, time and again, puts Donald back together again after another verbal explosion. A few examples from the last three years should suffice. Here's Jeffress on Fox News defending President Trump for calling certain African nations "shithole countries." Smiling, capable, smooth, Jeffress says, "Apart from the vocabulary attributed to him, President Trump is right on target in his sentiment."

---

1. Mooney, "Trump's Apostle."

This pattern of the president making outrageous statements and Rev. Jeffress rushing to his defense has become routine and expected. Who else could pull of such a contorted sentence that mildly chastises the president for using the word "shithole," and then saying, in effect, the president is correct and those countries are "shithole" nations?

When Trump had Michael Cohen pay Stormy Daniels $130,000 for her silence, Jeffress said, "Obviously we don't support hush-money payments, but what we do support is this president's excellent policies."[2] When Trump said Democrats would use violence to overturn all his accomplishments, Jeffress demurred that the president simply meant that a Democratic congress could undo his good policies.

President Nixon had Billy Graham, but no president has had a preacher who functions as ad hoc press secretary, defense minister, and interpreter like President Trump has with Robert Jeffress. While Paula White is the television preacher, prosperity gospel evangelical who is a paid member of Trump's staff, it is Jeffress who is the pope of the movement. Historian John Fea says, "Robert Jeffress seems to have secured a place at Trump's right hand."[3] In a photo of the president signing an executive order on religious liberty, he is surrounded by a cadre of evangelical leaders, and Jeffress is at the president's right hand. In another photo, evangelicals huddle around the president and lay hands on his head. I'm sure the president was thinking, "Watch the hair, the perfect hair." Images of Hur and Aaron holding up the arms of Moses float through the air.

John Fea, in a column for *The Washington Post,* holds up Jeffress as the prime contemporary example of a "court evangelical," his term "for a Christian who, like the attendants and advisers who frequented the courts of monarchs, seeks influence through regular visits to the White House."[4]

Jeffress had a lot of heads shaking when he said he wanted the toughest possible president—a son of a bitch. He as much as said he couldn't vote for Jesus because Jesus was soft on terrorism. He didn't want a candidate who would govern the nation on the basis of the Sermon on the Mount, but on the basis of Romans 13:1–6. He insisted that God gave President Trump permission to bomb North Korea. "In the case of North Korea, God has given Trump authority to take out Kim Jong-Un. I'm heartened to see that our president—contrary to what we've seen with past administrations who have taken, at best, a sheepish stance toward dictators and

2. Young, "A Guide to Robert Jeffress' Excuses."
3. Fea, *Believe Me,* loc. 1555.
4. Macon, "Why the controversial."

oppressors—will not tolerate any threat against the American People."[5] Jeffress later tried to walk back the statement on North Korea, but mostly he speaks with absolute certainty that every word he utters is not only biblical but also the truth. Some would be more inclined to agree with Raney, in the Clyde Edgerton novel, when she insists that the ideas of Charles, her husband, do not form in her head like gold.[6]

For all this President Trump reciprocates with praise: "I was watching television with Melania, and I saw Pastor Jeffress, and I said, 'Look at his mouth move! Look at how quickly that mouth moves. It's like a machine gun! I would never want to see that used against me someday!'"[7] Jeffress is the tower that reaches to heaven in defense of the president. He is Trump's Amaziah defending him against prophets, the media, the liberals, and all the perceived enemies hiding in halls of power. All others pale in comparison.

Historically, preachers have often seemed oblivious to the mercurial favor of kings and presidents, but Jeffress has embraced his new role wide-eyed, eager, and with enthusiasm. He seems oblivious to all historical warnings of the dangers on the path he has taken. The master of Wakefield once opined, "Are we all hand-tamed by these gentry?"[8] Chaucer complained of "those shitty shepherds and their shitty sheep."[9] Preachers are always susceptible to the temptation of worldly power wrapped in White House visits and presidential compliments.

Jeffress has a political agenda shared with other evangelicals: A Christian America, the end of abortion, the end of gay marriage, religious freedom (as he defines it and the First Amendment), and conservative judges in the federal judiciary. He is helping to turn the Republican Party into the Evangelical Party.

Trump has delivered for Jeffress and that overrides any qualms he may have about Trump's character, verbiage, and actions. Here are examples of Jeffress downplaying character and dismissing ethos from the room: "We don't support extramarital affairs, we don't support hush-money payments, but what we do support are this president's excellent policies."[10] "The reason we supported President Reagan was not because we were supporting womanizing or divorce. We supported his policies."[11] "Evangelicals still believe

---

5. Young, "A Guide to Robert Jeffress' Excuses."
6. Edgerton, *Raney*, 70.
7. Mooney, "Trump's Apostle."
8. Marney, unpublished presentation.
9. Marney, *Priests to Each Other*, 10.
10. Young, "A Guide to Robert Jeffress' Excuses."
11. Young, "A Guide to Robert Jeffress' Excuses."

in the commandment: Thou shalt not have sex with a porn star. However, whether this president has violated that commandment or not is totally irrelevant to our support of him."[12] Jeffress has been clear on his reasons for supporting Trump: Strong and good policies; protecting America; making it safe; making America great again; protecting religious liberty. All of this can be by any means necessary for Jeffress and for Trump. This includes the use of spurious rhetoric. Jeffress and Trump are prolific users of hateful rhetoric. This is a major connection between Trump and the evangelical "trumpets"— the heralds of the gospel according to Trump. Incendiary rhetoric was always a staple of evangelical preachers in the twentieth century.

The shocking reversal of evangelicals on the issue of character (ethos) cries for a more critical and scholarly investigation. As Bonnie J. Dow argues, if the 2016 and 2020 elections were more about persona than prose, we might have had a turn toward ethos, but, in the case of evangelicals, the death of ethos. Without question, evangelicals have rewritten Aristotle and the entire tradition of rhetoricians on the subject of ethos as a necessary means of persuasion. They have assassinated ethos and replaced it with anti-ethos. It doesn't matter what this president says as long as his policies are excellent. Words no longer matter because there are alternative truths; reasons don't matter because "feeling good" matters; rational deliberation is no longer central to how American Christians make decisions.

Jeffress has a favorite rhetorical weapon: hyperbole. Evangelicals major in hyperbole because it relates to their apocalyptic worldview and their desire to really scare people. Jeffress, for example, wanted the nation to be really scared about the awful consequences if the Democrats won the 2020 election. "Once the left, if they succeed, they don't only want to dismantle our current police, they want to replace our current police with the *thought* police, who go around patrolling every thought that they find objectionable."[13]

And if the left ever gained control of this country, he predicted it would be like the French Revolution. "Bring out the guillotines, and execute every thought they object to, and every person who holds every thought that they object to."[14]

Jeffress, no stranger to audacious cause/effect arguments, is a master of fear-based exaggeration. Jeffress warned that the Democrats would start a "Civil War" if they were successful in removing Trump from office. He said on Fox News, "It will cause a Civil War-like fracture in this nation

12. Young, "A Guide to Robert Jeffress' Excuses."
13. Miciak, "Trump's Favorite Pastor."
14. Miciak, "Trump's Favorite Pastor."

from which this country will never heal."[15] Note that the upper case for "Civil War" makes it clear that Jeffress is not using a metaphor, but is deliberately referring to the Civil War of 1860 to 1865 that killed more than 750,000 Americans.

When confronted with his hyperbole, Jeffress gets testy. For example, after his Civil War-like fracture comment became a controversy, he said repeatedly that he was not attempting to incite or "advocate violence"; that, he said, "would be irresponsible." If you try to argue otherwise, "you're either dumb or dishonest. Either words mean something, or they don't. If they say I am calling for a civil war, they are lying. They are pulling something out of the air."[16]

Ken Ham, the Creation Museum creator, routinely blames the teaching of evolution for every disaster in the world since Darwin published *The Origin of the Species*. David Barton says that ACT scores of high school students declined when the Supreme Court outlawed prayer in schools (something the Court didn't do). Evangelicals preachers and hyperbole are a matched pair.

Jeffress is cut from the same rhetorical cloth: wildly exaggerated claims, false notions, false cause/effect, false and problematic claims. Yet these statements are accepted at face value in the evangelical community and repeated again and again by lesser lights of evangelical pulpits. These manipulations of the truth are accepted because they are wrapped in a smiling, easygoing, fast-talking, absolutely certain persona so that even some Texans don't see that Jeffress is "all hat and no cattle." Even more important, these words are spoken as if they come straight from a literal-truth Bible. The preachers and the Bible are granted literal truth status.

One Texan who was not fooled is Robert Hunt of Perkins School of Theology, who argued that Jeffress was offering a justification for violence. "To find an evangelical pastor turning himself into a political commentator is remarkable," said Hunt, who wrote in 2015 that Jeffress is "bad for Dallas" and its image as a tolerant, welcoming place. "He seems to live in a zone in which it isn't necessary to come up with evidentiary matter. He doesn't quote research. He has turned himself into a political commentator who has no basis in discernible facts."[17]

Jeffress preaches an end-time premillennialism, but his politics are postmillennial. How he holds these two in creative tension is a remarkable display of rhetorical agility. In *Countdown to the Apocalypse*, he says, "We

---

15. Wilonsky, "What Robert Jeffress meant."
16. Wilonsky, "What Robert Jeffress meant."
17. Wilonsky, "What Robert Jeffress meant."

are closer to the 'end of days' than we have ever been."[18] In line with his end-time preaching, Jeffress compares the USA to Sodom and Gomorrah: "If Sodom and Gomorrah were destroyed by fire and brimstone from heaven (Genesis 19:23–29), what can we in America expect?"[19] Jeffress takes no note of a different perspective on Sodom that comes from the prophet Ezekiel: "This was the guilt of your sister Sodom: she and her daughters had pride, excess of food, and prosperous ease, but did not aid the poor and needy."[20] He is strangely silent on political pride and the sin of not helping the poor and needy.

He begins his book, *Countdown to the Apocalypse: Why ISIS and Ebola Are Only the Beginning*, by sounding more like a person reading from a traditional grocery list of sins than a preacher reading from the Bible. He lists all the horrific wickedness that will herald the end of the world: ISIS, Ebola, the Middle East crisis, the breakdown of the family, the redefinition of marriage, and the moral decline that has led to an avalanche of immorality in our day. His equating of terrorism with the redefinition of marriage suggests a weird sort of logic. Believing that this is all predicted in the Bible, he spices his preaching and his writing with an endless array of verses of Scripture as warrants for his argument. Over and over, he tells his readers that they should be afraid. "There are good reasons to be frightened these days."[21] He spices his remarks with words designed to engender fear and doubt: "Perhaps we are not as safe in the United States as we think." In an appearance on Fox News he reveals that the idea that Hillary Clinton might win the presidency was the fear that kept him up nights. One would think there are larger fears to keep a person awake at night.

Evangelicals are connoisseurs of fear, working in fear the way Ralphie's father worked in profanity in the movie *Christmas Story*, to paint a scary future. Their mastery of this emotional appeal makes them an evil Rembrandt painting pictures of hell and eternal damnation in the minds of Protestant Americans.

Jeffress backs up his claims about the second coming and his support for President Trump with the unmistakable characteristic of certainty. For example, he says, "But make no mistake. Jesus clearly predicts His eventual return to the earth. Matthew 24:2–31 cannot mean anything other than a literal, physical Second Coming of Christ."[22] The language of certainty

18. Jeffress, *Countdown*, 4.
19. Jeffress, *Countdown*, 4.
20. Ezekiel 16:49.
21. Jeffress, *Countdown*, 9.
22. Jeffress, *Countdown*, 15.

can't be missed: "clearly" "cannot mean anything other than." There is no ambiguity in Jeffress, no complexities, no contingencies.

When it comes to politics, Jeffress never talks about the subject in his pulpit. His appearances on national television reveal a different kind of preacher. What doesn't change is the note of certainty. I think that it is a crucial connection between Jeffress and Trump. Pronouncements are made as matter-of-fact certainties. There's no wiggle room in this austere dualism. Jeffress is right and good; the Democrats are evil and wrong. As he trumpets his complete support of President Trump, he seems to have forgotten that he has been preaching for years that "the very systems in which we have placed so much confidence will utterly fail; chaos will spread across the earth as men and women cry out for a leader to bring them peace and safety. In those frightful hours, a man of peace will rise up with a promise of deliverance for those who follow Him. Millions will do so to their eternal regret because that man will prove to be the ultimate false Christ, or as he is commonly referred to, the Antichrist."[23]

Yet Jeffress doesn't really believe that this is about to happen, because he has put all his trust in a man and a political party. He preaches the "end is near," but he is actually asking Jesus to postpone his return long enough for evangelical conservatives to rule the nation. He doesn't want Jesus to return because he wants the "meanest, toughest son of a you-know-what I can find." Prior to the election he announced that he couldn't vote for Jesus because Jesus wouldn't be strong enough. He insists that Donald Trump is that strongman who will stand up to the liberals and let them have it "with both barrels."[24]

Jeffress never misses an opportunity to paint Democrats as godless. He and his fellow evangelicals are the true believers, the real Christians. Everyone else is "godless." He sounds like a sixteenth-century Spanish inquisitor scouring the land for Protestant heretics. When the Pew Report noted that 70 percent of atheists were Democrats, Jeffress did math calculations that rival Kellyanne Conway's "alternative truth." Jeffress's math came out like this: "It is no coincidence . . . that 70 percent of atheists identify as Democrats and only 15 percent as Republicans. The Democrat Party has become a godless party. That is a true statement according to the Pew Research Center's 2014 Religious Landscape Study. (Considering how much has changed since then, I would strongly suspect that 70 percent number is quite a bit higher now.)"[25] That same study, however, also found that 84

---

23. Jeffress, *Countdown*, 17.
24. See Lyons, "First Baptist's Robert Jeffress"; and Gettys, "Megachurch pastor."
25. Metha, "Robert Jeffress, Using Bad Math."

percent of Democrats believe in God in some capacity. (Seventy-six percent are absolutely or fairly certain God exists!) In other words, the Democratic Party is not a "godless party" by any stretch of the imagination. Even if 100 percent of atheists were Democrats, the party as a whole would still be more than 70 percent religious. Yet Jeffress rushes to judgment: "Well, listen, quite frankly I think President Trump hit out of the ballpark when he talked about Joe Biden and by extension, the Democrats by saying they're against God and they're against the Bible. I think that's not an overstatement. It is no coincidence, . . . that 70 percent of atheists identify as Democrats and only 15 percent as Republicans. . . . The Democrat party has become a godless party and so that's why you find such animosity against conservative Christians and against the Bible."[26]

When Jeffress is not attacking Democrats as godless, he berates liberal Christian pastors for being crazy, unbiblical, and untruthful. To hear Jeffress tell it, most of our problems are caused by liberal clergy. He says that liberal pastors have departed from the Christian faith. "These are the leaders who, in the name of religious unity, deny the truthfulness of the Bible, deny the necessity of Christ's death for our sins, deny the virgin birth of Christ, deny the reality of eternal hell, and deny that those who die without Jesus Christ are lost forever. They turn away after fads and popular social causes and pander to the powers that be. They support abortion, the redefinition of marriage, and the right of pornographers to practice their evil trade. They do not preach the message of Christ's salvation, because they do not even believe the gospel. They are wolves in sheep's clothing."[27]

Here Jeffress sounds like a fundamentalist who has somehow wandered back from the nineteenth century to attack pastors who disagree with him. Nineteenth-century versions of Jeffress believed that the modernist, higher critics of the Bible were a conspiracy of intellectuals. There was a strong predisposition that the biblical critics with their speculations about the Bible had arisen because they were "men who have poisoned their nervous systems and injured their minds by the use of narcotics and other poisons."[28] Unable to imagine otherwise, these biblical purists and keepers of the faith could only conclude that anyone disagreeing with them had to be under the influence.

Sounding the same discordant notes of criticism, Jeffress has maligned liberal churches: "There are some churches that deserve to die.

---

26. Jeffress, interview by David Asman.
27. Jeffress, interview by David Asman.
28. Hauerwas, *Unleashing the Scripture*, 32.

Liberal churches that are changing God's message to fit the culture."[29] Take note that a pastor who has a Fourth of July celebration with patriotic hymns, music, the Pledge of Allegiance, and a speech by Lt. Colonel Oliver North, with fireworks in the sanctuary, has a lot of nerve to say that liberal churches are fitting the culture.

When the Democrats announced that Union Seminary Vice President Derrick Harkins would lead the party's 2020 faith outreach efforts, Jeffress mocked and scorned the Democrats and Rev. Harkins. Jeffress began with an odd sort of statement: "I am not a Republican or a Democrat, so I don't say this from a partisan perspective." He is, of course, using paralipsis: "I'm not saying I'm partisan, but I am partisan." Then he turns his rapid-fire delivery on the Democrats: "But the truth is that when you talk about righteousness and unrighteousness, it is becoming clearer and clearer that the Democrat Party has truly become a godless party. It is a godless party." He says, "Today, they are actively working to remove 'so help me God' from their oaths of office," he stressed. "The problem runs much deeper than that. They are promoting policies and values that are completely antithetical to the Christian faith."[30]

Satisfied that he has eviscerated the Democrats, he turns his mocking rhetoric to Dr. Harkins: "You have seen lately, in fact even this week, that the Democrats are realizing that they have a God problem in connecting with voters.... They don't want to completely write off faith voters, so they have hired this week a faith outreach director."[31] Speaking about Harkins, Jeffress called him a "Trump-hating pastor" that comes from a "liberal seminary that is filled with liberal professors who couldn't find God if their life depended on it.[32]

Jeffress completely ignores the reputation and credentials of Rev. Harkins, who earned a Master of Divinity from Union Seminary in 1987, and began his career at Abyssinian Baptist Church in Harlem, where he was a seminarian intern before becoming assistant minister.

Harkins was also Vice President with the North American Baptist Fellowship of the Baptist World Alliance and has been a guest lecturer on the church and social action at a number of colleges and universities, including Bucknell, Cornell, Iona College, and Harvard's Kennedy School of Government. He served as senior pastor for seventeen years at Nineteenth Street Baptist Church in Washington, DC. As a fellow American Baptist, I can testify

29. Jeffress, "Fox News' Pastor Robert Jeffress."
30. Quoted in Kuruvilla, "Evangelical Pastor."
31. Kuruvilla, "Evangelical Pastor."
32. Kuruvilla, "Evangelical Pastor."

that Harkins doesn't need to be searching for God. He has been a faithful servant of God his entire career. Jeffress trashes him, it seems, for the joy he receives from trashing people who disagree with him.

Jeffress warns his Fox News audience: "When they talk about God, they are not talking about the real God—the God of Abraham, Isaac and Jacob, the God who revealed Himself in the Bible. They are not talking about the real God. These liberal Democrats are talking about an imaginary God they have created in their own minds: a god who loves abortion and hates Israel. The true God of the Bible, the real God, is a God who hates abortion and loves Israel."[33]

The major flaw in all these liberal pastors, according to Jeffress, is that they are not fundamentalists. He sounds as if he just arrived in Dallas from 1925 to disinter the worst literalism and certainties of the fundamentalist movement. Not content to resurrect his Lord and Savior, the Fundamentalist God, Jeffress is attempting to disinter a far more discredited creed: the one that is known as biblical literalism. Jeffress takes upon himself the task of instructing liberals in the forgotten doctrines of fundamentalism. In his view, the deepest problem we face is the influence of liberal preachers, their lack of belief in the gospel. He suffers from no such lack; his faith in fundamentalism is of the blind, unquestioning variety.

Jeffress fails to note that he belongs to a part of the church—the evangelical wing—that is frequently opposed by the more moderate and liberal wing of the church that includes millions of faithful Christians, pastors, and seminary professors. Jeffress, casually pushing aside the differences, goes with the absurd notion that he's on the right side and all other Christians are wrong. The contrast has never been clearer than on the day when President Trump did his photo op at St. John's Episcopal Church by waving a Bible. Jeffress fawned over the president's action: "I thought it was completely appropriate for the president to stand in front of that church. . . . And by holding up the Bible, he was showing us that it teaches that, yes, God hates racism, it's despicable—but God also hates lawlessness."[34]

On the other hand, The Rev. Gini Gerbasi, an Episcopal priest, told *HuffPost* that she was in the crowd of people that was tear-gassed and driven away by police. She called what happened "grotesque and offensive and sacrilegious."[35] Bishop Mariann Budde, leader of the Episcopal Diocese of Washington, told *HuffPost* that she was "outraged" about Trump's appearance. "I am going to do everything in my power to disassociate our church

---

33. Kuruvilla, "Evangelical Pastor."
34. Coleman, "Trump Photo."
35. Beer, "Before Trump's Photo-Op."

from what the president did tonight," she said. "He did not pray when he came to St. John's," Budde said. The president also failed to acknowledge the agony of people of color who are "rightfully demanding an end to 400 years of systemic racism and white supremacy. In no way do we support the president's incendiary response to a wounded, grieving nation."[36]

Roman Catholic Archbishop Wilton Gregory also offered a different perspective from Rev. Jeffress, commenting on the occasion when a Catholic facility was co-opted for Trump's purposes. He said, "I find it baffling and reprehensible that any Catholic facility would allow itself to be so egregiously misused and manipulated in a fashion that violates our religious principles, which call us to defend the rights of all people, even those with whom we might disagree." Saint Pope John Paul II, known for opposing communism in his native Poland during his papacy, was an "ardent defender of the rights and dignity of human beings," the archbishop said. "He certainly would not condone the use of tear gas and other deterrents to silence, scatter or intimidate them for a photo opportunity in front of a place of worship and peace."[37]

Jeffress is the culmination of one hundred years of evangelical resentment and ressentiment. Evangelicals have been saddled with deep insecurities about being considered "dumber than dirt." They have longed for a way to stand up to the liberals and be transformed from a ninety-eight-pound weakling having the sands of secularism and liberalism kicked in their face, into a strong and powerful force that can deliver serious blows to the liberals. Jeffress, believing that at last he has a savior in Donald Trump, has launched a full-scale offensive against the liberals for how his people have been treated for the last century. Now, that's residual resentment as deep as that of Joseph, when his brothers showed up in Egypt and Joseph toyed with them and had Benjamin arrested for stealing.

## Sermonic Artifacts

There are rhetorical artifacts available for inspection that can allow us to demonstrate more accurately the method and message of Rev. Robert Jeffress. Like two stars crashing into one another in space, Robert Jeffress, white evangelical preacher, and Jeremiah Wright, Black progressive preacher, offer sermons that serve as models for the disparate visions of America that exist in our polarized culture. Drawing on rhetorical theory and biblical hermeneutics, I argue that

---

36. LeBlanc, "Bishop at DC church outraged."
37. Hamilton, "Archbishop Gregory."

Jeffress is not a prophet, not even a fake prophet; Wright is a prophet in the Old Testament and Black theological model.

Here we are offered the opportunity to see from a vantage point "the great chasm that has been fixed" between Lazarus (representing the Others—nonwhite, immigrants, poor, foreigners, gays, women) and a rich man (white evangelicals). Here are two visions of America, two ideas about political leaders and governments. One goes with Christian nationalism and Donald Trump, the other with prophetic realism.

I am acutely aware of the hazards of suggesting sermons as artifacts capable of carrying the weight of issues of such grave concern in our politically charged culture. By themselves the sermons are not enough to constitute the mythic narratives, but instead serve as enthymematic markers of well-known stories. Preaching has fallen on hard times, reduced, in many minds, to "chicken soup for the soul," weekly pop psychology lessons, interesting speeches the preacher has culled from this month's *Atlantic*, or scary diatribes about the impending destruction of the planet. Ellen F. Davis offers a chilling observation that many clergy "no longer consider it necessary to speak in careful response to the Bible text" and "no longer feel the steady 'pressure of the church's experience of Scripture' weighing upon their own hearts and minds."[38] Yet, Jeremiah Wright's sermon not only speaks in response to Scripture, but it senses the steady pressure of the Black church's entire history. The sermon under scrutiny produced a response from then-Senator Barack Obama, a candidate for the Democratic nomination to be president. It is not a normal sermon that earns a critique from a powerful voice in the nation.

These sermons are rhetorical artifacts for the division we face as a nation. It's the white privilege trope vs. the Black suffering and oppression trope. It's history as it happened and history as Jeffress wishes it had happened. It's whiteness vs. blackness. It's white anger and rage vs. Black suffering, crying out of oppression.

Dr. Jeremiah Wright's sermon was reduced to a short video clip of him saying "God damn America," and that was repeated on an endless cycle by the news media. There was nothing in the clip that dealt with the biblical and prophetic context of Dr. Wright's sermon. When sermons are already complex rhetorical creations, it is a risky proposition to allow them to be edited, reduced, and misrepresented by the media.

In all events, we begin with a sermon from Rev. Jeffress.

---

38. Davis, "Critical Traditioning," 165.

## Robert Jeffress Sermon: "America Is a Christian Nation"

Jeffress preached this sermon in his church as part of an event dubbed Freedom Sunday. It was delivered in the context of patriotic music, a salute to the US military, fireworks in the sanctuary, and a special message from Lt. Col. Oliver North, combat-decorated marine, best-selling author, small business owner, and holder of three US patents. Advertisements for Freedom Sunday offered a free gift—a DVD of two Jeffress sermons, "America at the Crossroads" and "America Is a Christian Nation."

The dominant rhetorical trope in the sermon is "American exceptionalism." Jennifer Mercieca identifies "American exceptionalism" as one of the six major rhetorical strategies of President Trump. Evangelical preachers have sounded the same distorted view of history since the Mayflower landed on these shores. Exceptionalism fueled the nativism of J. Frank Norris, the civic religion of the Eisenhower years, and the John Birch Society. Claire Conner, in *Wrapped in the Flag*, says that political discourse sounds now like it did in 1958 when the John Birch Society first entered the American scene. "All across the country newly awakened Birchers rallied to take our country back."[39] The trope is the religious/political philosophy that America has unique status among other nations in the world. Hauerwas suggests that it means that some American Christians assume a righteousness that other nations lack. Mercieca says, "Appeals to American exceptionalism rely on Americans' pride and their desire to believe that their nation is the best among others, that it is chosen by God (News to the Jews?), and that it has a heroic destiny to spread democracy and enlightenment around the world."[40]

"We are in a competition with the world," Trump insisted at his big America First economic policy speech in Detroit, Michigan, on August 28, 2016, "and I want America to win. When I am president, we will."[41] American exceptionalism was and is a big part of Trump's rhetoric. "Make America Great Again" oozes American exceptionalism. This theme is an evangelical dream come true because it combines the hope of American greatness with the belief that Trump will restore the principles that a secular culture has abandoned. Evangelicals seem not to notice that Trump believes that what makes America great has nothing to do with morals, ethics, founding principles, or God. For Trump greatness is winning and never losing.

---

39. Conner, *Wrapped in the Flag*, 1.
40. Mercieca, *Demagogue for President*, loc. 521–80.
41. Charles, "Transcript."

Trump's political jeremiad is a facile promise of national salvation. "It is a puerile discourse of redemption by demolition and deal-making. It prompts followers to emote—to express uninhibited feelings of fear, anger, and hatred. It is a seductive spectacle of the wrecking ball well adapted to a media culture of fast-paced, combative entertainment."[42] Evangelicals, predisposed to embrace exceptionalism, even in a form that suggests a presidential con, fell over themselves to push their own version of American exceptionalism, and the leader of the band was Robert Jeffress.

No secular event could have even approached the depth of American exceptionalism and patriotism of FBC Dallas worship. The blustering certainty and overweening confidence of Jeffress that America really is God's nation and mostly white evangelicals are God's new chosen people is hard to miss. This is a sermon wrapped in red, blue, and especially white. The danger in the sermon is that patriotism is a species of melancholy.[43] It disallows evangelicals confronting the nation's violent, racist past. Rather than working through melancholia as a step toward "inventing a society that remembers, rather than unconsciously repeats, a murderous and authoritarian past," evangelicals wave the flag, recite the creed, and give God's blessing to the feast of idolatry.

Jeffress has a previously constructed audience that already views itself as honest, hard-working, patriotic, good Americans. Together they participate in the legitimizing fantasy as the patriarchal patriot dangles a dramatic vision of a godly and patriotic congregation before their adoring eyes. They already know they are "God's people." There are no doubts in their minds. For the congregation there is a deep angst that an elite has dishonored a historically, culturally, geographically, divinely (but not diversely) constituted people. The American way of life is under siege—its memories, origins, common territory, deep beliefs, ways of life, even God. They are the chosen people, and this is how the enemy is created and the apocalyptic conflict unleashed. If the people were more diverse, less white, more negotiable, more open to rhetorical truth claims from other sources, then the enemy would be less visible, and there would be questions to answer about the identity, privilege, and standing of the people. But Dr. Jeffress doesn't allow such interventions in this epideictic celebration of American exceptionalism.[44]

The words of John the Baptist to a similarly constituted people of God, with self-assurance and certainty of their patriotism and standing in hand, would never cross their minds. "Do not presume to say to

---

42. Ivie, "Trump's Unwitting Prophecy," 708.
43. Biesecker, "The Rhetorical Production."
44. See Lee, "The Populist Chameleon."

yourselves, 'We have Abraham as our ancestor'; for I tell you, God is able from these stones to raise up children to Abraham."[45] No analogical imagination would allow such a reading at the First Baptist Church of Dallas; there would only be cognitive dissonance.

Kenneth Burke, concerning the use of rhetoric, sees political address and dramatic acting as two forms of the same thing. In both cases, argued Burke, speakers aim for what he calls consubstantiality, a super-identification of the audience with the actor/orator in which listeners suspend their sense of individuality and see the speaker as a projection of themselves as a group. "For instance, consubstantiality describes how flags waving together can make alliances real."[46] Jeffress and his audience achieve consubstantiality as easily as a Catholic priest and his congregation creates transubstantiation.

At the outset, Jeffress attacks the enemies who have caused our government "to acknowledge any acknowledgment of God . . . in the public square."[47] His rhetorical move here is to make his congregation both spatially and culturally distinct from their enemy. The development of the "people" and the "enemy" is a symbiotic process. The two polar opposites engage in a dance of perversion designed to unmask and humiliate the enemy. What is at stake here is identity—the identity of this congregation as the faithful people of God. The identification is complete between preacher and people—they experience what rhetorical scholars name as feeling themselves to be "substantially one" with one another. In this relationship, "the leader is sublime, beyond anything negative, a pure expression of the true identity of the followers."[48] Judgment is abdicated to the leader. Belief and obedience are almost automatic. "Followers accept and believe that the past was as the leader portrays it [America was founded as a Christian nation], the present is as he depicts it [America is a Christian nation], and the future will be as he predicts it [Jesus will rapture the holy people of America]. And they follow without hesitation his prescriptions for action."[49]

Jeffress says America "is ceasing to acknowledge any kind of acknowledgement of God in the public square."[50] No prayer in public schools, no display of the Ten Commandments in public buildings, no nativity scenes at the malls, no saying "Merry Christmas" because there's a war on Christmas, no teaching of the Bible in public schools—the entire dubious case is laid

---

45. Matthew 3:9.
46. Burke, *A Rhetoric of Motives*, 21.
47. Jeffress, "America Is a Christian Nation."
48. Roberts-Miller, "Charisma Isn't Leadership," 102–114.
49. Willner, *The Spellbinders*, 7.
50. Jeffress, "America Is a Christian Nation."

out. Jeffress then says, "We are told repeatedly that our country's fathers were secularists, deists, sprinkled with a few Christians who came to this nation seeking above all other things to build an unscalable wall between the government and Christianity. And most importantly, they want to compartmentalize Christianity to the state and the home."[51]

"Listen long enough to any . . . left-wing group and you'll believe [the secular] history of America," Jeffress said. "You will come to believe that America was founded by men with a large diversity of religious belief . . . all united by one dream. They wanted to build a secular nation. . . . Their goal was to build a large unscalable wall around this country . . . that would protect this country from any religious influence seeping into public life."[52] Jeffress ignores that the verdict of actual historians disagrees with him and he blames the view of history that he despises on left-wing groups. There is no such group among American historians.

The heart of the sermon contains an appeal to nostalgia that relies on illusions, significant erasures, and an assortment of false historical claims. The sermon may be seen as the fruit that has come forth from the soil of David Barton's revisionist vision of America. Barton's statistics, Barton's misleading stories about the Supreme Court and the government are sprinkled throughout the sermon. Jeffress, using a ploy often used by conservative writers, fills his sermons with what he confidently presents as the facts of the matter, but the source for nearly every claim is David Barton, and Barton has been shown to be a fabricator of sayings of the "Founding Fathers."

Jeffress uses David Barton's material and Barton uses James Kennedy's material but they are all attempting to drink from "cracked cisterns that can hold no water."[53] John Fea concludes, "The belief that the United States was founded as, and continues to be a Christian nation (Christian nationalism) undergirds much of evangelical politics today."[54]

Jeffress's sermon has the appearance of a scholarly, "footnotable" piece but it is filled with ahistorical references, each as problematic as the others. For example, he says with his unique brand of absolute certainty that fifty-two of the fifty-five signers of the Constitution were "evangelical believers." False. He trots out false information about the purpose of the First Amendment. This leads him to the conclusion that America is a Christian nation and that other religions should not be treated equally with Christianity. Once this list of spurious claims leaves the barn, an entire herd

---

51. Fea, *Believe Me*, 135.
52. Fea, *Believe Me*, 135.
53. Jeremiah 2:13.
54. Fea, *Believe Me*, 12.

fills the sermon. In one sweeping generalization he swears that the removal of school prayer by the Supreme Court has produced increased violence, illegitimate births, divorce, and lower SAT scores.

His sense of American exceptionalism is a seamless match for the rhetoric of President Trump. The patriarchal patriotism drips from every sentence of the sermon. The themes of nativism, nationalism, triumphalism, and militancy play over and over like a praise tune with only nine words. Lurking in the background of all this flag-waving, patriotic singing, and sermonic jeremiad, are the archetypal tropes of evangelicalism: whiteness, maleness, and racism. The echoes of J. Frank Norris ranting about Roman Catholics, alcohol, and immigrants add to the cacophony of a decades-long litany of woe.

Jeffress, implicitly acknowledging that his argument is on shaky ground, says, "I realize is it incorrect to say this, but it is nevertheless true. America was not founded as a Muslim nation. America was not founded as a Hindu nation. America was not founded as a nation that is neutral toward Christianity. America was founded as a Christian nation, and today we are going to discover that truth from history."[55] He doesn't, however, acknowledge that his discovery from history will not include the work of any actual American historians.

Traditional Christian values are defended in the sermon with the zeal a man would defend his wife and children from a band of brigands. America is strong; other nations are weak. America is righteous; other nations are wicked. "This is a Christian nation," Jeffress insists. "Every other religion is an impostor, an infidel."[56] Jeffress studiously insists that his politics and his pastorate are separate. "We don't check green cards or passports at First Baptist Dallas," he's fond of saying. When he's at the podium in church, he seldom utters a word about the president.[57] This rather insipid defense doesn't change the reality that Jeffress and Trump both employ apocalyptic, demolition rhetoric with the use of the "rape-of-the-nation" trope. Both are undergirding their version of populism with gender, strengthening its diverse manifestations. Their performed political masculinity supports and connects them to conservative social and political and religious gender norms. While Jeffress operates in an evangelical culture that offers him an "anointed authoritarianism," Trump operates in the theatre of an emerging "populist authoritarianism." One of the members of FBC, a black mother in her thirties, says of Jeffress, "He

---

55. Jeffress, "America Is a Christian Nation."
56. Jeffress, "America Is a Christian Nation."
57. Mooney, "Trump's Apostle."

is so right. It is time to stop being wimpy about Christianity. I wish more Christians had the heart for the Lord that he does."[58]

There is, of course, a symbol of the deep commitment than many Christians have to American exceptionalism—the American flag. When the American flag is more honored than the cross, Christians should know that something has gone badly awry. Its verbal speech act counterpart is the Pledge of Allegiance to the United States. Theologian Roger Olson says that a gentleman in one church said that if someone removed the flag, he might do something violent about it. In another church some people in the congregation kept returning the American flag to the worship space when the pastor moved it elsewhere in the church building. It seems that during the past few decades, any criticism of our American war efforts have been greeted with the same condemnations as a blatant heretic would be treated in an orthodox church.[59]

Perhaps critiques of why Rev. Jeffress is a loyal spokesperson of President Trump finally settle on the sense of empowerment that Trump gives him and his fellow evangelicals. They now have someone who can and will fight for them—a warrior for the cause of righteousness. Maybe it is as simple as Jeffress wanting a president who is the meanest son of a bitch in the world. Instead of being mild, kind, and good, they can unleash the monster who will stomp all over the liberals and give victory to them. Behind the smile and the smooth words, Rev. Jeffress seems to hold a residual resentment against all the perceived enemies that distort and damage his primary trope of American exceptionalism.

## Jeremiah Wright Sermon: "Confusing God and Government"

Jeffress's sermon "America Is a Christian Nation," clashes dramatically with a sermon by the Rev. Dr. Jeremiah Wright, "Confusing God and Government." Even the title of the sermon seems to condemn the Christian nationalism of Jeffress. These two preachers with contrasting visions also happen to be a white preacher of American exceptionalism and a Black preacher of the Black prophetic tradition.

Dr. Wright's sermon, preached during Obama's first campaign for president, produced moral outrage from conservative evangelicals. No surprise here because as far back as 1967, outrage erupted across all theological and political spectrums when the Rev. Dr. Martin Luther King, Jr. criticized

58. Mooney, "Trump's Apostle."
59. Olson, "Stanley Hauerwas, America and war."

America in a sermon. When King spoke out against the war in Vietnam, he said, and this is a quote, "America[n government] is "the greatest purveyor of violence in the world today."[60] This was in 1967 at Riverside Church. King was almost universally condemned for this sermon. His sermon, like Wright's, stands in the prophetic tradition of truth speaking to power. Cornel West, speaking of the killing of an African American jogger, evoked the memory of Dr. King: "When I saw those pictures there of Atlanta, you could see Brother Martin right there in Atlanta, saying: 'I told you about militarism. I told you about poverty. I told you about materialism. I told you about racism in all of its forms. I told you about xenophobia.' And what you're seeing in America is those chickens coming home to roost. You are reaping what you sow. And in this instant, you have Brother George [Floyd]—it is so clear—it was a lynching at the highest level. Nobody can deny it."[61]

The condemnation that King faced, and the condemnation Wright later faced, come down to one factor: A Black preacher condemning a white nation—and this would not go without a devastating counterattack. It wasn't the use of the language by Wright; it was the audacity of Wright to attack white America and its delusions of an America that doesn't exist, has never existed, and will never exist.

The *Washington Post* wrote that King had "diminished his usefulness to his cause, his country, and his people."[62] The *New York Times*, opining on "Dr. King's Error," reminded King that his proper battlegrounds were "in Chicago and Harlem and Watts." It said King, as an individual, was of course free to *think* about Vietnam, but, as a leader of Black people, he had an obligation to stay in his lane, i.e. to "direct [his] movement's efforts in the most constructive and relevant way." *Life* magazine called the speech "demagogic slander that sounded like a script for Radio Hanoi."[63]

King makes it clear that he stands in a Black prophetic tradition much older than the Vietnam War by quoting Langston Hughes: "O yes, I say it plain America never was America to me, and yet I swear this oath—America will be!" Even earlier there is the fierce, unrelenting critique of Frederick Douglass. In 1847 Douglass made it clear: "I have no love for America, as such," he announced in a speech he delivered that year. "I have no patriotism. I have no country."[64] Douglass let his righteous anger flow in metaphors of degradation, chains, and blood. "The institutions of this country

60. King, "Beyond Vietnam."
61. West, "Cornel West Says."
62. Pierre, "Martin Luther King Jr."
63. Both cited in Robbins, ed., *Against the Vietnam War*, 109.
64. Blight, "Frederick Douglass's Vision."

do not know me, do not recognize me as a man," he declared, "except as a piece of property." All that attached him to his native land were his family and his deeply felt ties to the "three millions of my fellow-creatures, groaning beneath the iron rod . . . with . . . stripes upon their backs."[65] Such a country, Douglass said, he could not love. "I desire to see its overthrow as speedily as possible, and its Constitution shivered in a thousand fragments."[66] Six years later, as the crisis over slavery's future began to tear apart the nation's political system, Douglass intensified his attacks on American hypocrisy and wanted to know just *who* could be an American. "The Hungarian, the Italian, the Irishman, the Jew and the Gentile," he said surveying the huge waves of European immigration, "all find in this goodly land a home." But "my white fellow-countrymen . . . have no other use for us [Blacks] whatever, than to coin dollars out of our blood." Demanding his birthright as an American, he felt like only the "veriest stranger and sojourner."[67]

The distance between Jeremiah Wright and Frederick Douglass shrinks to a pair of overlapping lines: 1866, 2020—still we struggle with America's identity, especially now with a president and power broker for whom white supremacy is not a notion but a reality. Emotionally, materially, the same despair that Douglass felt in the shadow of slavery is the same that Wright felt—I'm saying that Wright and King and Douglass had hearts that beat as one with Moses and his impassioned "Let my people go."

In the last great speech of his life, "Lessons of the Hour"—an excoriating analysis of the "excuses" and "lie" at the root of lynching—Douglass betrayed a faith "shaken" and nearly gone. Disenfranchisement and murderous violence left him observing a nation mired in lawless horror. Lynchings were "lauded and applauded by honorable men . . . guardians of Southern women" who enabled other men to behave "as buzzards, vultures, and hyenas." A country once endowed with "nobility" was crushed by mob rule. His dream in tatters, Douglass begged his audiences to remember that the Civil War and Reconstruction had "announced the advent of a nation, based upon human brotherhood and the self-evident truths of liberty and equality. Its mission was the redemption of the world from the bondage of ages."[68] We would be deaf not to hear the cries of the African Americans in the streets of Minneapolis, Portland, and Louisville today.

The criticism of America by African Americans causes the trouble, not disagreement with the prophetic tradition in the Bible. America is the

---

65. Blight, "Frederick Douglass's Vision."
66. Blight, "Frederick Douglass's Vision."
67. Blight, "Frederick Douglass's Vision."
68. Blight, "Frederick Douglass's Vision."

sacred cow, the golden calf, maybe even the snake on a stick still hanging out in the temple at the time of King Hezekiah. Idols never die easily, especially when they are denied. Literalists to the core would say that we are finished with idols because the idols described in Scripture are made of stone and wood, and literalists are sure they don't have such gods. This ignores the idols that are nonmaterial, the idols that are represented by what people love more than God.

Jeremiah Wright attacked those invisible, denied idols and paid a huge price for so doing. Wright was raised in Philadelphia's Germantown neighborhood. His father was a prominent Baptist minister and his mother a respected educator. In the early 1960s, Wright signed up with the US Marine Corps, and later transferred to the Navy and served three more years as a medical technician. Later he earned his undergraduate degree from Howard University and went on to earn degrees from Chicago Divinity School and United Theological Seminary.

Wright became the pastor of Trinity Church (Chicago) in 1972. At the time, it was a struggling congregation with only eighty-seven members—it currently exceeds 6,000. Rev. Wright's efforts to address the needs of the community has made Trinity one of the most politically active and socially conscious churches in the nation. (In early 2008, Wright retired after thirty-six years as the senior pastor at Trinity and is now pastor emeritus.)

Trinity Church grew in size and influence under Wright's leadership. He and his congregation made pilgrimages to Africa, welcomed women leaders and gay members, and made Trinity a social force with over seventy ministries addressing community needs ranging from youth groups to day care.

Rev. Wright attacked the "sacred cows" of evangelicals; American-bred sacred cows of national perfectionism, national superiority, and exceptionalism. The preacher pulled no punches. Here are some of the words Americans should have heard and taken to heart and then repented, but these are not the words that made it to the media declaration: "And the United States of America government, when it came to treating her citizens of Indian descent, she failed. She put them on reservations."[69] "When it came to putting her citizens of Japanese descent fairly, she failed. She put them in interment prison camps."[70] "When it came to putting the citizens of African descent fairly, America failed. She put them in chains. The government put them on slave quarters. Put them on auction blocks. Put them in cotton fields. Put them in inferior schools. Put them in

69. Wright, "Confusing God and Government."
70. Wright, "Confusing God and Government."

substandard housing. Put them in scientific experiments. Put them in the lower paying jobs. Put them outside the equal protection of the law. Kept them out of their racist bastions of higher education, and locked them into positions of hopelessness and helplessness."[71]

Then the Rev. Wright, fired by the power of his gospel-laced proclamation, brought the argument to the house: "The government gives them the drugs, builds bigger prisons, passes a three strike law and then wants us to sing God Bless America. Naw, naw, naw. Not God Bless America. God Damn America! That's in the Bible. For killing innocent people. God Damn America for treating us citizens as less than human. God Damn America as long as she tries to act like she is God and she is Supreme."[72]

Steeped in the not-so-great history of America, Wright spoke the truth of the gospel through the lens of American civil rights leaders. We can learn much from how Wright uses history in his sermon. Wright spares no portion of our history as a people of oppression and he is not interested in going back to some golden age of American greatness. He is calling us to go forward in hope and to live up to the principles of our nation. Wright gives a no-holds-barred, clear-eyed presentation of the past. And yet, even in the midst of all this injustice, Wright still proclaims the goodness of God, the hope of the future, and the trustworthiness of God. There's hope and humility in his view of American history.

Wright sets the scene for his denunciation of the military with a narration of the biblical story of Jesus raising Jesus from the dead. After setting the biblical scene, Wright makes a dramatic shift: "Let me help you with something. Let me help you, let me help you. The military does not make for peace. . . . War does not make for peace." And Wright deplores the idea of revenge. "Peace is not on your mind. Payback is the only game in town. You just bide your time and you wait for your opportunity, but somebody is going to pay dearly."[73] Here Wright is on solid biblical ground. In Zechariah 4:6 we read: "Not by might, nor by power, but by my spirit, says the Lord of hosts." Jesus says, "My peace I give to you."

Jesus, according to Dr. Wright, tells the people, "You did not see the meaning of my ministry. You are missing the real things that make for peace. You are confusing external appearances with external power."[74] The implication that the evangelicals have confused God with government is clear. "A lot

---

71. Wright, "Confusing God and Government."
72. Wright, "Confusing God and Government."
73. Wright, "Confusing God and Government."
74. Wright, "Confusing God and Government."

of people still confuse God with their Government."[75] Wright spends considerable time and energy making the case from the Bible and from history that the first-century Jews confused God with government. Evangelicals are also confusing God with their government.

Wright touches a vital nerve with evangelicals when he points out that our military acts in the same way as Muslim "jihadists." Now, the understanding that evangelical leaders have of Muslims contradicts Wright, especially when we consider Jeffress and Franklin Graham. Even if the "God damn" portion of the sermon had been different, Wright would have received condemnation for his remarks about Muslims and "jihadists." These are buzz words for battle among evangelicals. Jeffress has claimed, in one of his sermons that "The deep, dark, dirty secret of Islam: It is a religion that promotes pedophilia—sex with children. This so-called prophet Muhammad raped a 9-year-old girl—had sex with her." He has also called Islam an "evil, evil" religion and said the religion was both "oppressive" and "violent," and was inspired by Satan and was a "false religion."[76] Franklin Graham has claimed that the Islam religion was "behind the violence" around the world.[77]

Dr. Wright, reflecting on the sermon later, and using words from Jesus about not being judgmental, says,

> We can't see the speck . . . because we equate our government with our God. We confuse government and God. When you start confusing God and government, your allegiances to government—a particular government and not to God, then you're in serious trouble because governments fail people. And governments change. And governments lie. And those [were the] three points of the sermon. And that is the context in which I was illustrating how the governments biblically and the governments since biblical times, up to our time, changed, how they failed, and how they lie. And when we start talking about my government right or wrong, I don't think that goes. That is consistent with what the will of God says or the word of God says that governments don't say right or wrong. That governments that wanna kill innocents are not consistent with the will of God. And that you are made in the image of God, you're not made in the image of any particular government. We have the freedom here in this country to talk about that publicly,

---

75. Wright, "Confusing God and Government."
76. Tripathi, "Robert Jeffress."
77. Goldstein, "Billy Graham's Preacher Son."

whereas some other places, you're dead if you say the wrong thing about your government.[78]

Dr. Wright's sermon strikes at the heart of Christian nationalism. The reaction of the clergy to his use of the words "God damn" were hollow spitballs of self-righteousness. The real anger is that Dr. Wright connected the "God damn" to America. This the evangelicals can't abide. While this causes many evangelicals to label him as unpatriotic, it doesn't make him unpatriotic or un-Christian. William Sloane Coffin, Jr. said that a true patriot carries on a lover's quarrel with the nation.

Jeremiah Wright broke out the Old Testament "prophet" on an entire nation, a nation that feels it is God's chosen people. The parallels between Wright's preaching and that of Amos are striking. Wright's sermon serves as condemnation of all that evangelical Christian nationalism holds dear. The evangelical disdain for a "prophet" reeks of irony because evangelicals revel in their prophetic genius. The problem is that their definition of prophet differs dramatically from the biblical definition of prophet. Jeremiah Wright is a prophet in the line of the Old Testament prophets.

Amos offers the paradigmatic rhetoric for prophets required to speak difficult words of criticism to the nation: "Alas for those who are at ease in Zion, and for those who feel secure on Mount Samaria, the notables of the first of the nations, to whom the house of Israel resorts! Alas for those who lie on beds of ivory, and lounge on their couches, and eat lambs from the flock, and calves from the stall; who sing idle songs to the sound of the harp, and like David improvise on instruments of music; who drink wine from bowls, and anoint themselves with the finest oils, but are not grieved over the ruin of Joseph!"[79]

In chapter 7 of his book, Amos employs a powerful metaphor to drive home the judgment of God against the nation: "This is what he showed me: the Lord was standing beside a wall built with a plumb-line, with a plumb-line in his hand. And the Lord said to me, 'Amos, what do you see?' And I said, 'A plumb-line.' Then the Lord said, 'See, I am setting a plumb-line in the midst of my people Israel; I will never again pass them by; the high places of Isaac shall be made desolate, and the sanctuaries of Israel shall be laid waste, and I will rise against the house of Jeroboam with the sword.'"[80] Now, hear the predictable response from the king's priest: "O seer, go, flee away to the land of Judah, earn your bread there, and prophesy

---

78. Moyers, interview with Jeremiah Wright.
79. Amos 6:1–2.
80. Amos 7:7–9.

there; but never again prophesy at Bethel, for it is the king's sanctuary, and it is a temple of the kingdom."[81]

Amaziah condemns himself out of his own mouth: "It is a temple of the kingdom." Not a temple of Almighty God. Not a temple of righteousness. A temple of the kingdom and of this kingdom, which is destined to fall. Amaziah is high priest. How many evangelical pastors and churches have become Amaziahs of flawed kingdoms/temples?

Dr. Wright got the Amos treatment from evangelicals. Rev. Jeffress and other evangelicals managed to make Dr. Wright America's "boogeyman" with the effective use of "devil terms."[82] While they routinely use the rhetoric of declension to denigrate America, they are actually merely blaming liberals and their allies for the demise of America. They separate their vision of the mythical America created in their minds, with the flesh-and-blood, flawed, and imperfect nation inhabited by a people of "unclean lips." They confuse moral progress in race relations and human sexuality with moral decline. It's a strange world when "up" becomes "down" and "down" becomes "up."

Later in his sermon, Wright turns his attention to the deepest convictions of the evangelicals: God sent them to America, gave them America, anointed America to be "a city on a hill." "He sent us to take the country from the Arawak, the Susquehanna, the Apache, the Comanche, the Cherokee, the Seminole, the Choctaw, the Hopi, and the Arapaho. We confuse Government and God." "We believe God ordained African slavery."[83]

Wright challenges the American exceptionalism that is bedrock ideology for evangelicals. When he cries out, multiple times, "God damn America," it's as if he has gone into his freezer, pulled out four or five frozen slush balls (snow and ice mixed with clay and rocks), that he's been saving since the last snowball fight in February, and throws every slush ball, right into the face of everything evangelicals hold dear. For Wright, this is not a case of resentment but an outburst of righteous anger.

Then a controversy emerged from video clips of Wright's sermon that threatened to turn the Obama campaign into a footnote to history. Excerpts from the sermons of Reverend Jeremiah Wright were aired on ABC's *Good Morning America*. Brian Ross introduced the segment by noting that "Senator Obama has been a member of the same church in Chicago for twenty years, where his pastor has been Reverend Jeremiah Wright, the man who performed the Obamas' marriage ceremony, and

---

81. Amos 7:12–13.
82. Weaver, *Language Is Sermonic*.
83. Wright, "Confusing God and Government."

the man Obama credits for the title of his book, *The Audacity of Hope*." Politically Obama felt a need to not be part of the gospel message of Dr. Wright.[84] Beneath the stinging rebuke of Wright there was the complicated sense of race. Jeremiah Wright, a Black man, had a lot of nerve, talking down to white America, according to his critics.

It was not the first time that Wright had emerged as a potential political liability, but this time the response was, in Obama's own words, a "firestorm."[85] The story was picked up by every major news outlet, and its circulation on the Internet dwarfed the previous controversies by several orders of magnitude. On the day after the ABC report, Obama posted a response at the widely read *Huffington Post* Blog, in which he stated, "I vehemently disagree and strongly condemn the statements that have been the subject of this controversy. I categorically denounce any statement that disparages our great country or serves to divide us from our allies. I also believe that words that degrade individuals have no place in our public dialogue, whether it's on the campaign stump or in the pulpit. In sum, I reject outright the statements by Rev. Wright that are at issue."[86]

Obama also posted a video on YouTube, in which he repeated this statement almost verbatim and ended by asking his supporters to "please forward this video on and get this message out to everyone you can."[87] But the controversy continued to build until it became clear that a more dramatic response was required. It is rare for a politician to give a speech that is a rhetorical critique of another person's speech. Obama did this to Wright's sermon. Prophets are without honor even among their famous church members.

Dr. Otis Moss, Jr., in his sermon, "A Prophetic Witness in an Anti-Prophetic Age," gives voice to the treatment of prophets. Rev. Moss argues that we don't like prophets: "And let me [say], we ought to remember that the community, the world does not like prophets, and neither does the church. The world does not like prophets. Prophets disturb us. They shake us out of our dogmatic slumber. Prophets override our contradictions and put to shame our mediocrity. The world does not like prophets and the church often refuses to celebrate them."[88] We don't like prophets because prophetic rhetoric is social and material. It is the social gospel and Donald Trump is attempting to destroy what's left of the political aspect of the social gospel—the platform

---

84. Allen, "How Jeremiah Wright."
85. Murray, "Have I Missed the Competition?"
86. Baker, "What Should Obama Do About Jeremiah Wright?"
87. Krauthammer, "The Speech."
88. Quoted in Gilbert, *A Pursued Justice*, loc. 3163.

and politics of Franklin Roosevelt. The prophetic rhetoric is political and sociological. It's not pie in the sky by and by. It's not the Gnosticism that gave birth to anti-Semitism and then to white nationalism and the racism that trailed in the wake of both those powerful storms. Prophetic rhetoric is not welcome now; it has never been welcomed.

Wright's sermon seems tame when compared to some prophetic actions. Isaiah walked naked and barefoot in the streets for three years to visualize the people being led away in captivity, "naked and barefoot, with buttocks uncovered."[89] God commanded Ezekiel to cut his hair in three pieces and burn one part in the city, smite a second piece with a knife, and scatter the third part in the wind. Startling, inappropriate, unexpected, but it was the symbolic action of a true prophet. Jeremiah was instructed by God to "Make yourself a yoke of straps and bars, and put them on your neck."[90] The attempt by evangelicals and Republicans to place Rev. Wright outside of the biblical mantle of the prophet fails.

Like Israel and Judah, the USA doesn't much care for prophets. Moss says: "There is no danger in the sermons we preach, no challenge, and no threat to anybody in particular . . . But Jesus almost got killed on his first sermon—perhaps, his first public sermon."[91] Jeremiah Wright has a prophetic rhetoric that disturbs the status quo. Jesus would be shocked at the idea that people would have liked his sermon in Nazareth. He offended his own family. He offended his friends and neighbors. The gospel can be offensive; that doesn't make it wrong.

This disdain for the prophetic voice is not a new-fangled expression of religious people. There's always been a "bull" market for putting down, taking down, and taking out prophets. "We don't like prophets." Moss outlines how badly Martin Luther King, Jr. was treated. "He was not wanted in his hometown. So, bombed in Montgomery; jailed in Birmingham, Albany, and St. Augustine; stoned in Chicago; invited out of town in Cleveland; and unwanted in Atlanta."[92]

Wright's sermon is consistent with the language of condemnation used by the Hebrew prophets. Abraham Joshua Heschel writes that the prophets "speak and act as if the sky were about to collapse because Israel has become unfaithful to God." The prophet's "words are outbursts of violent emotions. His rebuke is harsh and relentless."[93]

89. Isaiah 20:5.
90. Jeremiah 25:2.
91. Moss, "A Prophetic Witness," 778.
92. Moss, "A Prophetic Witness," 779.
93. Heschel, *The Prophets*, 5.

Wright got into political trouble for this kind of preaching. Interestingly, the same ideas, presented in the scholarly language of Stanley Hauerwas, doesn't cause the same kind of trouble. "In this sense," Hauerwas says, "the church has not conquered America; America has conquered the church." Hauerwas is white and has made a career of using salty language and reminding his audiences that he is the son of a bricklayer.

For example, Hauerwas gave an address at the Youth Academy at Duke Divinity School. He admits that his purpose is not to shock the young people that he admits to not understanding. He then adds, "I do not want to make Christianity easy. I want to make it hard." Hauerwas, in the prophetic stream where Wright swims, tells the youth that he is not sure that the Christianity that made them Christian is Christianity. This is a direct assault on American nationalists, previously known as evangelicals.

He then offers them a test:

How many of you worship in a church with an American flag?

How many of you worship in a church where the Fourth of July is celebrated?

That recognizes Thanksgiving?

That celebrates January 1 as the "New Year"?

That recognizes Mother's Day?

Each time he answers, "I am sorry to tell you your salvation is in doubt."[94]

Hauerwas bemoans the use of faith to underwrite American pretensions that we are a Christian nation possessing righteousness that other nations lack. Hauerwas blisters the Episcopal Church in Kennebunkport for saying the Pledge of Allegiance in worship with the president in attendance. Hauerwas points out, "The Christian pledge is not the Pledge of Allegiance, but rather is called the Apostle's Creed."[95] He insists that this was idolatry. Admitting that his judgment is harsh, Hauerwas insists that it is "one that needs to be made if we are to recover faithful Christian practice."[96] Hauerwas says he knows President Bush is sincere and a very serious Christian. "The problem is not his sincerity. The problem is that the Christianity about which he is sincere is not shaped by the gospel."[97]

---

94. Hauerwas, *Working with Words*, 116.
95. Hauerwas, *Working with Words*, 118.
96. Hauerwas, *Working with Words*, 118.
97. Hauerwas, *Working with Words*, 118.

Hauerwas argues that this is "but one instance of the general failure of the church in America to be the church."[98]

Hauerwas makes startling claims that are just as provocative as Jeremiah Wright's sermon. The response to Hauerwas is mild compared to what Wright faced after his sermon and for at least the next dozen years. What is going on here? Why is Jeremiah Wright the scapegoat?

Will Campbell, no less of a critic of American nationalism, wrote, "For certain, our nation has done it share of killing children. From the Trail of Tears to Dresden to Hiroshima to My Lai to Waco. Ah, we have killed children."[99] Campbell also, in a larger passage worth citing in full, argues:

> I believe God made the St. Lawrence River, and the Rio Grande River, China Sea and the English Channel, but I don't believe God made America, or Canada, or Mexico, or England, or China. Man did that ... It is doubtful that there has ever been a nation established for bad reasons. Nations are always established to escape tyranny, to combat evil, to find freedom, to reach heaven. Man has always been able to desire to build a heaven. But it seems he has never been able to admit that he didn't pull it off. So, he keeps insisting that he did pull it off. And that is really what patriotism is all about. It is the insistence that what we have done is sacred. It is that transference of allegiance from what God did in creating the whole wide world to what we have done with a little sliver of it. Patriotism is immoral. Flying a national flag—any national flag—in a church house is a symbol of idolatry. Singing "God Bless America" in a Christian service is blasphemy. Patriotism is immoral because it is a violation of the First Amendment.[100]

Neither Hauerwas nor Campbell drew heavy fire from evangelicals for their incendiary remarks. Is it because they are white? Is it because Hauerwas is a bricklayer's son from Texas, Campbell the son of a Mississippi poor working man? Is it because they didn't say, "God damn America?" While neither Hauerwas nor Campbell made their profane remarks in the heat of a presidential campaign, there is still the nagging sense that the deeply embedded racism of our nation gives a pass to white preachers and theologians that is less likely to be granted to African American preachers like Jeremiah Wright. In any event, the combination of "God damn" with "America" must be the key, because Hauerwas and Campbell said, "God

---

98. Hauerwas, *Working with Words*, 118.
99. Campbell, *Soul among Lions*, 31–32.
100. Campbell and Goode, eds., *Crashing the Idols*, 55.

damn." Campbell once told a seminarian persistent in questioning Campbell about his beliefs, "I believe in Jesus God dammit, I believe in Jesus," so the profanity is not the issue.

What we have is that "God bless America" comes face-to-face with "God damn America." Two visions clash like two opposite weather systems that create tornadoes over Kansas. The rhetorical trope, "America is a Christian nation" undergoes radical deconstruction in Wright's sermon.

Lerone A. Martin, assistant professor of the History of American Religion and Culture at Eden Theological Seminary in Saint Louis, sheds some light. "Wright indicted an entire country," he said. "What Wright did; Wright used the old style of preaching rooted in the ways of the prophet narratives of the Old Testament. Because the nation has done wrong, God will present judgment unless you repent. This is what God will do. [Wright] indicted an entire country for the things America has done."[101]

Wright's sermon, or at least the "sermon bytes" that appeared on the news cycle, were a visible threat to the nation's vision of itself, especially the vision of white evangelicals. Evangelicals, wishing to be washed as white as snow, did not wish to remember the pain they had caused and the harm they had done. In Doris Betts's short story, "This Is the Only Time I'll Tell It," a baby is baptized after being saved from drowning in a bucket of icy water on the back porch by her own father. They named the little girl Silver. They gave her to Zelene, the woman who saved her from drowning. The narrator's wife told Zelene, after the baptism, that Silver would never remember all of that early pain. Zelene shook her cropped brown hair. "The pain went in her." Zelene only ran one finger down the thin arm that crazy man had broken, "saying in silence that the mark was made, made deep, that water meant for drowning had gone inside this child, that no grown body—at any size—would ever be fully dry of that knowledge."[102] The pain that "went into" persons of color from the second century to the present remains a part of our heritage. There is an accumulation across time and "across both relatedness and interruptions in relatedness, becoming a palimpsest of force-encounters traversing the ebbs and swells of intensities that pass between bodies . . . Affect marks a body's belonging to a world of encounters."[103] For centuries it has been accepted that infliction of cruelty on the bodies of non-whites is a right of those bodies that are white. The acts of violence by white Americans on Native Americans and African Americans went deep, left eternal scars, and was felt. "In other words, an act of violence has to be experienced as cruel in

---

101. Allen, "How Jeremiah Wright."
102. Betts quoted in Ketchin, ed., *The Christ-Haunted Landscape*, 234.
103. Gregg and Seigworth, eds., *The Affect Theory Reader*, 2.

order to be cruel."[104] Cruelty becomes what power feels like for the inflictors of it; it becomes what power feels like when cruelty sticks to the bodies of those who are non-white. Jeremiah Wright held up all that pain and suffering and he made white America look at it. He did this as surely as Moses made the people of God look on the bronzed serpent in the wilderness, that they might be healed and the scourge stopped.[105]

Evangelicals steadfastly refuse to look. Like the Israelites who worked the bronze serpent into their worship, evangelicals have worked their cruelty into their idolatry of American exceptionalism. Perhaps evangelicals need to sit at the feet of Wittgenstein's famous dictum: "To repeat: don't think, but look."[106] There can be no redemption of the past until we are willing to look on it. Somehow the Gnosticism within the evangelical strain of faith dissuades such looking at "America's flaws." Take, for example, a primary evangelical text—the born-again story of Nicodemus. Jesus said to Nicodemus, "Just as Moses lifted up the serpent in the wilderness, so must the Son of Man be lifted up, that whoever believes in him may have eternal life." Later Jesus insists that he must die by being "lifted up from the earth" so that he can draw all people to him. In order to live, we must look on this man's death.

This is where the Gnosticism, with its disdain for bodies, kicks in. We skip the dead man on the cross and go straight to the resurrection. This is why the cross in evangelical churches is empty. Gnosticism is irresistible. There is, however, no salvation in Gnosticism. If we are to live, we must look. If we are to be saved from our past sins, we must look on the bodies we have damaged, distorted, denied, and destroyed. This is why Wright's sermon created such outrage. Evangelicals didn't want to see, really see, because looking would mean participating in the lives of the others both in repentance, reparations, and then reconciliation. We are invited to look and see the body on the cross along with all the bodies we have hung and we are invited to partake of Jesus' body and blood.

Jeremiah Wright—his story, his body—contains the wounds that all descendants of oppressed people carry. In this sense, his sermon is not sacrilegious; it is sacramental. The wounds carried by the descendants of Native Americans and American slaves remain open. They are still living out the servant poem of Isaiah. The pain from the whips went in them, literally and metaphorically. No generation is ever clear of the cruelty. I push the metaphorical limits of Scripture here: They have borne our infirmities

---

104. Levina, "Whiteness and the Joys of Cruelty," 76.
105. Numbers 21:4–9.
106. Wittgenstein, *Culture and Value*, 24.

and carried our diseases; we accounted them as less than human, struck down by God, and afflicted. They have been wounded by our transgressions, crushed by our iniquities; upon them have fallen the punishments we have dished out. We have bruised them and oppressed and afflicted them, yet they opened not their mouth except to God and to one another in the language of unbearable pain. They have been like lambs led to the slaughter, and by a perversion of justice they were deprived of their native lands, families, and fortunes. Who could have imagined their future? For they were cut off from the land of the living, stricken by our transgression. Their unmarked graves are hidden everywhere across the lands as victims of our unrelenting violence.

Jeremiah Wright gave voice to that cruelty as his sermon carried within it the primordial screams of the Hebrew slaves, the African slaves, and the segregated Americans whose cries God at last heard. Wright gave anguished voice to all the Rachels, Awanatas, Chenoas, Rosas, Sojourners—voices of Jews, Native Americans, African Americans—"A voice is heard in Ramah, lamentation and bitter weeping. Rachel is weeping for her children; she refuses to be comforted for her children, because they are no more."[107] Wright lifted up that Afrocentric prophetic tradition flowing from the Nile and the Mississippi through the experience of slavery and desegregation. The sadness is how some whites dismiss this as the ramblings of a crazy Black man. Wrapped inside the "God damn America" were the groanings of God's tortured children: "For the Lord would be moved to pity by their groaning because of those who persecuted and oppressed them."[108] "For my sighing comes like my bread, and my groanings are poured out like water."[109] "Because the poor are despoiled, because the needy groan, I will now rise up, says the Lord . . ."[110]

## Whither the American Vision: Jeffress or Wright?

This intense theological and historical attempt to understand the American vision and know who we are has been the burden of this story. Nicholas Lash says that the story the church tells is a story of sacrifice that is meant to challenge the stories of a world bent on sacrificing to false gods.[111] That puts it

107. Jeremiah 31:15; Matthew 2:18.
108. Judges 2:18.
109. Job 3:24.
110. Psalm 12:5.
111. Lash, *Theology on the Road*, 91–92.

right where I think it should be—in our laps as we try to see our involvement with false gods of success rooted in ancient rhetorics of racism, whiteness, and maleness. Upon reflection, I consider Wright's sermon an expression of who and what the church is meant to be. The church, as material alternative to a spiritualized Gnosticism, is all we have. Evangelicals, it turns out, for all their bluster about a literal Bible, are a bunch of symbolists.

Cornel West, defending Dr. Wright, calls his sermon the prophetic vision of the Black church. West argues, "Jeremiah Wright was the canary in the mine. The Black preaching tradition has been emptied out."[112] "The Black prophetic tradition has been the leaven in the American democratic loaf," West said. "What has kept American democracy from going fascist or authoritarian or autocratic has been the legacy of Frederick Douglass, Harriet Tubman, Sojourner Truth, Martin King, Fannie Lou Hamer. This is not because Black people have a monopoly on truth, goodness or beauty. It is because the Black freedom movement puts pressure on the American empire in the name of integrity, decency, honesty and virtue."[113]

Always in every era there are those ready to whitewash every moment of American history, to downplay the prophetic voice of Black liberationists, and to maintain the pretense of a righteous nation. James C. Scott argues, "The struggle is over the appropriation of symbols, a struggle over how the past and present shall be understood and labeled, a struggle to identify causes and assess blame, a contentious effort to give partisan meaning to local history."[114]

What was at stake in the Wright sermon response was the white evangelical outrage over Wright's "downing" of America. They don't wish to hear the story of American injustice from anyone, but especially not from a Black pastor. The evangelicals already believe that history teachers present a distorted, liberal version of American history. "Teachers intentionally made students feel bad about America's many crimes from its checkered past—slavery, the treatment of Native Americans, and the oppression of women."[115] Evangelicals stewed that students knew little about the triumphs of the new conservatism from the 1960s to the present. They weren't taught about heroes like Andrew Carnegie and John D. Rockefeller, who, in their view, embodied American greatness. Students were not learning about America's godly heritage. "In their estimation, civil rights leaders like the labor organizer Chavez and Supreme Court Justice Thurgood Marshall received too much

---

112. Hedges, "Cornel West and the Fight."
113. Hedges, "Cornel West and the Fight."
114. Quoted in Brueggemann, *Truth Speaks to Power*, 7.
115. Stephens and Giberson, *The Anointed*, 3.

attention for their meager achievements."[116] These Christians want to baptize American history and Christianize the American story with a different view of our past—founded as a Christian nation, and a different view of our present—America is Christian, and a different view of our future—God's chosen ones who will be raptured into glory. "God is no longer visible in American history," hyperbolizes David Barton.[117]

Not liking the stories of history, evangelicals "amid the thorns and thistles of the wilderness, long for Eden," said William Sloan Coffin in 1982.[118] The evangelical lust for Eden is not only an illusion; it is a denial of the words of the Bible they swear they believe is the literal truth of God. Read the words in Genesis 3 and have the courage to say goodbye to Eden.[119]

Kenneth Burke claims that "Eden" has more to do with power than faith. Andrew M. King says, "The beginning of the human drive for power is told in the Biblical story of the Fall. In Burke's term, with the fall from grace, humankind invented the 'Negative.' In order to learn the Negative, they had to acquire the gift from the forbidden fruit, Language. Now, capable of saying 'No,' humans started the long journey of the dialectic of History."[120] The garden exists in the trope of perfect America, maintained by the language of evangelicals. Frustrated by the disenchantment and weariness of a secular society that seems to beat them down, and disappointed in an end that refuses to come, the evangelicals have abandoned the present and the future for this golden age, this pristine past. Wright shattered that vision and paid a big price because people become violent when their American exceptionalism trope is deconstructed or revealed to be lies. No one likes others tampering with their primary tropes. Even for literalists, it's still about the symbols: Bible and flag.

Wright dared to speak truth to established power. Walter Brueggemann argues the power "traffics in established truth about which there is general agreement among the parties that matter: the state, the church, the corporate structure, the academy, and so on. The several institutions are skillful in articulating and maintaining truth that can readily be seen as allied with status quo power."[121] The gatekeepers of what is true are skilled in articulating and maintaining that truth even to the point of insisting on "alternative facts." There are, however, other versions of truth that arise from

---

116. Stephens and Giberson, *The Anointed*, 3.
117. Stephens and Giberson, *The Anointed*, 16.
118. Coffin, *The Courage to Love*, 7.
119. Genesis 3:24.
120. King, *Power and Communication*, 1–2.
121. Brueggemann, *Truth Speaks to Power*, 2.

below, from outside the structure of the power. James C. Scott speaks of "hidden scripts" devised by peasants that contain a truth linked to lived reality and kept mostly hidden from the power. In the Bible, this other truth is carried by prophets and poets.

For example, in the evangelical push for a sanitized, conservative view of American history, racism is the hidden script. There were much earlier attempts to influence history textbooks on behalf of African Americans who were insulted by the portrayal given by the authors of African Americans and Native Americans. When the new history in the 1970s gave truthful space to the stories of Others, the evangelical alarms went off everywhere. These are the same alarms that erupted when Wright attacked the evangelical vision of America. They rallied to protest these histories that made so much of the contributions of Others, that depicted the Civil War as a war over slavery, that depicted the South as traitorous.

According to evangelical leaders like David Barton, "teachers intentionally made students feel bad about America's many crimes from its checkered past [crimes rooted in racism, nationalism, colonialism, exceptionalism]—slavery, the treatment of Native Americans, and women."[122] History, for Barton, is more about feeling good than getting the truth of history recorded and taught to the next generation. Pathos as history seems an odd pedagogy, rife with distortions, lies, and the oppression of Others.

The tragedy of Barton's "American exceptionalism" trope, his revisionist history, is its attempt to silence the voices of non-white members of our history. In Barton's reading of history, the voices of the peasants, the slaves, the poor are reduced to anonymous contributors in the statistics of conscription, crop production, taxes, and demographics. Scott maintains that these groups have been denied the luxury of open, organized, political activity, and Barton and company would like to keep it that way.

History has usually paid attention to peasants only when they have engaged in futile political rebellions. Peasant rebellions are few and far between. The vast majority are crushed unceremoniously. This deeply ingrained silencing of the voices of the oppressed made the civil rights movement so traumatic. Now, the protests in our cities demonstrate the same tensions between those who want to keep the story of power intact, at any price, including violence, and those who wish, at long last, to have their voices heard and their concerns addressed. Make no mistake, Barton and company are attempting to fasten their dominant vision of control on Others even more effectively than their predecessors.

Has this been about affect all the time? Evangelicals want to feel good without making any changes. As Lauren Berland has proposed, "The Trump

---

122. Stephens and Giberson, *The Anointed*, 2.

Emotion Machine is delivering feeling ok, acting free."[123] Trump manages to convert evangelical shame of racism, nativism, homophobia, and the like into a felt sense of dignity. Trump, however, himself a stranger to repentance, has offered evangelicals "feeling good" without any moral transformation.

While Trump may be perceived as the product of "structural racism, institutional sexism, and a carnivorous right-wing media," he has also intuitively taken advantage of Americans' declining trust in national institutions, leaders, and each other.[124] Roderick Hart sees Trump as a product as well as a cause of the nation's political maladies. Trump, in Hart's analysis, is something of an "emotional revolutionary" who is proud of his feelings, unafraid to express them, and who understands and reaches out toward his supporters' emotions as well.[125] Trump and his followers share this sense of being shamed unfairly, of being persecuted, of not being given the freedom to feel good about their deep-seated mistrust and racism. Hart attributes Trump's electoral success and his ability to sustain support to that connection.

With or without Wright's use of profanity, America needs the sermons of Black preachers, but they will face an even more emboldened and hostile evangelical enemy. As John A. Williams laments, "The closer a black man comes to the truth of America in his writing and speaking, the more quickly, the more positively the nation's press close the doors against him."

The Rev. Dr. Jeremiah Wright presents a different vision of America. It is a sermonic form of the American history that evangelicals deny. Dr. Wright speaks an uncomfortable truth. Like Lazarus separated from the rich man, there is "a great chasm" that has been carved out between evangelicals and progressives. The two messages are polar opposites. Jeffress has one version; Wright has the other version. Historians and most Christian scholars are on Wright's side. Jeffress offers a non-prophetic yet strangely apocalyptic vision of America.

## Conclusion

Two preachers, one politician, two visions, even two Americas. Christian nationalism and prophetic tradition, reconciliationist and emancipationist, evangelical and social gospel. "America Is a Christian Nation" vs. "Confusing God and Government." Whither the vision of America? How will we decide the values by which we shall live as a people?

The vision of Robert Jeffress will not sustain Christianity or democracy. We see a rich Christian tradition in America desecrated in the name

---

123. Berlant, "Trump, or Political Emotions."
124. Hart, *Trump and Us*, 18.
125. Hart, *Trump and Us*, 18.

of a conservative worldview, a worldview Wright and Martin Luther King would be in direct opposition to. Wright is against Trump because of his neglect of the poor and the working class and because of the racism he embodies, because he is a war president. Cornel West says, "We are talking about crimes against humanity—Wall Street crimes, war crimes, the crimes of the criminal justice system in the form of Jim Crow, the crimes against our working poor that have their backs pushed against the wall because of stagnant wages and corporate profits going up. Abraham Heschel said that the distinctive feature of any empire in decline is its indifference to criminality. That is a fundamental feature of our time, an indifference to criminality, especially on top, wickedness in high places."[126] Trump and his evangelicals see the protestors in the streets as the criminal element, when the high crimes connect back to the White House. Jeffress is religious cover for the crimes.

"This is not personal," West said. "We are talking about an imperial system, manifest in Trump's disdain for the other institutions of democracy. We are talking about a corporate state and a massive surveillance and national security state. It operates according to its own logic. Profit on the one hand, and secrecy to hide imperial policy on the other."[127] Robert Jeffress is the head house preacher of the White House, just as Al Sharpton was the head house Negro on the Obama plantation. But there is a difference. Jeffress loves being the spiritual overseer of the Trump plantation. He will not say a critical word. It is sad and pathetic. We are living in the age of the sellout.

Our hope for a better future lies in the direction of Wright's prophetic realism. The Age of Trump has placed us at a critical decision-making intersection. We can refuse to marginalize the complexities of democracy, embrace our diversity, and mobilize all our citizens. As Sheldon Wolin puts it, democracy is "first and foremost about equality" made possible by "social cooperation."[128] In the face of deeply faced grievances, perhaps only a sermonic trope will suffice: Let us put our backs to our past and our faces to the future.

---

126. Quoted in Hedges, "Cornel West and the Fight."
127. Hedges, "Cornel West and the Fight."
128. Quoted in Ivie, "Trump's Unwitting Prophecy," 714.

# Chapter 5—An Alternative Set of Biblical Tropes

## Or Trump in a Lesser Light

Nietzsche claimed that truth was an "army of metaphors."[1] James C. Scott argues, "The struggle is over the appropriation of symbols, a struggle over how the past and present shall be understood and labeled, a struggle to identify causes and assess blame, a contentious effort to give partisan meaning to local history."[2] Politics in some measure is a process of "choosing one trope over another."[3] In other words, truth is contestable with many claims staked. In the contest with evangelicals over how to read and interpret the Bible, a battle of metaphors and tropes unfold.

In this metaphorical battle, I write sermonically from a life of practice. In fact, I find it impossible to write any other way. This means that I read the Bible imaginatively and symbolically. "Reading Scripture is an art—a creative discipline that requires engagement and imagination"[4] that goes beyond the strictures of literalism. Stanley Hauerwas puts it exactly right for me: "The sermon is at the heart of our ability to speak as well as sustain speaking Christian."[5] I hope it can be said of me that I only know how to write sermonically.

In this case it also means adhering closely to the narrative of the current political situation and exegeting that in sermonic form. The literary complexity of Scripture means that its language is often metaphorical and symbolic.[6] The garden of Scripture is a tropological paradise. My understanding of Scripture has its own text: "Therefore every scribe who has been trained for the kingdom of heaven is like the master of a household

---

1. Nietzsche, *Portable Nietzsche*, 46–47.
2. Scott, *Weapons of the Weak*, xvii.
3. Ivie, "Rhetorical Aftershocks," 62.
4. Davis and Hays, eds., *The Art of Reading Scripture*, xv.
5. Hauerwas, *Working with Words*, 93.
6. I have addressed this issue in a previous work, *The Creative Power of Metaphor*.

who brings out of his treasure what is new and what is old."[7] The challenge, among readers of the Bible, "is whether or not that symbolism is open to radical reinterpretation. Interpretation of symbols is the church's most serious and most consequential business."[8] This methodology mirrors, in reverse, the rhetorical arguments of conservative evangelicals who use biblical passages and characters to give divine approval to and Christian support for President Trump. While we all see through a mirror darkly, it is hard not to lose patience with the captious and fatuous reading habits of evangelical literalists. There are other ways of reading Scripture.

This section responds to the ways that conservative evangelicals have drawn specific connections between President Donald Trump and Old Testament concepts and kings. This is a major way in which they have given birth to this president. Trump is the progeny of their preaching and ideology of Scripture. In the language of the King James Version, conservative evangelicals "begat" Donald Trump. While our secular age has little interest in the Bible, if the evangelical conservatives are to be understood, the Bible has to be part of the picture. While it may be very difficult to engage conservative evangelical Trump supporters in meaningful ways, the only road to any dialogue is the Bible. As many evangelicals learned in Vacation Bible schools, "The B-I-B-L-E, that's the book for me."

Even this attempt to engage the evangelical with the Bible has serious obstacles. There is much in the evangelical "love" of the Bible that has little to do with the actual texts of Scripture. It's as if the Bible is only symbolic, as if appealing to it as if it were a black leather binding with no words, or announcing, "The Bible says . . ." is enough to grant authority to the preacher's word. There may have not been a more powerful expression of this reality than the photo op of President Trump holding up a Bible in front of St. John's Episcopal Church in Washington, DC. No words spoken. The Bible was not opened. It was simply waved in the air. A discussion with a symbol defended by literalists may be futile. Evangelicals seem unmoved that their adumbrations may be unhinged from historical reality.

Evangelical preachers have laid down a fierce protective fire for the president that would resemble bombers protecting advancing troops in a war. The jeremiads of evangelical preachers warning of moral decay clash with their adumbrations of making America great again. Conservative evangelicals produce jeremiads of American decline with weeping, groaning, and gnashing of teeth.

---

7. Matthew 13:52.
8. Davis and Hays, eds., *The Art of Reading Scripture*, 13.

Evangelicals have weaponized the Bible and taken literally the metaphor that the Bible is the "sword of the Lord." Evangelicals, unconsciously infected with the democratic notions of common sense and freedom, also tend to believe they can read the Bible spiritually and individually. As Stanley Hauerwas argues, "They assume that they have all the 'religious experience' necessary to know what the Bible is about."[9] This frees them to use the Bible politically while ignoring that the Bible has its own politics. Their minds are voices of the possibility that their biblical analogies of Trump are inapposite and overly imaginative. The arguments of evangelicals in defense of Trump seem inapposite to a movement long aligned with morality. Their elliptical style hides a sinister desire for control and power, even as their leaders portray an effervescence of goodness. They are as bubbly as a bottle of cheap champagne.

There are reasons why the Bible is the chosen weapon of evangelicals. This is their history, their comfort zone. The Bible, especially the defense of it, defines their existence. James McClendon suggests that Baptists have produced so few great theologians because, among other reasons, the Baptists have expended so much energy fighting about the Bible, about its nature, its inspiration, its importance.[10] Writing good theology becomes a challenge if energy is directed to "defending" the Bible.

Critiques of this particular way of reading the Bible as literal, as absolute authority, have been challenged by thoughtful evangelical scholars, but this collection of mostly university professors lack the media platform to reach millions of people. Evangelical preachers are masters of all forms of media. Spokespersons for an alternative approach to reading Scripture don't have a media empire. For instance, if Stephen E. Fowl, Chair of the Department of Theology at Loyola College in Maryland, gave a series of lectures on his incisive work *Engaging Scripture: A Model for Theological Interpretation*, he might draw a crowd of forty persons. A televangelist preaching on "God Caused Hurricane Katrina to Punish Gays" would have an audience of 6,000,000. Dr. Fowl's nuanced arguments, powerful analogies, and the usual ambiguities that populate scholarly writing doesn't get a lot of traction in a popular world that revels in simplicity, dualism, and authority.

Compare Paula White's book, *Something Greater*, which is at number 3,674 on the Amazon best-seller list, with Ellen F. Davis and Richard B. Hay's edited volume, *The Art of Reading Scripture*, which is at #476,349. White is a prosperity preacher and spiritual advisor to President Trump who writes fluff and asked her followers to send their entire January salary

---

9. Hauerwas, *Unleashing the Scripture*, 3.
10. McClendon, *Ethics*, x.

to her ministry; Davis and Hays, professors at Duke Divinity School, are noted scholars and authors who write significant works on the Hebrew Scriptures and the New Testament. Neither Davis nor Hays "sit at the helm of a media empire or has enough clout with conservative groups to counter the simple and straightforward appeal of leaders invoking biblical authority for their positions, no matter how suspect."[11]

Underlying all of this is the belief that the preacher's statements are "biblical." As Kathleen C. Boone puts it, "They believe what they believe because the Bible tells them so."[12] There's no ambiguity in the proclamations. There's right and wrong. There are no gray areas.

Now, this establishes a direct line of authority: God—the Bible—the pastor. President Trump was afforded the anointing that is given to the pastor. Or in the case of some television evangelists, the anointing they have self-proclaimed. Having said they were not electing a senior pastor as president, evangelical leaders proceeded to anoint Trump as senior pastor of the nation and endow him with the authority of senior pastor. He is right; everyone else is wrong.

There is a sense in which this is also true in the larger audience, the universal audience of all conservative evangelicals. Boone posits an "interpretive [fundamentalist] community" that establishes hermeneutical norms and even 'writes' the text itself."[13] The frequent use of "Bible" as an adjective as well as the use of jargon, clichés, and shibboleths adds to the sense that the only intermediary between oneself and the Scriptures is the Holy Spirit. Hauerwas suggests that "North American Christians are trained to believe that they are capable of reading the Bible without spiritual and moral transformation. They read the Bible . . . as democratic citizens who think their 'common sense' is sufficient for 'understanding the Scripture.'"[14] Something of American exceptionalism has invaded the evangelical reading of the Bible—any ordinary person can read and interpret the Bible well. This willingness to give a roseate tint to reading the Bible without the benefit of teachers produces interpretations that are off the wall and outside the realm of reason. No literary critic would allow the interpretation of Hamlet by an untutored person, yet supposedly even an unchurched, biblically illiterate person can happen upon a Bible, read

---

11. Rosin, "Rock of Ages."

12. Boone, *The Bible Tells Them So*, 1. See also Enns, *The Bible Tells Me So*; and Maltby, *Christian Fundamentalism*.

13. Boone, *The Bible Tells Them So*, 61.

14. Hauerwas, *Unleashing the Scripture*, 15.

it, and make sense of it. As a character in the movie *Metropolitan* insists, "You don't have to read a book to have an opinion."[15]

I am arguing that evangelical support of President Trump originates in notions of the Bible, the interpreters, and the authority of the pastor. In this instance, conservatives needed biblical support, so they started with Trump and then applied the biblical idea of anointing to him, and compared him favorably to Old Testament kings and leaders.

By now, even the secular media has caught on to the creative exegesis of evangelicals posturing President Trump as King Cyrus or King David, or King Solomon or even Samson. Paula White suggested Trump was Queen Esther but that violates the heteronormative analogies so beloved by evangelicals. The other biblical defenses offered by evangelicals have been a rendering of Romans 13 as justification for President Trump's policies, the evangelical insistence that Trump is God's "anointed," and that Trump is the "strongman."

Rather than rehashing the well-known evangelical biblical attempts to present Trump as "God's anointed," as King Cyrus, as King David and the "Strongman," here are alternatives using the same Bible evangelicals use. For example, the idea of anointing is not as clear-cut as evangelicals make it in their haste to anoint President Trump. Trump has retweeted quotes from one of his more sycophantic—and unhinged—followers, Wayne Allyn Root, calling Trump the "King of Israel" and "the second coming of God."[16] Later that day, when speaking to reporters, Trump embraced the prophet identity again, calling himself "the Chosen One," in response to a question about trade dealings with China. Whether or not Trump was serious, his followers certainly are. They do believe Trump is "God's anointed," and Trump, with his usual paralipsis can say that he's not really saying it, but he's saying it. Plausible deniability—that he might be joking, that these are just metaphors—is as Donald at it gets.

The idea of God actually speaking to preachers or politicians and anointing them is as foreign to most mainline Christians as it is the norm for evangelicals. In Peggy Payne's delightful novel *Revelation*, the highly educated, respected senior pastor of a university town Presbyterian church, actually hears God's voice in his backyard. The novel then unfolds as the crisis of a preacher attempting to explain to his congregation that he has literally heard the voice of God. The natural skepticism of the congregation and the resulting spiritual crisis for the pastor highlights how difficult the idea of God actually speaking is for those outside the evangelical

15. https://www.quotes.net/movies/metropolitan_7465.
16. Santucci, "Trump promotes claim."

bubble. When the Rev. Swain Hammond finally tells the congregation that God has literally spoken out loud to him, Payne shows us the reaction of the pastor's best friend, Bernie, as the reaction most mainline church members would have—incredulousness. The church's governing board thinks the pastor needs therapy.[17]

Peggy Payne's book wouldn't make sense to most evangelicals. Routinely they hear their preachers say, "The Lord spoke to me last night and told me . . ." The preacher is the direct conduit between God and the people. After all, God spoke to Moses; therefore, God speaks to evangelical pastors today. There appears no deeper reading of the Bible, no concept that direct communication with God was so frightening in the time of Moses, that the people begged for God not to speak to them again. Evangelicals would be stunned if they read Hebrew scholar Richard Friedman's *The Disappearance of God*, in which he chronicles divine recession in the Hebrew Bible. Samuel was the last person to whom God is said to have been "revealed"[18]; Solomon the last person to whom God "appeared." God's words then became remembered and were written down to be repeated by preachers and priests.[19]

Biblical anointing is tied to faithfulness and obedience to God. It is not a license to run havoc over others. It is linked to a covenant with God. The anointing of kings was always a liturgical experience in which the king was expected to give unconditional loyalty to God. The anointing could be removed if the king was unfaithful, and this happened to King Saul.

Silence is not an alternative for pastors, scholars, politicians, or citizens who care about the integrity of the Bible. Centuries of biblical scholarship is being trashed by preachers with little understanding of the Bible. When citizens are less biblically informed today, it is even more imperative that options to the evangelical "misuse" of Scripture be offered. Voices must be raised; truths need to be spoken; dissent needs to be sustained. Call this a statement of resistance to the rhetorics of racism, whiteness, maleness, ressentiment, and enemies. While progressive pastors have been speaking with courage and wisdom, they haven't often made the news with alternative metaphors or ways of reading Scripture. Robert Hunt at Perkins School of Theology in Dallas has been a progressive voice speaking in dissent of Robert Jeffress; Randall Balmer has numerous essays published in daily newspapers speaking out against the perversions of evangelicalism. But the tribe is small.

---

17. Payne, *Revelation*, loc. 389.
18. 1 Samuel 3:21.
19. Taylor, *When God Is Silent*, 53.

"Donald Trump is an idiot who wants you to be in his reality show. The challenge is not to let him dominate your life," said Stanley Hauerwas.[20] Progressive voices such as the presiding bishop of the Episcopal Church, Michael Curry; Jim Wallis, former editor of *Sojourners;* or the Rev. William Barber II, the voice behind Moral Mondays in North Carolina are interviewed infrequently by national news networks, but this is a drop in the bucket compared to the constant appearances of Robert Jeffress on Fox News.

There is an alternative reading to the Trump is "Cyrus" metaphor. Evangelical prophets claim they were miraculously led to read Isaiah 45 because Trump was the forty-fifth president. Putting aside that kind of mystery reading, the context of the biblical witness concerning Cyrus is attempted. This includes the entire forty-fifth chapter of Isaiah, and portions of 2 Chronicles, Ezra, Isaiah, Daniel, Bel and the Dragon, and 1 Esdras, because in the progressive mind, context makes all the difference in the world. We learn from these additional biblical passages that Cyrus initiated humane practices in opposition to the inhumane Babylonian practices. Perhaps Cyrus, like God hearing the cries of the Israelites in Egyptian slavery, heard the voice of deep despair in the Israelites in Babylonian captivity: "By the rivers of Babylon—there we sat down and there we wept when we remembered Zion. On the willows there we hung up our harps. For there our captors asked us for songs, and our tormentors asked for mirth, saying, 'Sing us one of the songs of Zion!'"[21] It is by no means axiomatic that kings or presidents will hear the screams of pain from the oppressed of their lands: "Our bones are dried up, and our hope is lost; we are cut off completely."[22]

The despair of the people, the pain and agony of discrimination, incarceration, imprisonment, and violence warrants more biblical attention than Trump allows. Frustration runs deep among a people who are harassed, bullied, and hurt by whiteness. Condign punishment has been rare when the person accused of murder is a white policeman. Attention to the bodies in pain, the African Americans who are being choked and shot and harassed by the police, gives a different feel to Isaiah 45.

Cyrus, hearing the voice of pain, reacted differently from Trump, who hears only the whining of evangelicals in his ears. Cyrus enacted policies that helped the exiles in need, instead of policies designed to harm and criminalize immigrants. He replaced the Babylonian politics of displacing

---

20. Cited in Maule, "Stanley Hauerwas Slams Trump."
21. Psalm 137:1–2.
22. Ezekiel 37:12.

and dislocating people by returning people to their homelands and provided them support as they rebuilt their homes and temples.

Compare the policy of Cyrus with President Trump's policies on displacing and relocating people. Immigration was the key to Trump's campaign and his time in office. Trump mistrusted and demeaned foreigners at every opportunity. Trump's announcement that he was running for president concentrated on immigration as the issue and the building of a wall as the dominant metaphor. Reporters, according to Jennifer Mercieca, "thought Trump sounded racist when he said things like 'when Mexico sends its people, they're not sending the best . . . . They're sending people that have lots of problems and they're bringing those problems with them. They're bringing drugs. They're bringing crime. They're rapists.' And finally, reporters thought that he sounded like a charlatan when he said, 'I would build a great wall—nobody builds walls better than me. . . . And I would have Mexico paying for that wall.'"[23] President Trump was no Cyrus in this policy area. "Thus, says King Cyrus of Persia: The Lord, the God of heaven, has given me all the kingdoms of the earth, and he has charged me to build him a house at Jerusalem, which is in Judah. Whoever is among you of all his people, may the Lord his God be with him! Let him go up." "Let him go up" sounds a more positive note than "Send her back." This is a far cry from the Trump executive order sending DACA students back to their home countries. Even when the Supreme Court reinstated DACA, the Trump administration openly defied the Supreme Court ruling.

Cyrus possessed a more generous spirit than President Trump. Cyrus's policies gave financial support to those who left. (This is clear from the biblical books of Ezra and Nehemiah.) If people returned home, he funded rebuilding. Trump's policies offer no financial support to those whom he will forcibly remove from the USA. Trump sends people, not back to a city where they can build a wall providing safety and a church where they can worship, but to a fate that includes starvation and death. The big, beautiful wall didn't even have to be taken literally by Trump supporters.

Trump's idea of helping is to build a huge wall. The "wall" remains the primary metaphor of Trump's entire campaign: "Make America Safe Again." "America First." Protect the evangelicals from the horde of enemies that include more than immigrants but also liberals, socialists, professors, scientists, Democrats, progressive pastors, and others. "Build the wall!" Evangelicals are accumulating metaphors by the busload: "The Bible," "the wall," "law and order," "the flag," "the Pledge of Allegiance," "statues of Confederate generals," "Cyrus," "David," "Samson."

---

23. Mercieca, *Demagogue for President*, loc. 190–91.

The irony is that the wall was never meant to be the metaphor of Trump. His campaign staff gave him the "wall" as a simple mnemonic device so that he could remember to talk about immigration in his campaign speeches.[24] Call it the "accidental" metaphor that gained epistemic power through Trump disciples embracing what the "wall" meant to them. It has always been about security, protection, and power.

King Cyrus himself brought out the vessels of the house of the Lord that Nebuchadnezzar had carried away from Jerusalem and placed in the house of his gods.[25] Cyrus returned the gold and the silver and the vessels from the temple to the Jews. This can't possibly be about President Trump who is not known for his charity and is on record as not paying his bills, refusing to pay contractors in his real estate business. He is currently being sued by Scotland for not paying a court-ordered fee of $840,000. At least ten cities where President Trump held rallies in 2019 have not been reimbursed for security costs.[26]

Cyrus fits the teachings of the Hebrew Bible about the treatment of aliens, sojourners, and strangers. Randall Balmer has written presciently and prophetically about the treatment of migrants.[27] God is on record consistently for instructing his followers to "welcome the stranger." Consider Leviticus 19:33–34: "When an alien resides with you in your land, you shall not oppress the alien. The alien who resides with you shall be to you as the citizen among you; you shall love the alien as yourself, for you were aliens in the land of Egypt: I am the Lord your God."

To complicate the evangelical interpretation, consider Leviticus 19. Old Testament professor Ellen Davis explains that the tradition contains two apparently contradictory commands about the treatment of aliens. The oldest tradition insists that one's neighbor is a fellow Israelite. A later addition to the text comes to a different conclusion. Verse 34 instructs the Jews to treat the alien as neighbor. The two texts are left there by the editors, perhaps so each new generation can debate the meaning of *neighbor*. In any event, the evangelical turn away from the inclusiveness of "neighbor" suggests a refusal of the teaching of Jesus about the Good Samaritan, an oddity for evangelicals indeed. The Hebrew Bible often instructs the Israelites to treat strangers with kindness and compassion precisely because they were once aliens themselves. The corollary here is that United States has often

---

24. Sumner, "Advisers dreamed."
25. Ezra 1:7-11.
26. Kumar and Forgey, "Unpaid bills."
27. Balmer, "The story of Christmas makes it clear"; and "What the Bible Says about Immigrants."

been described as a nation of immigrants, which suggests that all of us (Native Americans excepted) once were foreigners.[28]

President Trump continued to portray refugees as threats to American security after his election. It is an interesting juxtaposition for evangelicals to weaponize the Bible and criminalize the immigrants the Bible means to provide for and protect. Dorian, a Category 5 hurricane, battered the Bahamas for two days with unprecedented intensity. Winds lashed the islands at 200 miles per hour and storm surges caused extensive flooding. In the most affected areas—the Abaco Islands and Grand Bahama Island—entire neighborhoods were obliterated, and infrastructure, including hospitals and public buildings were destroyed. The United Nations estimates that 76,000 were left homeless, and the majority of the population lost any means of livelihood as businesses were swept away. President Trump refused to allow hurricane refugees into the United States by using his usual fear-mongering rhetoric.

Furthermore, the application of the word *anointed* to a king doesn't guarantee that the anointing will be permanent or that the anointed one will be righteous. Isaiah, the prophet who says Cyrus was anointed by God, also says, "Ah, you who make iniquitous decrees, who write oppressive statutes, to turn aside the needy from justice and to rob the poor of my people of their right."[29]

President Trump is no Cyrus when he pushes the elimination of "dozens of long-standing federal programs that assist the poor, fund scientific research and aid America's allies abroad."[30] Squaring justice for the poor with massive tax cuts for the affluent and attempts to deprive the poor of access to healthcare doesn't speak of altruism, generosity, or caring.

In short, Cyrus put in place a humane foreign policy. Cyrus's policy of resettlement may not have been altruistic—but it was humane. It gave Israelites in exile—like many other nations in exile at the time—the opportunity voluntarily to remain where they were or to return home, rebuild their homes and temples, and live as their grandparents had. It was for his actions that Cyrus was deemed anointed by the prophet. The anointing came after the action of liberation. Evangelicals gave President Trump a one-way anointment in advance with nothing to go on but a slogan, a bumper sticker: Make America Great Again, and a red trucker's hat. Trump received all the protection, privilege, and authority of anointing without the ethical responsibility. This, of course, is exactly the way Trump liked it, because this is how

---

28. Balmer, "What the Bible Says about Immigrants."
29. Isaiah 10:1–2.
30. Paletta and Mufson, "Trump Federal Budget 2018."

he has always done business. Brian Beutler, in the *New Republic*, decides that "impunity" may be the best descriptor of Trump, since he has functioned his entire adult life without being held responsible.[31]

Anointing was not granted in advance for a license for paranoia, incompetence, and recklessness. There's no anointing of a president of the United States to undermine the courts, the media, the Congress, the FBI, the Secret Service, and other federal agencies. There's no anointing for the dismantling of President Obama's legacy. There's no anointing for what amounts to a Seinfeld presidency, a television show about nothing, without the humor.[32]

Cyrus gave hope and courage to a displaced and oppressed people; President Trump produces fear, anxiety, and despair. Cyrus supported the practice of the religions in his empire. Trump, in the name of "religious freedom," attempts to give protection to evangelical conservatives and their bid to make Christianity the only religion that is accepted in the US. Trump's antagonism toward Muslims alone is enough to disqualify him from being God's anointed.

Cyrus, as it turns, out is a mere cipher of imperial power. There is always a Cyrus at the center of power. Cyrus could have been any king, or all of them. Because if you have seen one holder of power, you have seen them all. Cyrus is not even the subject of Isaiah 45.

God is always the subject and always we are reminded that God is God and we are not. What really matters in Isaiah 45 is not the mention of Cyrus, but that twenty-four times God speaks the divine "I." It carries the same power as God speaking to Moses at the burning bush.

> "I am the God of your father, the God of Abraham, the God of Isaac, and the God of Jacob." Then the Lord said, "I have observed the misery of my people who are in Egypt; I have heard their cry on account of their taskmasters. Indeed, I know their sufferings, and I have come down to deliver them from the Egyptians, and to bring them up out of that land to a good and broad land, a land flowing with milk and honey." God said to Moses, "I am who I am." He said further, 'Thus you shall say to the Israelites, "I am has sent me to you." God also said to Moses, "Thus you shall say to the Israelites, 'The Lord, the God of your ancestors, the God of Abraham, the God of Isaac, and the God of Jacob, has sent me to you': This is my name for ever, and this my title for all generations."

31. Beutler, "This Single Concept."
32. Stephens, "The Vertigo Presidency."

The primary pronoun keeps repeating in the chapter. God is the great "I" while most kings speak the "I" only as ego, as selfish greed, as power. Isaiah 45 is no more about Donald Trump than it is Cyrus. It is about God. God is God and we are not. Isaiah 45 speaks of God. Conclusion: Donald Trump is nowhere to be seen or heard in Isaiah 45. In this reading of the biblical texts, God is God; and Trump is not Cyrus.

# Chapter 6—An Alternative Pair of Kingly Tropes for Trump

There are other biblical kings than Cyrus that provide additional alternative readings and more accurate metaphors for President Trump: Saul and Solomon. Embedded in Scripture there's a second narrative that offers a counter-truth to the palace press releases. This counter-truth, hidden, ironic, and revolutionary, tells a different story of kings.

In other words, anointing, like milk left out in the heat, can go bad and become rancid, a stink in the nostrils of God. Anointing is not permanent. The person anointed can fail to keep covenant with God and lose the anointing. King Saul was anointed and look at the tragic events that ended his life. Saul goes mad, has a witch conjure up the ghost of Samuel, and is killed in battle. This never seems to be a consideration for conservative evangelicals.

President Trump seems more like Saul than Cyrus. In 1 Samuel 18 we have a character study in how power can be insecure, fearful, and destructive.

> As they were coming home, when David returned from killing the Philistine, the women came out of all the towns of Israel, singing and dancing, to meet King Saul, with tambourines, with songs of joy, and with musical instruments. And the women sang to one another as they made merry, "Saul has killed his thousands, and David his tens of thousands." Saul was very angry, for this saying displeased him. He said, "They have ascribed to David tens of thousands, and to me they have ascribed thousands; what more can he have but the kingdom?" So Saul eyed David from that day on."[1]

Steve Bannon could speak to this biblical story. He was fired by Trump, because Bannon could not win with this White House: he is not one to cede the stage, the spotlight, the megaphone to Trump, and Trump has never learned to share.

---

1. 1 Samuel 18.

Saul, a man with a huge ego but riddled with insecurity, could not tolerate someone else getting more credit than him. Nothing rattled Saul like the song of the women, "Saul has killed his thousands, and David his tens of thousands." How Donald! Saul is the most powerful man in the nation. He is king over all the people. Yet he is consumed with anxiety. This anxiety made Saul fearful. In his fear, Saul resolved to kill David. On the one hand he respected David, but on the other hand he could not imagine another person getting credit that Saul believed belonged only to him.

The Scripture doesn't comment on the irony that the one with all the power is the most anxious in irrational ways. Saul's anxiety and fear lead to self-destructive decisions that go against Saul's own needs. Unrestrained power has a way of gnawing at a person's self-esteem, undermining their decision processes and becoming destructive not only to the one with all the power but also to those subject to that power. Eventually Saul is reduced to a king wearing the clothes of a common man, sneaking into the hills, to enquire of a conjurer, the witch of Endor. He becomes a sniveling, sneaky, paranoid shell of his former self, and has the "anointing of the Lord" ripped from him and given to David. No doubt Saul never saw it coming, but there are no more tragic words for a politician than these: "The Lord said to Samuel, 'How long will you grieve over Saul? I have rejected him from being king over Israel. Fill your horn with oil and set out; I will send you to Jesse the Bethlehemite, for I have provided for myself a king among his sons.'"[2]

The anointing is not permanent; a crown freely granted can be snatched away. Anointing can go badly wrong, become tainted, and become a blasphemy against God's name. The story of King Saul is at least a suggestive humility about claiming to be anointed. Anointing is contingent on holiness, not "beautiful policies." Character matters for kings and presidents, for better or worse. Americans used to know this, thanks to the likes of Washington, Lincoln, and Roosevelt. But liberals dropped the idea with Bill Clinton and conservatives dropped it with Trump.

Is Donald Trump God's anointed? Progressive Christians say absolutely not.

## Trump as Solomon

In this study of Solomon and his place in the larger consciousness of Israel, Walter Brueggemann considers what Old Testament narratives regarding David's heir reveal about the aspirations and ideals of the ancient Israelite people. Brueggemann examines assertions about Solomon, a man praised

---

2. 1 Samuel 16:1–3.

for his wealth, wisdom, and power and depicted as an example of enormous human achievement. Looking beneath the surface of these claims, however, Brueggemann notes that an irony permeates the tradition and invites critique of accepted beliefs. Through close attention to nuances of the biblical text, he exposes the competing interpretive voices that claim to offer a reliable rendering of Solomon.

There are two narratives about Solomon in the texts. The official text, from the royal historian, pictures Solomon as wealthy, wise, and powerful. The second narrative, the one from outside the court of the king, reveals a darker story: deception, lies, and murder. In this reading, Solomon is not so much anointed by God as he is made king by the skillful plotting, deception, and lies of his mother and the prophet Nathan. In other words, the narrative from "below" suggests that Solomon came by his crown in illegitimate, even criminal ways, outside the official propaganda of the state, suggesting that Solomon is an illegitimate king.

Trump faced suspicion that he was illegitimate as well. Not only did he lose the popular vote by more than three million votes, but there was evidence that Russia interfered in the election to benefit Trump. Congressman John Lewis refused to attend the inauguration saying that Trump was illegitimate. "I don't see this president-elect as a legitimate president," he said. "I think the Russians participated in helping this man get elected. And they helped destroy the candidacy of Hillary Clinton."[3]

President Carter has also stated that he views Trump as an illegitimate president. Speaking at a Carter Center event at a resort in Leesburg, Virginia, the former president was asked by moderator Jon Meacham, "So, do you believe President Trump is an illegitimate president?" Carter paused, prompting some in the audience to laugh. He then replied, "Based on what I just said, which I can't retract, I would say yes."[4]

Trump's presidency has affinities with the ironic and unofficial text concerning Solomon. The unofficial text admits that Adonijah would be king, but Adonijah seemed to have limitations in the area of political intrigue and made mistakes that doomed his prospects.[5] He exalted himself; he put on a splashy announcement ceremony: chariots and horsemen and fifty men to run before him. The storyteller drops a hint of the likely outcome by inserting a comparison: "He was also a very handsome man, and he was born next after Absalom."[6] He didn't invite the people who controlled the power of the king-

---

3. Wang, "Trump's inauguration."
4. Stracqualursi, "Jimmy Carter suggests."
5. 1 Kings 1:5–8.
6. 1 Kings 1:6b.

dom to his coming-out party. The text shows no mercy in revealing the likely fate of his would-be king. No good comes from this kind of politics. Luke's Gospel delivers the opinion of Scripture, as sure and steadfast as a verdict of the Supreme Court: "For all who exalt themselves will be humbled, and those who humble themselves will be exalted."[7]

## Wealth and Power

When the subject is wealth and power Solomon is the patron saint. Solomon is wealth and power, all the wealth and power in the world. He is ruthless power, aggressive, accumulating power. Solomon is the *Forbes* Richest Man in the World, *People* magazine's Sexiest Man Alive. Solomon is the wisest man in the world.

The Solomon drama in 1 Kings 3–11 is an act of interpretative imagination by the scribes of Solomon's court. This is the work of ancient press secretary, communication staff, and public relations experts. Beneath the official account lies a different account, an account rich with irony. In the ironic reading, there are questions about how Solomon came to power, how he practiced power, and how he lost power. This second narrative doesn't present Solomon as God's anointed. Nor does it present him as God's gift to women. Nor does it consider him a wise and compassionate ruler.

Kings and queens from around the world were astounded at Solomon's wisdom and his wealth. Queen Sheba came for a state visit, for it seems King Solomon would entertain any dignitary that came bearing gifts, and the narrator tells us that Solomon "took her breath away." First Kings 10:5 reads, "There was no more spirit in her." Solomon was neither the first nor the last ruler to believe he was God's gift to women.

Almost as an aside, a heteronormative brag, we are told that Solomon had more wives than any man in the world. The king's loyal followers would have said, "It was just Solomon being Solomon."

The danger for us is to believe the press notices that fly above the facts on the ground. Those who take the reports of power at face value, who worship the ground that a hero walks on, who buy all the propaganda of the ruler, will never see the truth that jeopardizes all power. Such naïve readers will neither see nor hear the truth that comes up from the soil, the truth of the weak, the obscure, the unknown.

Solomon became king because his mother, Bathsheba, and the court prophet, Nathan, plotted to deceive King David. Solomon is made king as flattery, seduction, and manipulation do their time-dishonored work. The

---

7. Luke 14:11.

appointment of Solomon is one of deception, not of legitimacy. Solomon was actually an illegal king.

## Prophet, Queen, and King Conspire

The kingship of Solomon is contestable. Brueggemann says that Solomon came by the crown "by a carefully choreographed subterfuge, designed to deceive David and get him to proclaim that Solomon will be king in his place. There are two primary agents in the deception: The prophet, Nathan and the mother, Bathsheba."[8] Nathan has become the court prophet, and has much political clout with David.

Nathan hatches the plan for making Solomon king. Solomon's mother, Bathsheba, carries it out to perfection. His playbook for the royal claim for Solomon involves a deceptive duet engaging with King David and tricking him into declaring Solomon will be the king.[9] The scheme plays out exactly as Nathan had mapped it. The mark, King David, is completely fooled by his wife and prophet. He declares "Your son Solomon shall be the king." The political power play to make Solomon king puts even the machinations of the Underwoods in *House of Cards* in the shade. Deception, duplicity, and lies rule the narrative.

In chapter 2, King David becomes active in the battle plan to secure the throne for Solomon. Having promised the crown to Solomon, David, showing no indication that he knows he has been deceived, offers Solomon political advice—hard, tough advice about getting rid of opponents. In the same set of instructions David tells Solomon to worship God and kill Joab. Then David tells Solomon that Shemei also has to be killed. As chilling as this is, note that the killings are linked to wisdom: "according to your wisdom," and "You are a wise man."[10]

With others having secured the throne for Solomon, it is now up to Solomon to dispense with his brother and his brother's chief supporters. Deception only goes so far in the grasp for power. Now the violence follows in the wake of the deception. Solomon, with his first official lie as king, (perhaps the *Jerusalem Post* kept a running total), says of Adonijah, "If he proves to be a worthy man, not one of his hairs shall fall to the ground; but if wickedness is found in him, he shall die."[11] Solomon leaves himself deniability in case Adonijah later meets with tragedy.

8. Brueggemann, *Truth Speaks to Power*, 49.
9. 1 Kings 1:13ff.
10. 1 Kings 2:13–46.
11. 1 Kings 1:52.

The anointing of God now exits stage right, the wisdom of Solomon no longer attaches to a mother and her baby, and godly wisdom is now replaced with political pragmatism—knowing that people have to die and violence and wisdom become partners. David's words about wisdom provide the cover, the thin veneer of decorum and propriety maintained.

Bathsheba seems involved in a second scheme and this one leads to the death of Solomon's chief rival to the throne. Adonijah came to Bathsheba and asked her to go to Solomon to request that he be given the concubine Abishag. This sounds innocent enough until we realize that such a request would have been tantamount to handing over the kingdom to Adonijah, because Abishag had been King David's favorite. Surely Bathsheba, expert in royal intrigue, knew that taking this request to Solomon meant signing a death warrant for Adonijah. The text makes no mention except to say that Bathsheba made the request and the result is the death of Adonijah.

Three times in chapter 2, words of violence and death appear: "Then the king commanded Benaiah son of Jehoiada; and he went out and struck him down, and he died."[12] Adonijah, Joab, and Shemei all killed. Three times the lines sound like clods falling on a casket. The demolition of Solomon's rival and enemies takes place as the result of the earlier deception. Brueggemann makes it clear: "The establishment is accomplished by deception and violence, the twins of unfettered power. But a throne cannot be sustained finally by only deception and violence. It requires, eventually, more legitimacy than that. That legitimacy is enacted through the required royal liturgical performance: a Gihon."[13]

Nathan enters the narrative for his second major role in the establishment of Solomon as king. "The king went to Gibeon to sacrifice there, for that was the principal high place; Solomon used to offer a thousand burnt-offerings on that altar." Thus, three acts constitute the making of Solomon as king: an act of deception, three acts of violence, and a liturgy of legitimacy.

And now the dangerous part: Solomon covers all this deception, aggression, and violence with religious veneer. Whenever a regime claims to be righteous and finds a pack of yapping dog preachers to proclaim that national righteousness, we are in serious danger. Solomon builds a temple for God. The official narrative returns in 1 Kings 3:3—"Solomon loved the Lord." Yet in verse 1, it is reported that Solomon married Pharaoh's daughter, and thus married into and committed to the mode of exploitative rule and abusive economics that Israel had previously experienced from Pharaoh long before. So, we have a king making a verbal commitment to God

---

12. 1 Kings 2:25, 34, 46.
13. Brueggemann, *Truth Speaks to Power*, 55.

but ruling like God's sworn enemy, Pharaoh. Solomon offered up long and brilliant prayers to God in the Temple, while robbing his people blind. Solomon must have looked in the mirror and said, "I'm smart, really, really smart. They will never catch me."

Like the story of Pharaoh, Solomon's is one of accumulation. How we can read this narrative and not shudder is an indication of how deeply embedded we are in the same sequence of anxiety, scarcity, accumulation, monopoly, violence, and envy of the wealthy. He gets away with it because he has the blessing of religious authority. Solomon's wealth would make a television evangelist and the billionaires of the world envious. Solomon built his wealth on taxes, cheap labor, and the sale of military arms.[14] He accumulated women, property, and pawns in political alliances. Wendell Berry has observed that the treatment of women and the management of land are usually equivalent in a social practice, so that if one is abused, so is the other.

Now let me show you something we all missed in Sunday school about truth. Scattered through the Solomon report is the testimony of the Torah truth-tellers. These faithful ones manage to leave their trace of conscious critique and warning that destabilized the power of Solomon. They all speak the same truth: "If you will walk in my ways, keeping my statutes and my commandments, as your father David walked, then I will lengthen your life."[15]

No one could stand up to Solomon in public. Nobles, priests, prophets—all were afraid of him. The only way to voice truth was quietly, almost in a sneaky way. The truth-tellers stuck the truth in between all the greedy, violent, hypocritical moves of the king. And Solomon was undone by the truth. Power can't overcome truth.

The irony is that Solomon accrued all this popularity and success and reputation for being so wise and so wealthy. In reality, he was duping his own people. Solomon's deceptive ways obscure the destruction he caused. Solomon's wisdom hinges on a story of his decision about the real mother of a baby. No king ever got so much credit for dealing with a baby. No wonder politicians kiss babies. Solomon brought about his rule through demolition and deal making. He brought fame, wealth, power, and glory to his kingdom at the expense of his own people. Solomon, while receiving credit for being a king of the people, was actually exacerbating income disparity and financing militarism.

While President Trump claims to be the savior of the people, as Robert L. Ivie points out, "Lurking in the background of Trump's deception [are]

---

14. 1 Kings 10:28–29.
15. 1 Kings 3:14.

initiatives to lower the taxes for the super-rich, dismantle Wall Street regulations, reduce healthcare and other safety-net programs for people in need, defund public education, and minimize job-creation projects."[16]

Trump, like Solomon, is rich. Trump's campaign depended on the accoutrements of wealth from the opening announcement that he was running. The announcement was made at the Trump Tower, the symbol of wealth (as close to a biblical tower of Babel as possible), with its gleaming orange-and-pink marble and gold interior. Trump, the ultimate marketing genius and branding expert, branded himself, as he and Ivanka rode down the golden escalator from above, brandished his wealth and fame as the only real qualifications necessary to be president. He may have sounded hyperbolically arrogant to the media, but to his followers he was sounding the trumpet of truth when he said, "I'm really rich." Throughout the campaign and at his rallies, the Trump faithful passed back and forth stories of how rich Trump was, his private jet, "Trump Force Once," with its golden interior. The warm-up preachers at Trump rallies praised the miraculous wealth with which God had anointed Trump. Paula White and the prosperity gospel preachers were beaming to the bank and back insisting that Trump was living parabolic proof of the prosperity gospel—the message of getting right with God and getting rich.[17]

Kate Bowler, in her balanced and important study of the prosperity gospel, *Blessed*, demonstrates how millions of Americans Christians come to measure spiritual progress in terms of their wealth. The movement has ebbed and flowed under a number of labels—Word of Faith, Health and Wealth, Name It and Claim It, but mostly it is called the prosperity gospel. Bowler shows how it has come to dominate much of the contemporary religious landscape. Her work is beyond the parameters of this study, but I extend her study by arguing that the prosperity gospel has also come to dominate our political scene. The advances of the "Market God" as our Savior, the increasing worship of wealth, the consumption-based culture, the advertising of wealth, and the influence of billionaires have all joined the party as if the Roaring Twenties have roared back to life. Political campaigns are less about votes than dollars. In the campaigns for national office, only the wealthy need file papers to run. With the advent of Donald Trump, the prosperity gospel has a new patron saint.

All the warnings of Scripture about the dangers of wealth are lost in the razzle-dazzle, golden aura of Trump riches. God and Mammon have merged. Greed is a virtue in the Age of Trump. No one in a Trump rally is

---

16. Ivie, "Rhetorical Aftershocks," 66.
17. Mercieca, *Demagogue for President*, Introduction.

worrying about Jesus saying that God and money can't be worshiped together. No one gives a single care to the warning that the rich will have a hard time getting into heaven. There's no one at a Trump rally thinking that if a person is rich there's really big trouble on the horizon. The Scripture insisting that if you are rich you have a problem is a minor distraction if it comes up at all.[18] Donald Trump impresses with his wealth and along with his whiteness he becomes president of the United States. Coates insists that Trump became president simply because he was a white man following the first black president, a wealthy white man with no other credentials. Coates dubs him "America's first white president."[19]

In addition to his dazzling wealth, Solomon builds the temple in Jerusalem. Thus, our Sunday school lessons give us Solomon the great builder. Building the temple may seem beyond the grasp of Donald Trump, but his evangelical credentials went through the roof when he moved the American embassy to Jerusalem. That's close enough to the temple in American Israeli politics and in the minds of premillennialists to count for almost everything. With the American embassy in Jerusalem, somehow the premillennialists have renewed hope that the Muslims will soon give up the Dome of the Rock, have it razed, and then the new temple of the Jews can be built after which, voila, Jesus returns.

Solomon offers a chilling analogy for Trump's blaming immigrants for economic decline, and exploiting terrorism to legitimize military budget increases and legitimizing endless warfare. Trump, pretending to be a populist, is actual just the "next one up" in a line of crony capitalists. More particularly, Robert L. Ivie says, "In adopting the persona of the populist, he advances the agenda of a corporate capitalist. His act is political theater."[20] No more apt label could be ascribed to the narrative of Solomon, King of the Jews, a story of tragedy wrapped in wealth and unbridled power.

Ivie labels Trump's rhetoric as an "apocalyptic trope of demolition." A Trump speech is an all-out offensive. He tosses ideological grenades and demolition tropes as if someone is whispering in his ear, "Fire at will." Torpedoes of terror. Bombs of braggadocio. Rockets of revenge and resentment. "It is a seductive spectacle of the wrecking ball,"[21] with its repeated themes of resentment, nativism, nationalism, triumphalism, and militarism accompanied by mannerisms of outrageous statements, intolerance, conspiracy-mindedness, celebrity worship, and overt displays of patriotism. It is a movement grounded

18. Hauerwas, *Working with Words*, 126–29.
19. Coates, "The First White President."
20. Ivie, "Trump's Unwitting Prophecy," 708.
21. Ivie, "Trump's Unwitting Prophecy," 708.

in a mixture of economic angst, racism, religious bigotry, antifeminism, and hostility toward science, the mainstream press, and the establishment itself—all of it designed to placate the feelings of wounded, shamed white males. This apocalyptic rhetoric hides the reality of our crisis of democracy, an impending catastrophe, or in more secular terms, widespread destruction and devastation, such as visions of nuclear winter, global warming, economic collapse, pandemic, etc. The four horsemen of the apocalypse are characterized from the book of Revelation as pestilence, war, famine, and death. Trump pretends to be the strongman who is holding back the four horsemen on behalf of the people. In reality he is perpetuating the system that favors the super-rich.

In other words, Trump is running a con on the people to whom he is attached. Trump's hustle is marked by his allegiance to the upper class. In Alison Hearn's words, Trump provides himself an alibi for a "failing political economic system marked by perpetual crisis, where traditional jobs are disappearing and employment is every more precarious."[22] The alleged populist president is a corporate capitalist. His brazen use of the White House for personal gain is emblematic of his agenda of using his followers to advance his personal wealth. His promise of salvation is fake as the very, very, very rich are going to get very, very, very richer and his followers are going to fight for the crumbs that trickle down from above. Trump looks more like bad Solomon every week.

Americans desperately long for the wealth, wisdom, and power of Solomon even as our nation becomes increasingly secular. We are still a people addicted to wanting God's blessings, and acts of divine approval for those we elect and empower. As it was in the time of Solomon, so it is in the USA. When Billy Graham preached the sermon at the inauguration of Lyndon B. Johnson, he began with the story of the liturgical act that legitimated the kingship of Solomon. Graham reminded President Johnson, "No government rules except by the will of God." Graham preached the pre-inaugural sermon for Ronald Reagan and he called attention to the realities that God never changes. Nowhere in his sermon did Graham equate Reagan as God's anointed. He preached about God and about the need for repentance. Graham believed our hope is in God and not in the person who is elected president.

The Rev. Andy Stanley preached at the second inauguration of Barack Obama. He said that the president should be "the Pastor-in-Chief" of the nation. Stanley moved from that to telling the story of Jesus washing the feet of his disciples. "The takeaway: What do you do when in a position

---

22. Hearn, "Trump's 'Reality' Hustle," 658.

of power? You leverage that power for the benefit of other people in the room. Mr. President, you have an awfully big room." Stanley prayed that the POTUS would "continue to leverage this influence for the sake of our nation and the sake of the world."[23]

Franklin Graham, at the service for President George Bush, echoed words heard in three previous preinaugural sermons given by his father, the Rev. Billy Graham. He called the nation to God. He preached repentance. He invoked the struggles and successes of King David and implored the president to know the gravity of the moment.[24]

The Rev. Gardner Taylor gave the sermon at President Clinton's 1993 inaugural prayer service. President Clinton said, "I'll never forget his sermon at my inaugural prayer service in 1993, when he said that 'the things that unite us will obliterate the things that divide us.'"[25]

"Let me seek my footing now in the Word of God," Taylor begins. He reads the story of the Good Samaritan. "We have come again to Camelot with the accents of the Ozarks," as he made the connection between Kennedy and Clinton. He spoke of neighbors and mutuality across regions and races. "Divinity belongs only to God." "People can be brought together." "An open democracy with liberty and justice for all." Here is a vision for a country in the sermon of a Baptist preacher. He appeals to our founding document—the Declaration of Independence. It didn't make any exceptions. "All people." "This nation is not divine, but it is divinely appointed." "'This do and thou shall live.'" Unequivocal. "It's springtime in America. As we enter this new era, and we shall be solely, proudly, gloriously Americans." Drop the hyphens from whatever we are and make us Americans.

Dr. Taylor, summoning the magnificent and best practices of the Black rhetorical preaching tradition, brings his sermon to this rousing conclusion: "Standing under this clear word, 'this do and thou shall live,' we can have confidence in some bright tomorrow in this land that the things that unite us will obliterate the things that divide us. Standing in the light of that confidence we can believe in some clear day unclouded by pride and prejudice, when every valley of disparity will be lifted up, when every mountain of obstacle will be brought down, when every crooked day of deception will be straightened out, when every rough place of delay will be removed; and all flesh will see it to the glory of God. We see a better, a brighter, a more glorious day in this land which God has given us

---

23. Zaimov, "Pastor Andy Stanley."
24. Graham, "Franklin Graham's Sermon."
25. Clinton, "Statement."

all. My eyes have seen the glory of the coming of the Lord. Glory, glory, hallelujah. His truth is marching on."[26]

These preachers exult in the grandeur of America without deifying the nation and they call us back to the purposes of God through repentance. They call America back to God; evangelicals call God to Trump. From a rhetorical perspective, the liturgical act designed to stamp the label of "legitimacy" on the presidency of Donald Trump occurred on the morning of the inauguration at St. John's Episcopal Church in Washington, DC. The court priest responsible for the liturgical act was the Rev. Robert Jeffress. The walls of that venerable Episcopal church had probably never heard such a sermon in its history. The sermon of Jeffress, court evangelical, is of one piece with the liturgical act of legitimacy by Nathan, court prophet.

## Liturgical Legitimacy to Deception

Jeffress opens his sermon with a rhetorical version of Solomon's sacrificing and offering incense at the high places of Gibeon. Leaving no doubt about the purpose of this sermon, Jeffress intones: "After our Wendy's cheeseburgers, I said that I believed that you would be the next President of the United States. And if that happened, it would be because God had placed you there." The stage is set for God to enter stage right and anoint Donald Trump as the legitimate president and as "God's man."

Robert Jeffress attempts to quell the controversy sparked by accusations that Trump's presidency lacked legitimacy because he didn't win the popular vote and he had outside illegal help from the Russians. In his sermon, Jeffress wipes out any remaining line between church and state. He makes the case that God has come down from heaven as he did when he came to Moses on Sinai. His rhetorical strategy is designed to insert God and God's purpose into the inauguration of Donald Trump. There's no doubt that God has been invited to the event.

Moving seamlessly between biblical texts and allusions and mixing them with the political occasion, Jeffress demonstrates the ease with which he forces biblical texts to relate directly to Donald Trump. "As the prophet Daniel said, it is God who removes and establishes leaders. . . . God has raised you and Vice-President-Elect Pence up for a great eternal purpose."[27]

When liturgical effort covers for deception, lies, and even murder, the sense of God's anointing evaporates in the air. Whether Solomon at Gihon, or Trump in Washington, the liturgical experience feels off-center, a performance

26. Taylor, "Preinaugural Sermon."
27. Jeffress, "Read the Sermon."

designed to hide truth and embrace power. Robert Jeffress, doing an imitation of the court prophet, Nathan, preached a preinaugural sermon that not only gave divine approval to Trump, but also gave God's blessing to Trump's "wall." Between the gospel proclamation of so many inaugural preachers and the political pandering of Robert Jeffress "a great chasm has been fixed, so that those who might want to pass from here to you cannot do so, and no one can cross from there to us."[28]

## Why the Strongman Trope Doesn't Ring True

The strongman trope is a wish-fulfilment dream. It is born of frustration and its mistake is that it goes against the grain of God's purpose: "Not by might, nor by power, but by my spirit, says the Lord of hosts."[29] The strongman trope has a basic fallacy: strongmen always fail because they choose instruments of self-destruction. The penultimate strongman in the Old Testament was Pharaoh. He's not given a name, only a title, because if you've seen one Pharaoh you've seen them all. He is powerful and wealthy and yet insecure in the deepest part of his heart. There's always anxiety with the pretensions of strongmen, indicative of the feet of clay they all possess.

Imagine yourself as a conservative evangelical Christian, constantly berated and criticized by the larger culture as being a right-wing wacko, hearing all the time that you have no compassion, that you are a racist, that you are hard-hearted and uncaring. Imagine feeling that your voice has been silenced, that you are being persecuted in what you deem a Christian nation.

In this sense, I believe that the angst and anger of conservative evangelicals is more akin to that of young Saul, the zealous Pharisee, than it is to any kind of righteousness that derives from God. In Acts 9:1, Luke describes the pathos of Saul: "Meanwhile Saul, still breathing threats and murder against the disciples of the Lord, went to the high priest, and asked for letters to the synagogues at Damascus, so that if he found any that belonged to the Way, men or women, he might bring them bound to Jerusalem." This biblical description fits evangelical attitudes like a fine leather glove—an amalgamation of at least a century of perceived persecution, bitterness, anger, revenge, and a need to strike out at the enemy.

Generations and generations of being the people of God, and now it's as if it never counted for much. All your family and national traditions, all that you have ever known and believed, now challenged and dismissed from the board. Every belief held dear, every moment toward which your

28. Luke 16:26.
29. Zechariah 4:6.

life is pointed, now meaningless? Everything that grandfather and father and now you believed, gone? Every stance your family has taken over the decades—opposition to integration, women in ministry, gay marriage—now discredited and left in shambles. After more than forty years of an antiabortion crusade, you have suffered through Republican presidents unwilling to push for the outlawing of abortion. Even when a conservative was appointed to the Supreme Court, it was as if he was baptized into a kind of liberalism that you find intolerable. For eight years, you had to tolerate a black man in the White House, and I suspect that this has created far more angst than imagined.

You have held your breath as telling lies didn't weaken your hero. Having that dust-up about porn stars and hush money was nothing. His use of profane language may be unsettling but certainly nothing to write home about. LBJ would have put Trump to shame. Russian interference had no impact. Even the Ukraine was not his kryptonite. Maybe, as conservatives now see it, Trump is unassailable, flawed but unquenchable.

Liberalism is the enemy, and you are ready to do anything to stop it from destroying the country you love. You are happy to merge America with your faith. You are ready to put the flag at the center of your faith instead of the cross, because liberals disrespect the flag. You are tired of being pushed around, ignored, and belittled. You feel that you are losing everything and that it is time to rise again in defense of the church, the family, religious liberty. It's time to put prayer back in schools and teach the Bible and get rid of evolution and those liberal history books. You need to hear people saying, "Merry Christmas," and nativity scenes need to once again dot the landscape of that American idol, the shopping mall. And on top of all that, those liberals want to take your guns. And they hate America. And you have been stewing in the juices of losing for so long, and now, in President Trump, you see a chance to stick it to the liberals.

So, you resolve to do everything in your power to protect your territory, drive back this liberal invasion, stop this erosion, and secure the borders. This is how you genuinely, honestly, sincerely feel.

Conservative evangelicals are convinced that their worldview is as close to the final truth about reality as possible for humans, that the liberal point of view is completely false, dangerous, and un-Christian, and that the war between us can only be resolved if, and only if, liberals return to the America of a simpler time. They probably know that doesn't have a snowball's chance in hell of happening. Women are not going back in the kitchen; Blacks are not going back to their place; gays are not going back into the closet. Immigrants are not going to stop coming to America. But they fight on and will fight until the end.

There's something far deeper than angst, anger, fear, nostalgia, and resentment. There's something in the evangelical psyche that exceeds issues like public prayer in the schools, and that something is the evangelical conviction that this is a war to dominate the culture. It is the ancient battle between truth and power; evangelicals have sided with power—hence the strongman argument. There will be no terms. This is war. The archetypal metaphor "life is war" dominates all of life.

I have only slowly come to grips with the depth of the passion that evangelicals feel. The deep-seated passion sears into their eyes and blinds them to evidence in science, history, politics, and the Bible. This is an issue of life and death for them. They have circled the wagons around President Trump and are prepared to fight on every front, for every issue, and fighting is what they do. While our armed forces have been at war now for almost twenty years, the cultural warriors have been fighting since the day they left the courtroom in Dayton, Tennessee carrying their hollow victory over the forces of evil in a coffin and nursing the mental defeat that had crushed their strongman—William Jennings Bryan.

Having once been the established power in the culture, especially in the South, they have no intention of not once again controlling church and state. This is a reason they have deserted the Baptist principle of separation of church and state. And they are certain, certain beyond belief, not just that they should be in control, but that God wants them to be in control in order to save America. Franklin Graham, one of the lesser of the "court evangelicals," claims God was absent from the Democratic convention. An even less known court evangelicals, Mario Murillo, says that Trump is like Jesus Christ and God had sent Trump to "rescue" Americans from congressional Democrats.[30]

Now, instead of sabers, they are wielding Scripture to warn that the liberals are tearing apart the fabric of our nation. Compared to the slavery that actually tore apart our nation or the economic collapse of the 1930s that almost did the same, or the civil rights movement and anti-war movement of the 1960s, their issues seem minor. But that would be an error in judgment. In one respect, the evangelicals are right: what is at stake is nothing less than the soul of our nation. To a far greater extent, I believe evangelicals have picked the wrong enemy in their decision to blame liberals for the demise of their cultural hegemony. Will Campbell insisted that poor southern whites picked the wrong enemy in the 1960s when they decided that African Americans were the problem. Evangelicals, imprisoned still in that

---

30. Ryland, "Evangelist Claims."

same straitjacket of racism, have made the same bad choice and now fight what can only be a losing battle.

By choosing the strongman trope, the argument can be made that conservative evangelicals have forgotten their own theology. Until they embraced Donald Trump, their tradition insisted that they didn't want or need a "worldly" foundation because they knew there was no foundation other than Jesus Christ. Anabaptist theologian James McClendon taught us how to do theology in a world without foundations long before conservative evangelicals decided that the foundation laid in Jesus Christ was no longer sufficient.

A strongman is unnecessary for those are not attempting to build and control a civilizational order. "Then the king will say to those on His right hand, 'Come, you blessed of My Father, inherit the kingdom prepared for you from the foundation of the world.'"[31] "For no other foundation can anyone lay than that which is laid, which is Jesus Christ."[32] Evangelicals know that the story of strongmen in Scripture always ends badly. The images of power in the Bible are not ultimately that of strong and powerful men who dismiss or ignore God. Line them up and check them off as failures. The hall of shame for strongmen: Pharaoh, Saul, Ahab, Herod, Pilate. Look at the strongman when the pretensions fall apart. Take the long perspective. Here's Pharaoh, his magicians long impotent, now helpless to keep his free labor supply, now bending his knee to Moses: "Take your flocks and your herds, as you said, and be gone. And bring a blessing on me too!"[33] There's Saul, disguised as a commoner, at the cave of the witch of Endor, trying to conjure up the spirit of Samuel—no strongman here. There's Ahab, after Naboth refuses to sell him his vineyard: "Ahab went home resentful and sullen. He lay down on his bed, turned away his face, and would not eat."[34] A pitiful, pouting king is no strongman. And then there's Pilate, muttering about truth and washing his hands in utter fear of Jesus.

Isaiah taunts the strongman sitting on the throne of mighty Babylon: "How you are fallen from heaven, O Day Star, son of Dawn! How you are cut down to the ground, you who laid the nations low! You said in your heart, 'I will ascend to heaven; I will raise my throne above the stars of God; I will sit on the mount of assembly on the heights of Zaphon; I will ascend to the tops of the clouds, I will make myself like the Most High.'

---

31. Matthew 25:34.
32. 1 Corinthians 3:11.
33. Exodus 12:32.
34. 1 Kings 21:4.

## CHAPTER 6—AN ALTERNATIVE PAIR OF KINGLY TROPES FOR TRUMP

But you are brought down to Sheol, to the depths of the Pit."[35] The strongman trope is an illusion.

In a *Christian Post* article Lance Wallnau has expanded his biblical imagination to say that Trump is like the penultimate biblical strongman, Samson.[36] "What does he have?" asks Wallnau, warming to his subject of Trump the strongman. "A torrid history with Philistine babes and he's piling up people that he's clubbing with the jawbone of an ass. And we're saying, 'oh no, this is not what we want, we want a more eloquent deliverer?' I have a problem with the church, frankly, because I see what Trump has done. I see the fruit. So, I say, where is the discerning? I don't care about the rough package God delivers the results in, I care about whether or not we can preserve the strength of this guy in his office while he is like Samson, keeping the gates open."

Trump as Samson leaves Wallnau open to a biblical critique that doesn't favor the president. Samson was deceived and conned out of revealing the secret of his strength by a woman named Delilah. "Now Samson went to Gaza and saw a harlot there, and went in to her."[37] Then Samson fell in love with a woman named Delilah. She was offered 1,100 pieces of silver to deceive Samson. (I wonder if that is equal to $130,000?) Then she lulled him to sleep on her knees, and called for a man and had him shave off the seven locks of his head. (Recall, whimsically, that President Trump brags about how his hair has to be perfect.) "Then she began to torment him, and his strength left him. And she said, "The Philistines are upon you, Samson! So, he awoke from his sleep, and said, 'I will go out as before, at other times, and shake myself free!' But he did not know that the Lord had departed from him."[38] Samson, like Saul, lost the anointing of the Lord. So much for anointed strongmen.

Samson, deprived of his hair, his source of strength, and blind, finally grew his hair back and his strength returned. He asked his captors to take him to their temple. "And Samson took hold of the two middle pillars which supported the temple, and he braced himself against them, one on his right and the other on his left. Then Samson said, 'Let me die with the Philistines!' And he pushed with all his might, and the temple fell on the lords and all the people who were in it. So, the dead that he killed at his death were more than he had killed in his life."[39]

35. Isaiah 14:12-15.
36. Showalter, "Trump Like Samson."
37. Judges 16:1.
38. Judges 16:20.
39. Judges 16:30.

The guiding trope of Trump's apocalyptic rhetoric is demolition. He's a political version of Samson. He has been a wrecking ball in undermining the courts, the media, the Congress, and the federal bureaucracy. His administration ignored the Supreme Court ruling to reinstate DACA. Trump attempted, at every turn, to undo President Obama's legacy. As Coates points out, "Trump has made the negation of Obama's legacy the foundation of his own."[40] Ivie suggests, "The spectacle of presidential incivility—the bull in the china shop—raises the question of whether a fragile US culture was broken beyond repair."[41]

Mark Andrejevic notes that Trump enjoys the tearing down, the dismantling of government and democratic aspirations in the name of his evangelical authoritarianism. Andrejevic says that "Trump's demagogic 'jouissance,' provides a kind of pleasure in spectacle that merges entertainment with politics, skepticism with fantasy, and violence with authoritarian tendencies."[42] Donald Trump stormed onto the political scene as the realization of the obscene figure of enjoyment that Slavoj Žižek associates with the decline of "symbolic efficiency." The symptoms of this decline include the debunking of representation associated with a fragmented and conspiracy-theory-ridden public sphere coupled with attempts to resuscitate direct access to the "real." Reality TV is one cultural manifestation of this combination and Trump has become its political avatar. "The demagoguery and resurgent forms of political violence associated with Trump's campaign demonstrate the authoritarian tendencies of this combination." Perhaps the shortest route to a portrayal of Trump's jouissance is his repeated description of his daughter Ivanka as a potential object of his erotic attention: 'She does have a very nice figure. I've said that perhaps if Ivanka weren't my daughter, I'd be dating her.'"[43] Andrejevic notes, "Trump's obscene enjoyment is a latter-day version of the strutting dictator as leering libidinal Ubermensch."[44]

This is my quarrel with the church that brought me the saving knowledge of Jesus as my Lord and Savior; they have chosen the wrong strongman, when they shouldn't be seeking a strongman at all. Like the ancient Israelites grasping at any secular, political warrior as the promised messiah, they have chosen President Trump. This goes against the entire corpus of Christian Scripture and history. The strongman metaphor dissolves in the knife of Ehud, the Benjaminite, into the fat belly of the wicked king Eglon; depicts the

---

40. Coates, "The First White President."
41. Ivie, "Rhetorical Aftershocks," 62.
42. Andrejevic, "The Jouissance of Trump," 651–52.
43. Andrejevic, "The Jouissance of Trump," 651–52.
44. Andrejevic, "The Jouissance of Trump," 652.

nightmares of Herod when he hears of Jesus and think he is John the Baptist, the beheaded preacher, back to hold him accountable; and demonstrates the cowardice of Herod as he shuffles Jesus off to Pilate.

Strongmen don't fare well in Scripture because God doesn't ordain the violent as the way of redemption. God's way is nonviolent, suffering love. The choice of a strongman as redeemer involves the choice of an atonement of violence. Evangelicals, choosing the violence of the strongman, have donned the soiled garments of the zealots of the time of Jesus, those religious warriors willing to die in an effort to defeat the Romans. The zealots had foolishly counted on the intervention of heavenly armies to save them and those angels never came. Jesus had warned them at least forty years in advance: "For if they do this when the wood is green, what will happen when it is dry?"[45]

Evangelicals seem prepared to pay the price for the illusion of salvation by the violence of a strongman. They are trying too hard to create this "heaven on earth" with a Republican trademark on the front doors of this new Eden. Having been left outside so long, they have now entered the corridor of power and taken their seats at the banquet table and they will not willingly let go of that power.

By refusing the Trump-is-the-strongman metaphor I am being true to the side I chose in 1968, when I embraced the image of Jesus as a pacifist and nonviolent Savior. I stand with the words of the Apostle Paul: "God's weakness is stronger than human strength."[46] "God chose what is weak in the world to shame the strong."[47] "Let the same mind be in you that was in Christ Jesus, who, though he was in the form of God, did not regard equality with God as something to be exploited, but emptied himself, taking the form of a slave, being born in human likeness."[48]

More provocatively, I offer an alternative reading to Trump the strongman. In fact, my bias moves front and center in saying that Trump's biblical parallels reside more with the bad kings of Israel and Judah, more with the "Racha." Andre Chouraqui, Jewish theologian speaks of "Racha" as the devil: "It is not long before we meet the Prince of Darkness on the path of wickedness. The Psalter provides him with a frightful identity card that includes no less than a hundred and twelve names, surnames, titles, and qualities. He is the very entity of evil under all its various visages. He is the opulent, the wealthy, the despoiler, the worker of sin, the man with the heart puffed up. . . . He is

---

45. Luke 23:31.
46. 1 Corinthians 1:25.
47. 1 Corinthians 1:27.
48. Philippians 2:5–7.

the enemy of justice, the man oblivious to God; the oppressor, the adversary of peace.... The father of nothingness he incarnates a radical inadequacy, and emptiness and his works are the perfect likeness of the one who fathers them. His every word consummates a lie; his every action, a deed of violence."[49] To use Trump's own favorite rhetorical ploy, paralipsis: I'm not saying Trump is the devil. I'm just saying that he looks, talks, and acts like the devil. In other words, I'm not saying, I'm just saying.

---

49. Cited in Hauerwas, *Working with Words*, 11n7.

## Chapter 7—**Aristotle to the Rescue**
### Or Alternative Rhetorical Tropes for Evangelicals and Trump

After one hundred years of revivalist, populist, demagogic, televangelism preaching, what has this carnival of preachers produced? From Billy Sunday, vaudeville and the manly man, to J. Frank Norris, the circus and populist rhetoric, to Jerry Falwell, Sr., television and the rhetorics of ressentiment and racism, we arrive at Donald Trump. Rhetorical scholars have not been kind in evaluating the rhetoric of Donald Trump. Bonnie Dow says that the election of Trump threatened her teaching of rhetoric with the "conviction that words matter, that reasons matter, and that rational deliberation should be central to how American culture makes decisions."[1] Paul Johnson has argued that Trump's incoherent vacillations between strength and victimhood enable his white audiences to disavow hegemonic whiteness and align themselves with a marginalized, politically exiled subjectivity. Trump, he argues, reframes his audiences' generalized sense of human vulnerability as if it were the experience of structural racial oppression. Marginalization in the form of reverse discrimination and unfair treatment frees his supporters of any kind of debt or civic obligation to a seemingly cruel and hostile polity.[2] Robert Ivie focuses on demolition as the "guiding trope" of Trump's apocalyptic rhetoric.[3] Jennifer Wingard portrays Trump as the "product of a spoiled bunch" rather than just a "spoiled apple in the barrel."[4] Ryan Skinnell says, "Donald J. Trump is a notorious liar."[5] Anna Young labels Trump "a populist," and many call him a demagogue.[6] Trump's constant disavowals, his reliance on *paralep-*

---

1. Dow, "Taking Trump Seriously," 136.
2. Johnson, "The art of masculine victimhood."
3. Ivie, "Rhetorical Aftershocks," 69.
4. Wingard, "Trump's Not Just One Bad Apple."
5. Skinnell, "What Passes," 77.
6. Young, "Rhetorics of Fear," 23.

*sis* and *occultatio*, his transgressions, his denial of consensus reality, are all underwritten by a perverse form of enjoyment that frees his supporters from legal, rhetorical, and psychic strictures. Trump's jouissance: physical or intellectual pleasure, delight, or ecstasy.

Michael J. Steudeman: "Trump's rhetoric operates demagogically." It is "centered on the preservation of a conception of American identity rooted in whiteness, masculinity, and heteronormativity. He makes sweeping condemnations of media, politicians, and public figures based on their perceived alignment with" liberals.[7] "He practices what Roberts-Miller calls "naïve realism, offering up a worldview of simple truths and falsehoods." "I argue that a duplicitous claim of victimhood lies at the heart of Trump's demagoguery."[8]

The secular world offers alternatives to the evangelical preoccupation with Trump being like biblical characters. Since Trump has little history with the Bible, secular characters are more acceptable tropes for understanding the character of Trump: HBO's mafia don, Tony Soprano, the South's ubiquitous good ole boy, and the Russian dictator, Vladimir Putin. Since metaphors possess epistemic power, and since we live in an oral-video age of social media, the choice of tropes takes on even more significance.

## Trump as Tony Soprano

Tony Soprano in *The Sopranos*[9] is the best cinematic example of the man who occupied the White House. (Or, considering Trump's own braggadocio about his relationship with women, perhaps the theme song of *Two and a Half Men* should play at the beginning of a Trump rally.)[10]

*The Sopranos* debuted in 1999 with Tony Soprano (James Gandolfini), as a northern New Jersey Mafia captain. Soprano offers a vivid picture of American masculinity. "He was hulking and sweaty; he radiated a meaty, sweaty physicality, as if he were made of the slices of deli-case gabbagool that he would stand in front of his fridge and shove into his mouth. He was brooding and dangerous. But he was also self-pitying and nostalgic. Tony was void of empathy and the pain of others much like Donald Trump. He surrounded himself with sycophants but convinced himself that their sucking up was genuine. He demanded loyalty but felt no obligation to return

---

7. Steudeman, "Demagoguery," 8.
8. Steudeman, "Demagoguery," 15.
9. See Poniewozik, *Audience of One*.
10. https://www.lyricsondemand.com/tvthemes/twoandahalfmenlyrics.html.

it."¹¹ "This thing is a pyramid, since time immemorial," he told his captains, angry that they were not bringing in enough cash. 'Shit runs downhill, money goes up.'" This recalls Donald Trump saying, "Black guys counting my money! I hate it. The only kind of people I want counting my money are short guys that wear yarmulkes every day."¹²

Tony Soprano ruined people and went on his way. He wanted the prerogatives of traditional manhood but he didn't want to have to earn them. He whined and threw tantrums, yet wondered without irony to his therapist: "Whatever happened to Gary Cooper, the strong, silent type. He wasn't in touch with his feelings. He just did what he had to do." Trump said that he preferred the Ted Turner channel "that shows nothing but old movies, made in the days when Hollywood knew how to provide the public with heroes and glamour."¹³

Tony was neither admirable nor ethical; he was entertaining. He was a monster and a badass. He was petty and powerful. He was a winner. In the season 2 episode "Bust Out," Tony took advantage of the gambling addiction of his high school friend Davy Scatino to bleed his sporting goods store dry. Tony said, "It's my nature. Frog and the scorpion, ya know?" Trump takes feral delight in reading the poem of the kind woman who gave shelter to a venomous snake (the Democrats and immigrants). When the snake bit her, he declared: "You knew damned well I was a snake before you took me in."

There was no softening of Tony throughout the run of *The Sopranos*. But neither does Tony ever get his just desserts. Tony's evil was rationalized, accepted by his wife and family, defended by his team. The lesson of the drama: "Crime pays." If there was to be judgment on Tony, God would supply it, and *The Sopranos* would not supply it. If Trump ever faces judgment for his transgressive romp through the presidency, it will be in spite of the protection he gets from the Republican Senate, Attorney General William Barr, and the cover he receives from the Rev. Robert Jeffress and the carnival of evangelical leaders.

## Trump as Southern "Good Old Boy"

Nothing surprised me more during the research and writing of this project as much as the persistent image of Donald Trump playing the role of a southern Good Old Boy. He has convinced white males that he is one of them. Rodney Clapp first alerted me to the influence of the South, in his work *Johnny Cash*

---

11. Poniewozik, *Audience of One*, 111.
12. Cooper, "What Donald Trump Has Said about Jews."
13. Poniewozik, *Audience of One*, 111.

*and the Great American Contradiction*. In many ways, this book is a sermon with the words of Clapp as canonical text: "The young ones may consider it 'country,' and the Yankees 'call it dumb,' but now southern identity, like the Mississippi in flood, has surged well beyond the banks of the South as a region. In so much of its culture, religion, politics, and society, all of America now speaks with a southern accent."[14]

Flannery O'Connor once observed, "By and large, people in the South still conceive of humanity in theological terms. While the South is hardly Christ-centered, it is most certainly Christ-haunted."[15] O'Connor's words carry a frightening set of implications now. The old-time religion of evangelicals has long dominated the South to the extent that church and culture were one. As Alfred Kazin has argued, religion was "the most traditional and lasting form of southern community." This religion is tied up in land, slavery, and defeat in war. For southerners, the "loss of the Civil War was a religious crisis," Kazin argues.[16] There's always been an obsession with blood, pain, and sacrifice in the Christian story and in the southern story. The experience of failure and disgrace after the Civil War combined with the bitterness and resentment of Reconstruction to create a hard-core conviction of being misjudged, mistreated, and humiliated. All these deeply divisive emotions were then swallowed up by strict literal understandings of the Bible.

Conservative evangelicals, going into the 2016 national election, were feeling demoralized, weak, and defeated. The Supreme Court declaring gay marriage legal seemed to be the final nail in the coffin of ongoing losses in the culture war. After all, gay marriage completely deconstructs the "stern father" metaphor of evangelicals. For conservative evangelicals, especially those from the South, this decision must have felt like Lee at Appomattox. And to suggest that a southerner in 2016 didn't still feel the sting of losing the Civil War, is to be ignorant of what it means to be from the South.

Trump's rhetorical ability to speak southern includes the skill of scaring people (especially men) with doomsday scenarios in ways that would shame a hellfire and brimstone evangelist. Trump has managed to scare white men with persons of color and women while at the same time assuring them they are as powerful and strong as they dream. As southern whites once feared free Black men as a threat to the imagined purity of the white bloodstream through miscegenation, white males now fear women and persons of color as threats to their power base. Therefore, they have

---

14. Clapp, *Johnny Cash*, 1.
15. O'Connor, *The Habit of Being*, loc. 420.
16. Cited in Ketchin, ed., *The Christ-Haunted Landscape*, xi.

devised rhetorical strategies to manage the threat posed by women and persons of color.

Southerners had to face the reality that God had deserted them. It is hard to overestimate the immense depth of the belief that God was on their side that permeated the South. After Appomattox, spiritual depression set in—insecurity, guilt, violence, resentment, and, above all, alienation. The South retreated into a mythic "Lost Cause" and the revisionism of producing a kindly Robert Lee and a belief that the Civil War was not over slavery but states' rights. Connelly calls it "the long anger."[17] Charlie Daniels Band held out the hope in their hit song, "The South's Gonna Do It Again."

Fundamentalists and the evangelicals many of them became had to face the reality that they were not going to be the established church, that modernism would be the doctrine of the seminaries, and that they would be left to work out their own salvation in their parallel culture of Bible schools, universities, and seminaries that would keep the old faith. They retreated into a theological bubble that almost completely rejected the mainline churches and had little or nothing to do with secular politics for more than fifty years. They slowly hammered out revisionist ideas about science, history, America, and the future. Creationism, American exceptionalism, and the rapture became the rallying tropes of the movement. Above all, they honed their populist skills at creating enemies, powerful and seemingly invulnerable enemies who were trying to destroy America.

Evangelicals managed to create a president in their own image. They have spent the better part of the last two decades trying to undo the public school curricula of science and history. From the time they backed Richard Nixon, deserted and betrayed fellow evangelical Jimmy Carter for Ronald Reagan, to their full-throated support of the Bushes, and their votes for candidates McCain and Romney, they had the bad taste in their mouths that they were still losing. There were enemies at the gates of the church: women, persons of color, immigrants, and gays. Attempts to undo the laws on abortion, stop gay marriage, and put prayer back in public schools faltered and failed as surely as they failed in the effort to stop evolution and modernism at the courthouse in Dayton, Tennessee. At times evangelicals must feel that it is Groundhog Day every day as they keep getting the same non-results in every battle they fight.

Donald Trump now carries the flag of evangelical faith. Trump has managed to mobilize a circuit of shame and dignity, "in which supporters—especially white supporters—who feel ashamed find, in his verbal and

---

17. Connelly, *Will Campbell*, 25, 28.

visual style, a repudiation of shame."[18] As Schaefer notes, "Shame saturates contemporary politics. Bodies that once felt like the unchallenged masters of their space—white bodies, male bodies, cis bodies, straight bodies, rich bodies, citizen bodies—are being confronted, more and more, with a demand to respond to the violence trailing in the wake of the comforts and pleasures they enjoy."[19]

Trump is their undisciplined, unmanageable child and they are stuck with him and his braggadocio, his rhetoric of division and demolition, and his utter disregard for decorum and propriety. After four years of his presidency, evangelicals have decided to remain doting parents of a spoiled brat. They will stand or fall with Donald.

## Trump in the Image of Putin

Since evangelicals gravitate toward the strongman metaphor, perhaps a more appropriate analogy for Trump is Vladimir Putin, president-for-life of Russia.[20] Eskil and Wood offer a concise analysis of Putin. They claim that gender undergirds populism and demagoguery, particularly masculinity, strengthening its many faces. Putin's political performance projects a right-wing populism that hides in an "ostentatious masculine posturing that has the virtue of being relatively malleable."[21]

"Trump is Putin" has more of the ring of truth. Having made such a statement, I offer the following comparisons as edification and justification for my choice of this trope.

Trump inclines toward the imperial, thus his kidding around about wanting to be president for life, like his soul mate Putin, for whom he has a love-crush. Putin and Recep Erdogan had "openings for a more charismatic leadership based on populist appeals to their populations. For elites in both countries an appeal to the image of 'tsar' or 'sultan' has proven to be an alluring form of political PR."[22] The danger in embracing this populism is the potential for undermining institutions of democracy in favor of a charismatic form of undemocratic politics. The performance is a series of staged events forming a spectacle that divert attention away from the damages being done to democratic institutions, standards, and traditions.

---

18. Schaefer, "Whiteness and civilization," 1.
19. Schaefer, "Whiteness and civilization," 11.
20. See Eksil and Wood, "Right-wing Populism."
21. Eksil and Wood, "Right-wing Populism," 733.
22. Eksil and Wood, "Right-wing Populism," 737.

Not all the credit for Trump's "maleness" rhetoric can go to evangelicals. In the dozen years prior to Trump's election, there was an international "manly man" star—the president of Russia, Vladimir Putin. Trump loves Putin's rhetoric of manliness. Two streams, at ideological opposite ends—evangelical Christianity and Russia oligarchy—merge to influence Trump. Evangelicals and Putin provided Trump a game plan for winning the presidency of the United States: right-wing populism and gendered performance.

Putin's campaign for president of Russia had three main rhetorical markers: First, he presented himself as a populist image as a man of the people—an outsider renegade who was a transgressive, angry leader who would put matters to rights in Russia. Second, he rejected politics and parties in favor of a nativist discourse that castigates outsiders as deficient in terms of their masculinity. And third, he presented himself with a male-dominated and conservative set of ideas that appear to restore an imagined and idealized gender order based on male dominance. Putin promised to make Russia great again.

Putin's image as a real man's man went mostly unnoticed. Tim Alberta in *American Carnage* suggests, "What Bush and his Republican peers failed to understand was the degree to which Putin had become an appealing figure for many on the American right—for masculinity he radiated in such sharp contrast to his U.S. counterpart."[23] In September 2013, Marin Cogan wrote in *National Journal Magazine* about the cult following Putin was amassing on the American right with his macho exploits: tranquilizing a tiger, hunting a gray whale with a crossbow, riding war horses, catching gigantic fish. "He was always shirtless and never afraid, Rooseveltian testosterone oozing out of every pore."[24] Gayne C. Young, a Texas-based writer and blogger for *Outdoor Life*, interviewed Putin. He says, "People really liked him, at least on our comments section on *Outdoor Life*. Given the demographics of the readership, most are die-hard Republicans, and when they saw Putin hunting, he says, they were like, 'Obama wouldn't do that.'"[25]

For example, Putin became Russia's second elected president with speeches about defense of the Motherland as "a man's affair" and with rejection of public debates on the grounds that he did not need to engage in public debates on which was better, "Tampax or Snickers."[26] He told voters that he did not want anyone to make "a sweet, syrupy image" of him as a

---

23. Alberta, *American Carnage*, 322.
24. Cogan, "Vladimir Putin's American Fan Club."
25. Young, "One-on-One."
26. Eksil and Wood, "Right-wing Populism," 742.

candidate. He spoke to the nation at the time of the Beslan school crisis, quoting Stalin—"we showed weakness and the weak get beaten." Putin constantly refers to the "greatness of Russia." Over and over he also insists that Russia is the object of predators, of massive enemies out to destroy her. The goal of these foreign powers, Putin argued, was "to tear off a fatty piece." Putin presented himself as the strong man who would not show weakness and would not let others show it.[27]

He told Russians they would no longer be "second-class citizens" in their own home." In 1999, he claimed, "Russia can rise from its knees and fight back as it should." And he claimed that he was the only man strong enough to be the champion for the nation. He claimed he would "rub out the bandits in the outhouse." As one member of the Russian government said, "No politician has even been so fantastically vulgar. Ordinary people love it because it's the way the speak themselves."[28]

Trump imitates or at least follows in the macho wake of Putin. "Our country is in serious trouble," Trump says, as he begins his prepared remarks. "We don't have victories anymore. We used to have victories, but we don't have them. When was the last time anybody saw us beating, let's say, China in a trade deal? They kill us. I beat China all the time. All the time."[29] This is not simply a Trump promise of an economic turnaround. It also suggests an affective state shift. Trump insists we are humiliated, but he will deliver dignity. "When do we beat Mexico at the border?" Trump continued. "They're laughing at us, at our stupidity. . . . The US has become a dumping ground for everybody else's problems."[30]

Putin promoted his masculine imagery by linking his role as president with savior of the nation. The mayor of Moscow introduced Putin as a rally in the largest stadium in Moscow as "a real man, a leader, a person of word and deed." Putin told his rally crowd: "We won't allow anybody to interfere in our internal affairs because we have our own will, which has helped us to be victorious at all times." He implied that protesters were being paid by foreigners.[31]

Trump wants to be Putin. He idolizes him, imitates him, talks like him. I just hope we never see Trump shirtless riding bareback on a stallion. His golfing images are awful enough.[32] If Trump needed a model for

27. See Wood, "Hypermasculinity"; and Eksil and Wood, "Right-wing populism."
28. Eksil and Wood, "Right-wing Populism," 744.
29. *Time*, "Here's Donald Trump's Presidential Announcement Speech."
30. *Time*, "Here's Donald Trump's Presidential Announcement Speech."
31. Pavlova, "A real man."
32. See Houck, "Putting His Ass in Aspirational."

how to captivate people with masculine performances, there was already an international politician on hand to offer lessons in being a manly man: Vladimir Putin of Russia.

## Rhetorical Arguments as Resistance

Addressing the question of repairing the breaches in religion and politics, there is "no way out of the rhetorical surround. Any solution will be a rhetorical one." In other words, words still matter even in our post-truth, postmodern phantasmagoria. Even in the face of alternative truth, fake news, and deceptive politics, someone must insist that reasons matter, and rational deliberation is essential to a democracy. In the age of Trump, "it is easier to debase civic virtue, blame racial Others, fantasize about violence and revenge, and wallow in self pity than it is to live up to the lofty democratic ideals to which the nation normally aspires."[33] Hence, a revival of logos over pathos, and the return of ethos; in other words, Aristotle to the rescue. Politics in some measure is a process of "choosing one trope over another."[34] Replacing the ongoing processes of demolition unleashed by the evangelical-Trump alliance—ressentiment, enemies, nationalism, racism—is a necessary remedy to the demolition trope of Trump. The demonizing of opponents, the fingering of scapegoats, the mocking, insulting tweets and nicknames, the sleazy rhetorical strategies of ad hominem, ad populum, American exceptionalism, paralipsis, ad baculum, and reification has to be reversed.

Trump's rhetoric plays a chaotic tune and his followers dance in delight, especially evangelicals, which provide Trump with a sizeable and dependable base of support. Trump is playing their tune, "Onward Christian soldiers, marching as to war." The simplicity, the impulsivity, and incivility are standard marks of a certain kind of evangelical preaching that rages against the darkness.[35] Ivie describes Trump's rhetoric in vivid terms: "The rawness is visceral and verbal. Message and manner converge. One can sense the rhythmic swing of the sledgehammer in Trump's speech and tweets."[36] While Trump presents himself as a builder of builders, he is more a demolition expert blowing up the pillars of democracy. The demolition force of Donald Trump and his evangelical warriors has to be resisted.

33. Kelly, "Trump and the Rhetoric of *Ressentiment*," 24.
34. Ivie, "Rhetorical Aftershocks," 62.
35. Ivie, "Rhetorical Aftershocks," 61.
36. Ivie, "Trump's Unwitting Prophecy," 710.

There are rhetorical strategies available to help resist. A resistance movement is required so as not to be overwhelmed with the right-wing media propaganda machine. Trump and his renegade/outsider evangelicals have unleashed the four horsemen of the Trumpian apocalypse—"racism, nationalism, xenophobia, and militarism"—with "a polarizing rhetoric that is coarse, non-deliberative, illiberal, deceitful, and destabilizing."[37] Ivie offers a series of damaging reflections on Trump's reign of terror: "paranoia, incompetence, and recklessness;" "the bull in the china shop;" a "clown act."[38] One way to respond is to know the enemy.

Trump evangelicals are, in the phrase used by Benedict Anderson, "an imagined political community."[39] It is imagined because the majority of the members will have never met, or even have heard of one another, yet, with the power of social media, the community exists in the minds of each follower as an image of their shared communion. Trump has invented an audience—an imagined, universal audience that lives, breathes, and speaks as one voice even when there are variegated differences and opinions among the followers that are submerged in the interest of power. The community is an imagined community exercising a political power through the auspices of one person—Donald Trump. This imagined community imagines a nation that is wholly Christian according to the parameters of a conservative evangelical faith. This desire for control is conceived as a deep comradeship. Once Christianity was imagined through the medium of a sacred language and written script. Now it is imagined through social and political constructs that find the Bible only useful as a symbol or some of its verses as air-tight defenses of social and political stances. Evangelicals have happily participated in the decline of sacred communities, languages, and liturgies, even while clinging to notions of a literal Scripture. They have replaced it with the secular. The church growth movements of evangelicals are glad to entice people to church whether they believe in God or not. I sympathize with the conclusion of Hauerwas: "No doubt they will be successful for a time, but the 'churches' that result from such strategies are nothing more than Christian paganism in disguise."[40]

The imagined community now has a substitute for morning prayer—social media. The liturgy is performed in private by an individual yet each communicant is well aware that the ceremony is repeated by millions of fellow believers. Facebook posts, for example, will often display an array of

37. Ivie, "Rhetorical Aftershocks," 61.
38. Ivie, "Rhetorical Aftershocks," 61–64.
39. Anderson, *Imagined Communities*, 1.
40. Hauerwas, *In Good Company*, 4.

fellow believers congratulating one another on being so right, so certain, and so good. If one person, not a member of the group, dissents, there will commence a ganging-up on this dissenter until the group senses that the dissenter is too demented, too demonic, and too ugly to be tolerated and the thread will be deleted and the conversation ended. There can be no dissent among true believers who gather on social media to reassure one another that what they believe really is the truth. This ceremony is repeated endlessly. "What more vivid figure for the secular, historically clocked, imagined community can be envisioned?"[41] At the same time, the social media consumer, observing exact replicas of his own ideas being consumed and replicated by his imagined neighbors, is continually reassured that the imagined world is visibly rooted in his own understanding. Thus, "fiction creeps quietly and continuously into reality, creating that remarkable confidence of community in anonymity."[42]

Another way to respond to Trump's rhetoric is to pay attention to his persuasive attempts. Exactly what is Trump asking people to do? What kind of nation does he want us to be? Where is this headed? By attending to these and other pertinent questions, we can study Trump's rhetoric as a secular apocalyptic deception. He is not really for the common people; he is a promoter of crony capitalism.

Jennifer Mercieca says that Trump uses three unifying strategies to connect with his supporters: ad populum arguments, American exceptionalism, and paralipsis. Trump uses three dividing strategies: ad hominem, ad baculum, and reification.[43]

Ad populum arguments appeal to the goodness, righteousness, and knowledge of his followers. Trump offers as facts what he says most people believe. He uses the large crowds at his rallies as a persuasive appeal. He emotionally manipulates the crowd with appeals to safety and security and law and order. He also makes them fearful of an almost invulnerable and powerful enemy. The appeal to the wisdom of the crowd and then the reverse claim that the crowd is weak and in need of protection reveal the deception at work. Trump's entire campaign and presidency were one long ad populum argument against political correctness. It is one continuous appeal to a crowd that knows political correctness is unfair, that it robs people of freedom of speech, and it shames people who have done nothing wrong. Trump told his followers that political correctness had made us weak. Evangelical leaders

---

41. Hauerwas, *In Good Company*, 36.
42. Anderson, *Imagined Communities*, 36.
43. Mercieca, *Demagogue for President*.

tell congregations that political correctness has feminized the church and threatened traditional marriage.

Another possible rhetorical approach is to consider how he appropriates a term or a phrase to convince his followers that they are victims. For example, Trump is fond of the term *witch hunt*. The term usually refers to people in a community who have been scapegoated. In the Salem witch trials, for example, women accused of witchcraft were poor, disowned, or enslaved. They lacked power and voice. They had no resources to secure legal advice. As scholars Robert Ivie and Oscar Giner explain, the term *witch hunt* has long referred to instances in which 'others' in a community have been scapegoated in response to visceral fears.[44] In the "Red Scare" of the 1950s, the McCarthy "witch hunt" for communists pitted a powerful United States senator against a group of artists, teachers, and actors. The disparity in power was obvious. After 9/11, the "witch hunts" targeted religious and ethnic minorities and concentrated its xenophobia on Muslims.

Now, contrast the voiceless, powerless people facing "witch hunts" to a man who constantly brags about how wealthy he is, how strong he is, and how smart he is. A billionaire president holding the most powerful office in the land cannot easily make the case that he and his followers are victims. This, of course, doesn't keep the president from trying. He has, for example, insisted that he has been treated worse than any president in our history, even Abraham Lincoln, who was assassinated. Evangelicals have to account for their victory and their access to the White House and their ongoing claims of political exile. They are now in the center of power but continue to use the rhetoric of a people on the fringe, outcasts.

Another possible rhetorical response is the attempt to turn the discourse back to matters of policy and concrete outcomes. Instead of attacking Trump's rhetoric of "demolition," concentrate on whatever his actual policies are. How is President Trump actually alleviating the material challenges of people? For example, Trump constantly criticizes Obamacare, and yet he has been unable to overturn the legislation. Part of the reason is that the political discourse was turned away from Trump's criticisms to how healthcare was improving people's lives. Instead of Trump's rhetoric of victimhood, his voice was supplanted by a higher call of "I want this for us."

Eventually, there is no voice strong enough to censure President Trump as long as Fox News, the ethos of social media, the demonization of Democrats, a Republican Senate and party that mildly rebukes him in word but not deed, and a vast evangelical network that continues to feed the monster of "white male grievance," there's not much that can be done.

44. Ivie and Giner, "Hunting the Devil."

The people who have the power to stop President Trump's demagogic march will have to exercise it as the US Senate did to Senator McCarthy in 1954. In any event, it is incumbent on every one of us to keep reminding our elected leaders that they should not give voice to Trump's discourse of victimhood. "Not all claims of suffering are equal. Not all grievances deserve the same hearing. Not all pain can be traced back to concrete conditions of material hardship. To escape Trump's rhetoric of demolition, resentment, and anger, it is necessary to affirm these premises and declare that revenge is not a coherent political program."[45]

Another possible rhetorical strategy is to change the focus of the argument from Trump to his evangelical supporters. They don't possess the power he holds as president. They are more open to sustained, rational criticism. In other words, they are an easier target. Instead of insisting that Donald Trump is "one bad apple," perhaps it is time to accept that he is "a bad apple" in an entire barrel of bad apples. This is the approach of rhetorical scholar Jennifer Wingard, in her essay, "Trump's Not Just One Bad Apple: He's the Product of a Spoiled Bunch."[46]

This political variation of "bad cop," "good cop" works well for evangelicals in a related controversy—gay marriage. The most vile and despicable of all the anti-gay preachers in the United States for years was Fred Phelps of Topeka, Kansas. His website banner logos blasted: "God Hates Fags." Rebecca Barrett-Fox, in her work, *God Hates: Westboro Baptist Church, American Nationalism, and the Religious Right*,[47] argues that evangelicals have used Rev. Phelps and his church as their version of the "bad apple." Evangelical leaders who have antigay views as intolerable as those of Fred Phelps, and also have far more influence than Phelps, hide behind this Baptist preacher of a tiny church in Topeka. Barrett-Fox notes that the goal of the evangelicals is "to use Westboro Baptist Church as a foil to construct itself as compassionate to gay people but critical of gay sex. In other words, by characterizing Westboro Baptists as 'haters,' the Religious Right can recalibrate the scale of homophobia so that its own homophobia is seen as moderate—as, indeed, compassion rather than hate."[48] In this way Westboro Baptist Church serves as the scapegoat, keeps the antigay message alive, and serves the agenda of the Religious Right. Evangelicals criticized for being antigay can intone, "At least I'm not Fred Phelps."

---

45. Steudeman, "Demagoguery," 8.
46. Wingard, "Trump's Not Just One Bad Apple."
47. Barrett-Fox, *God Hates*.
48. Barrett-Fox, *God Hates*, 113.

When Robert Jeffress faced criticism for describing Mormonism as a cult and saying Mitt Romney was not a Christian, Jeffress deflected the criticism: "I am not a Jeremiah Wright on the fringe, making fanatical statements."[49] These attempts to isolate a "bad apple" and to blame others have nothing at all to do with the statements and actions of antigay preachers, Republican politicians, or evangelical leaders like Jeffress. Their arguments are completely irrelevant to their hateful rhetoric.

By concentrating on the way evangelicals have created, sustained, and upheld Donald Trump, it is easier to construct an argument that frames them as being less than honest, as being the same racist, overt bigots concerned about white male power as Trump. They created him; they own him and they are responsible for what he is doing to the institutions of democracy.

The forces of Trump that are gathering among us like storm clouds are deep and dark. They run the gamut from racism to homophobia. They must be named and refuted, and the presence in our own hearts of the same racism and homophobia needs to be negotiated. The possibility of persuasion should never be thrown out like trash because the resources of rhetoric as "a symbolic means of inducing cooperation in beings that by nature responds to symbols" give us the opportunity to have a larger, more inclusive community.[50] Negotiating with one another over the vast panoply of human tendencies to treat others as less than human is hard, ongoing, never-to-be-abandoned work. "It is a work that can only be accomplished by a democratic people. If we are to become such a people, we will need both to reject the temptation" to scapegoat Donald Trump and willingly acknowledge our own participation in the cruel methodologies of making others less than human. "For this work, we need each other, and as many of our Others as possible"[51] Truth, of the hard, but also caring, kind needs to be reinvented in American conversation. If we can admit to the risk of being vulnerable, of having an unwavering commitment and duty to democracy, and a determination to seek and articulate fundamental truths, perhaps we can take back democracy from focus groups, political consultants, poll takers, and other cynics. Maybe, on our own, we can find new ways to recreate American democracy where we are not automatically enemies to one another. This is a known reality—among evangelicals, we are the enemy. Every day I learn once again how many evangelicals feel about all Democrats. The attacks are scurrilous, insulting, and demeaning. Somewhere we lost the reality that we actually are fellow Americans and finding that core again will not be easy.

49. Jeffress, "Robert Jeffress on Mitt Romney."
50. Burke, *A Rhetoric of Motives*, 43.
51. Allen, "Who Owns Donald Trump's Antisemitism?," 73.

Rediscovering the "goods" that we have in common would at least be a step in the right direction.

A large part of my heart feels more like Frederick Douglass toward the end of his life, as described by historian David Blight: By the 1890s Douglass, aging and in ill health but still out on the lecture circuit, felt hard-pressed to sustain hope for the transformations at the heart of the "Composite Nationality" speech. He never renounced his faith in natural rights or in the power of the vote. But in the last great speech of his life, "Lessons of the Hour"—an excoriating analysis of the excuses and lies at the root of lynching—Douglass betrayed a faith "shaken" and nearly gone.[52] Disenfranchisement and murderous violence left him observing a nation mired in lawless horror. Lynchings were "lauded and applauded by honorable men . . . guardians of Southern women"[53] who enabled other men to behave "as buzzards, vultures, and hyenas." A country once endowed with "nobility" was crushed by mob rule. His dream in tatters, Douglass begged his audiences to remember that the Civil War and Reconstruction had "announced the advent of a nation, based upon human brotherhood and the self-evident truths of liberty and equality. Its mission was the redemption of the world from the bondage of ages."[54]

Having confessed to the dimming of the light of hope for a recreated America, I do confess that I hold out one bit of brightness, also courtesy of Douglass. Blight says that in an 1871 editorial Douglas took a position worth heeding today. The failure to exercise one's right to vote, he wrote, "is as great a crime as an open violation of the law itself."[55] "Only a demonstration of rebirth in our composite nation and of vibrancy in our democracy will again send thrills of joy and emulation around the world about America. Such a rebirth ought not to be the object of our waiting but of our making, as it was for the Americans, black and white, who died to end slavery and make the second republic."[56]

When hope drags in the dust, trailing behind us like a people in captivity crying, "How can we sing the Lord's song in a strange land?," perhaps we should take stock of what we are facing. No matter what efforts we make to bridge the great gulf fixed between us, there is the unalterable reality that has to be faced. Many Trump supporters have engaged in the act of "pure identification" with their leader. He can't be wrong or criticized or belittled.

---

52. Blight, "Frederick Douglass's Vision."
53. Blight, "Frederick Douglass's Vision."
54. Blight, "Frederick Douglass's Vision."
55. Blight, "Frederick Douglass's Vision."
56. Blight, "Frederick Douglass's Vision."

He is always right no matter what. Trump's followers have what is known as a "charismatic leadership" attachment to the president. In charismatic leadership, followers so emotionally identify with their leader that he becomes them and they become him.[57] The two are one and there is no breaking of that bond. The lesson here is that some large portion of our efforts at persuasion must be turned in the direction of those for whom Trump is not the charismatic leader, those who haven't yet made up their minds.

Identifying racism does not stop it. Denying it doesn't make it disappear. Apologizing for racist remarks and actions add insult to injury.[58] Apology has become a way of cloaking racism through rhetorical strategies of denial, bolstering, and minimization. Nor does it contradict Trump's overt bigotry. The question is how do we move forward? There is ample evidence that Trump supporters are not just suckers falling for a scam. Some may be uninformed, others prone to conspiracy theories, and others totally convinced that Democrats and all liberals are the scourge of the planet; this doesn't make them irrational or dummies. Many Trump supporters know that Trump is a serial liar, but they think the lies are necessary in order to win. The devil's tools for the victory of God seems to be the line of thought.[59]

Behind the perma-press smiles of evangelical preachers, and the eruptions of "God bless you, brother," I am haunted with a vision from Dostoyevsky's *The Brothers Karamazov*. Aware of how many preachers have reached for this story as the jewel of a sermon, I use it, not as illustration, but a dominant rhetorical trope of my interpretation of evangelical leaders. Part of my quarrel with evangelicals unfolds in the narrative of Dostoyevsky's story. "The Grand Inquisitor" is actually a story told by Ivan Karamazov to his brother Alyosha, in which Ivan imagines the return of Jesus to earth in Seville at the height of the Spanish Inquisition. Jesus is taken prisoner by the ninety-year-old Grand Inquisitor who then—like police interrogators before and since—details the suspect's crimes. The return of Jesus after fifteen centuries of absence interferes with the work of the church. Jesus preached a message of freedom, but the church has discovered that it is not freedom that humankind desires; it is authority. "Oh, we shall convince them that they will only become free when they resign their freedom to us, and submit to us," says the Inquisitor. "The most tormenting secrets of their conscience—all, all they will bring to us, and we will decide all things, and they will joyfully believe our decision,

---

57. See Roberts-Miller, "Charisma Isn't Leadership."

58. Holling, Moon, and Nevis, "Racist Violations and Racializing Apologia."

59. Hauerwas, in *Working with Words*, 119–20, makes a compelling case that Jesus, in refusing the gifts of the devil on the mountain, refused to use the devil's means to accomplish the purposes of God. Evangelicals suffer from no such reluctance.

because it will deliver them from their great care and their present terrible torments of personal and free decision."[60]

Admitting the difficulty of engagement is progress. Continuing to speak truth, as we experience it, remains our most important vocation. "There is an important space for frankness and candor in American politics if it commits to the virtues of parrhesia: risk or danger for the speaker, an unwavering duty to society, and the expression of fundamental truths. Perhaps this realization can help us recognize different ways to engage in American democracy—and American political discussions—moving forward."[61] Being a faithful witness to the virtues of parrhesia is an important step. For a pastor of a local congregation, this definitely involves risk as she/he attempts to help a congregation deal with the hidden and vicious nature of racism. A faithful preacher listens attentively for the word of God in Scripture and life. And when the word of God arrives, "he climbs up there where the fire is so hot it's ice, and ice so cold it burns like fire."[62]

A preacher of the gospel has no other alternative than to challenge the structures, systems, codes, and invisibility of racism. Doing so comes with attendant risks. When racism is challenged, the reaction of whites "is always severe"[63] and responses range from overt racism,[64] to entrenchment in white supremacy, to refusing to listen to others,[65] to actively denying the importance of racism and our complicity in it.[66] Furthermore, whites typically present themselves as moral and responsible social actors who would rather not be identified as racist and subsequently attempt to persuade others that they support equality and justice. Of all this and more the white cloak of invisibility is constructed as a rhetorical trope.

## Knowing the Enemy: The Cloak of Invisibility

Evangelicals hide behind words such as, "There is no systemic racism in America," "Maybe there's residual racism," "Everyone who knows me

---

60. Dostoevsky, *The Grand Inquisitor*, 7.
61. Skinnell, "What Passes for Truth," 97.
62. Ramsey, *Preachers and Misfits*, loc. 397.
63. Guillermo and Moras, "Defining an 'anti' stance," 383.
64. Rich and Cargile, "Beyond the Breach."
65. Fishman and McCarthy, "Talk about Race.
66. Warren and Hytten, "The Faces of Whiteness." See also Ramasubramanian, Sousa, and Gonlin, "Facilitated Difficult Dialogues on Racism"; Patton, "Reflections of a Black Woman Professor"; Ramasubramanian and Miles, "White Nationalist Rhetoric"; and Morrissey and Sims, "Playing the Race Card."

knows that I'm not a racist." Somehow evangelicals have borrowed Harry Potter's "invisibility cloak" and thrown it over the nation. It's solid white and the racism is now invisible. There's a cloak of invisibility that covers all signs of racism for evangelicals. Like a whiteout in Pierre, South Dakota or a fog-covered bayou in Louisiana, there is whiteness and nothing but whiteness. Racism can't be seen and therefore can be assumed not to exist. The cloak covers absolutely everything. Part of our task, theologically and rhetorically, is coming to terms with our own racism and grappling with the existence of the white cloak of invisibility.

More often than not, there are tears in the cloak and questions arise about our allegedly post-racist culture and our vaunted color blindness. For example, racial slurs in white American discourse continue to occur, especially the word "n****r".[67] Randall Kennedy[68] and others have taken note of the "special status" of the n-word as a racial slur, casting it the "all American trump card, the nuclear bomb of racist epithets,"[69] and as the only racial slur that has the "ability to tear at one's insides."[70] Recognizing the n-word as a "vestige of slavery" and white supremacy, in 2007 the National Association for the Advancement of Colored Persons (NAACP) conducted a mock funeral for the word at their annual meeting. As Nelson B. Rivers III, COO of the NAACP observed, "The N-Word is the most vicious of all racial insults. . . . [T]ime has come to celebrate the end of its wretched, destructive life."[71] Despite widespread agreement at the offensiveness of the slur, the term keeps popping up in our allegedly post-racist white culture.[72] In other words, racist stereotypes are deeply entrenched in white racial frameworks and repeated in a variety of cultural, political, and personal arenas.

While the "sun has set on the era of white Christian dominance," as Robert P. Jones argues in *The End of White Christian America*, the cloak hides even this slide into decline. The danger of living in such whiteness, another word for blindness, is that, as Slavoj Žižek puts it, "Now is the time for monsters."[73] Imani Perry notes that racism percolates through us, often outside our field of awareness. In the twilight of overt racism, a massive white

---

67. Hill, *The Everyday Language of White Racism*, 51.
68. Kennedy, *Nigger*, 28.
69. Chideya, *The Color of Our Future*, 9.
70. Hacker, *Two Nations*, 42.
71. NAACP, "Rap pioneers join NAACP."
72. Holling, Moon, and Nevis, "Racist Violations and Racializing Apologia."
73. Žižek, "A Permanent Economic Emergency."

cloak of invisibility—"an apparatus of instrumentalized racialization"—is used to elevate whites by enveloping others in shame.[74]

White supremacy, long associated with the KKK, white hoods, and robes, burning crosses, and lynch mobs, seems too grotesque to be admitted and so evangelicals put white supremacy in this "frozen-in-time" past that doesn't include their whiteness. This is a benefit of the cloak of invisibility. Zeus Leonardo explains that racially coded language appears neutral yet demonstrates "whites know how to talk about race without having to mention the word."[75] Such an ability to talk about race or racism without being explicit is a form of white racial knowledge, "comprised of a constellation of metaphors used to define whites' sense of self and group in oppositions to a denigrated other."[76] Therefore, masking racist violations such as saying the n-word, referring to Black men as "monkeys," or thinking of Black women as promiscuous contributes to minimizing pernicious racial epithets and/or stereotypes while implying a mere slip of the tongue. White people use coded language easily understood by other whites, and insulting to minorities. It's as if whites feel privileged to pretend it's all one big joke followed by apologies like "the remark I made was a mistake" or "an offense by accident." The alleged apology reinforces the original racist remarks under cover of the cloak of invisibility.

Eddie Glaude, Jr. attempts to pull back the cloak of invisibility: "The phrase white supremacy conjures images of bad men in hooded robes who believed in white power . . . but that's not quite what I mean here. On a broader level, white supremacy involves the way a society organizes itself, and what and whom it chooses to value. . . . A set of practices informed by the fundamental belief that white people are valued more than others."[77] Thomas K. Nakayama and Robert L. Krizek argue that whiteness is a rhetorical construct. This makes the white cloak of invisibility a visual metaphor of how racism can be ignored, denied, and discounted in a majority white culture.[78] As Abdul-Jabbar wrote: "African Americans have been living in a burning building for many years, choking on the smoke as the flames burn closer and closer. Racism in America is like dust in the air.

---

74. Perry, *More Beautiful and More Terrible*, 42.
75. Leonardo, *Race, Whiteness, and Education*, 114.
76. Leonardo, *Race, Whiteness, and Education*, 114.
77. Glaude, *Democracy in Black*, 6. Glaude here refers to "the thick fog of uncertainty."
78. Nakayama and Krizek, "Whiteness." See also Chakravartty, "#Communication SoWhite."

It seems invisible—even if you're choking on it—until you let the sun in. Then you see it's everywhere."[79]

## How Can We Make Progress?

In a polarized nation, the idea of common ground may seem naïve, but I believe that there are rhetorical resources available to guide us. For example, rhetorical theorist Celeste Condit calls us to be more "empathic" in our thinking, so that we may "locate pieces of common ground among various voices and to discover options for those compromises necessary for coexistence."[80] The "empathic" approach requires looking at one's own attitudes, becoming aware of the invisible ways that we are blinded by whiteness and racism. Increasing our ability to see is the heart of the matter.

Ludwig Wittgenstein postulated the possibility of "human beings lacking in the capacity to see something as something—and what would it be like? Would this defect be comparable to color-blindness?" He said, "We will call it 'aspect-blindness.'" The result, he claimed, would be a debased ethical disposition, and even more tragically a method for effective governance. We are all part of specific pedagogies that lead to "how one sees things."[81] To look, to see, to really see, the systemic racism, is never easy, especially if deceived by the message that political correctness is an elitist pedagogy designed to make evangelicals "feel bad" when they act in racist ways.

## The Cloak of Invisibility

The sharp denials of racism that suffuse the evangelical world raises questions about how people fail to observe incidences of racism. After a century or more of attempting to make persons of color invisible, white people have covered racism with a cosmic white sheet. Oxygen and whiteness coexist, unnoticed, on the planet. Whites don't notice it; they just breathe in and out and live their lives. I label this white sheet the "Harry Potter Cloak of Invisibility."

The invisibility cloak has multiple expressions as this macro-KKK white sheet makes racism disappear from sight but not reality. In a crucial early foray into the study of whiteness, Richard Dyer makes exactly this argument. White is at once nowhere and everywhere; it is everything and

---

79. Cited in Lee, "Kareem Abdul-Jabbar."
80. Condit, "The Critic as Empath," 189. See also Condit's *Angry Public Rhetorics*.
81. Wittgenstein, *Philosophical Investigations*, 213.

nothing. White people are "not there as a category and everywhere everything as a fact."[82] To use Roland Barthes's language, whiteness in the United States can be defined as "the social class which does not want to be named."[83] Thomas K. Nakayama and Robert L. Krizek point out that whiteness "wields power yet endures as a largely unarticulated position."[84]

Much of the impetus for these moves is part of a group that Blight labels as "reconciliationists," one of the three major visions coming in the wake of Reconstruction. It is to provide white people with a gospel that requires no recognition, no repentance, no reparations. When the president claims he needs no repentance and then offers to make his supporters feel good instead of shameful, we know that a gospel has been offered opposite of the one whose opening gambit is, "Repent and believe the gospel."

In Anne Tyler's *Saint Maybe*, Ian Bedloe, the protagonist of the novel, believes that he is responsible for the death of his brother in a car wreck. Ian encounters Rev. Emmett and unburdens on him his feelings of guilt. Earlier in the church service, Ian had asked for prayer. Now, he tells Rev. Emmett that he believes his prayer was answered. The pastor refuses to let him off the hook and informs him that real, material reparations must be made.[85]

## "This is not about Race; it's about History"

A favorite expression of the cloak, among those who insist that is little racism left in America, is to lodge race-based issues as being about history. There are attempts to silence the story, the cries of the oppressed. History, meant to save us from past mistakes, is being used as an invisibility cloak for racism. The "America was founded as a Christian nation" trope is part of the invisibility cloak. Suddenly, history lovers are coming out from under the woodpile of evangelical faith.

Senator Tom Cotton, in an attempt to cut school funding over the teaching of slavery by using the "1619 Project," is a prime example of an ongoing attempt to squelch any serious discussion of race. Sen. Cotton (R-AR) insists he isn't opposed to having students study America's history of slavery, but he has presented legislation that would cut funding from any public school that taught a curriculum based on The *New York Times*' 1619 Project. His complaint, he said, was that the "factually, historically flawed" collection

---

82. Dyer, "White," 46.
83. Barthes, *Mythologies*, 138.
84. Nakayama and Krizek, "Whiteness," 291.
85. Ramsey, *Preachers and Misfits*, chapter 4.

of essays is based on the premise "that America is at root, a systemically racist country to the core and irredeemable."

Cotton, offering questionable readings of history, argues, "As the Founding Fathers said, it was the necessary evil upon which the union was built, but the union was built in a way, as Lincoln said, to put slavery on the course to its ultimate extinction."[86] Racism survives on turns of phrases: "necessary evil," "three-fifths of a person," "the lower race of human being" (Jefferson Davis). The cries of oppression are squelched: "I have no love for America, as such" (Frederick Douglas); "I question America" (Fannie Lou Hamer); "the greatest purveyor of violence in the world today—my own government (Rev. Dr. Martin Luther Kings, Jr.)"; "Not God bless America, but God damn America" (Jeremiah Wright).

## "I Pledge Allegiance to the Flag" as Racist Trope

Perhaps the most insidious use of the white sheet of invisibility is the use of the flag as a quilt over the sheet. Since issues of race, religion, and nation are bundled together like a bunch of onions at Whole Foods, untangling racism from patriotism has proven to be complex. There's no affect like that of waving the red, white, and blue over issues of Black and white.

Protests of racism by professional athletes was a favorite Trump ploy. When a Black football player kneels during the singing of the National Anthem, he can be accused of being unpatriotic, of not loving America. Racists get two for one in this scenario. It's political genius. Supporters get to parade their patriotism, and no one will notice the implied racism. Evangelicals have wrapped the Bible in the American flag and now the president has wrapped the flag around racism. Red, white, and blue—the colors of our flag—are now being used for an unpatriotic, un-American purpose: to divide us and to create a new "place" where people can be excluded. Place is an important piece in the racist vision that President Trump offers. Even some of the placid supporters who defended the athletes' rights added, "The singing of the National Anthem is not the place for that sort of thing." Former NFL head coach Mike Ditka connected the protests of athletes during the National Anthem as "disrespectful" and insisted they should "get the hell out of the country."[87]

"Patriotism" makes a powerful cloak for racism because the word is universally accepted in America as a virtue. Every culture thrills to its favored words or concepts. In *The Ethics of Rhetoric*, Richard Weaver dubbed

86. CNN, "GOP senator."
87. Joseph, "Mike Ditka."

them "god terms."[88] They're the argument-ending, conclusive words that we find intrinsically persuasive because they express our deep prejudices about what's good and true and beautiful. In Weaver's nomenclature, "patriotism" is a God term.

President Trump, for example, tried to make an issue out of the false report that the Democrats had left "God" out of their reciting of the Pledge of Allegiance during their digital national convention. The president tweeted: "The Democrats took the word God out of the Pledge of Allegiance at the Democrat National Convention. At first, I thought they made a mistake, but it wasn't. It was done on purpose. Remember Evangelical Christians, and ALL, this is where they are coming from—it's done. Vote Nov 3!"[89] Actually, the Democrats said the Pledge and included "God" all four nights. Trump lied but, as usual, the lie didn't matter. The affect grew wings and reinforced what evangelicals already believe, as Rev. Jeffress made clear in his attack: "Democrats have a God problem."[90] When you have the president of the United States and a leading evangelical pastor claiming that the "God" of the Pledge of Allegiance is the God Christian worship, there should be an alarm that sounds. The Christian God is the Father, Son, and Holy Spirit, not the generalized deity affirmed in the Pledge. After all, "The Christian pledge is not the Pledge of Allegiance but rather is called the Apostles' Creed."[91]

## "Political Correctness is Killing Us" as Racist Trope

With "patriotism" as their "god" term, evangelicals and Trump added "political correctness" as the primary "devil" term. The invisibility cloak is strengthened with steel fibers of "political correctness." Trump's campaign and his election can be seen as a victory over "political correctness." Polls show that while people have no understanding of what political correctness even means, it is unpopular. A Fairleigh Dickinson University Public Mind survey found that 68 percent of all Americans and 81 percent of Republicans agreed that "being politically correct" was a "big problem in this country."[92]

Jennifer Mercieca argues that "Trump's campaign-long attack on political correctness was essentially one long ad populum appeal—it was one continuous appeal to the "wisdom of the crowd" against established

88. Weaver, *The Ethics of Rhetoric*, 212–22.
89. Chung, "Trump Attacked."
90. Kuruvilla, "Evangelical Pastor."
91. Hauerwas, *Working with Words*, 118.
92. Jenkins, "Trump Taints."

leadership—and it relied on preexisting mistrust and attempted to increase distrust between the people and their elected officials."[93]

Political correctness was the trope that most effectively established the "total identity" between Trump and his disciples. Trump's supporters could participate in the pleasure of violating the norms of political correctness and fighting corruption by championing their hero and using language like he did. Trump campaign rallies became "safe spaces" for Trump supporters to say whatever they had been suppressing due to the scourge of political correctness.[94]

Evangelicals hear "political correctness" and interpret it as liberal shame pedagogy. Shame saturates contemporary politics. Bodies that once felt like the unchallenged masters of their space—white bodies, male bodies, cis bodies, straight bodies, rich bodies, citizen bodies—are being confronted, more and more, with a demand to respond to the violence trailing in the wake of the comforts and pleasures they enjoy. This effect is amplified by the increasing mediation of society, that is, the way in which the density of social interactions is steadily increasing, underwritten by technological shifts. We live in an increasingly saturated shame panopticon. This has led some of the former masters to a state of shame-exhaustion, in which it becomes easier to repudiate shame altogether than respond to the moral demands placed on them.

Eve Sedgwick asks: "Can anyone suppose that we'll ever figure out what happened around political correctness if we don't see it as, among other things, a highly politicized chain reaction of shame dynamics?"[95] The insight of this framing lies in the way it stages political correctness as a pedagogy, a sweeping masterwork of shame designed to rip residual structures of degradation from speech. It is to be expected, then, that this chain of shame would provoke a shame response, a furious refusal of culpability. This is where Trump comes in.

When Donald Trump ran for president, one of the core pillars of his pitch to the voting public was this: Political correctness is a cancer eating away at the body politic. "We have to straighten out our country, we have to make our country great again, and we need energy and enthusiasm," Trump said during an appearance on *Meet the Press* in August 2015. "And this political correctness is just absolutely killing us as a country. You can't say anything. Anything you say today, they'll find a reason why it's not good."

---

93. Mercieca, *Demagogue for President*, loc. 669–845.
94. Mercieca, *Demagogue for President*, loc. 669–845.
95. Sedgwick, *Touching Feeling*, 64.

Kathleen Hall Jamieson and Doron Taussig identify Trump's rhetorical signature as demonization, evidence-flouting, and repudiation of institutions—these attributes "aided his cause as a candidate because it signaled a rejection of both the status quo and political convention to a constituency eager to see those things shaken up."[96] Ivie's conviction is that Trump inflamed "a collective fantasy that he will get things done by shaking up politics as usual."[97]

Evangelicals react to being shamed as a pedagogy, a sweeping masterwork of liberal shame designed to rip away the degradation of their free speech. The evangelical riposte: "How dare they!" Taking the side of whites who have been confronted with their complicity in racial disparity, Trump assures them that rather than feeling ashamed, they should take revenge on those who have tried to challenge their right to "feel good" about their divisive, hateful rhetoric. He alerts his followers that they should refuse to be shamed and he demonstrates how this works by violating decorum and then refusing to apologize. His followers are entranced by this tough man who exhibits no sense of blame, fault, or shame, even when he should, by never saying he is sorry. He uses his facial expressions—a sneer and a smirk—and his posture—no head bowed, no shoulders slumped—and his refusal to apologize as nonverbal rhetorical tropes for deconstructing political correctness.

Trump, the evangelist, offers his followers a new life of pride without the shame they have endured from those awful accusations of being racists, bigots, homophobes, and worse. Lauren Berlant has proposed that the political appeal of Trump does not rest in an ideological posture. "Trump's people," she writes, "want fairness of a sort, but mainly they seek freedom from shame. Civil rights and feminism aren't just about the law after all, they are about manners, and emotions too: those 'interest groups' get right in there and reject *what feels like* people's spontaneous, ingrained responses. People get shamed, or lose their jobs, for example, when they're just having a little fun making fun. Anti-PC means 'I feel unfree.'"[98]

Trump attacks political correctness like Billy Sunday thundering against "society women." A particularly nasty animus seems to motivate Trump when the perceived opponents are women. He even suggested that Senator Kamala Harris, now vice president, might not be a citizen of the United States—his favorite racist trope. His long history of sexism

---

96. Jamieson and Taussig, "Disruption," 641.
97. Ivie, "Trump's Unwitting Prophecy," 708.
98. Berlant, "Trump, or Political Emotions."

overshadows his public remarks about women. His hegemonic masculinity oozes from his speech.

Attacking "political correctness" became a part of the denial of racism. Now, the subject is not the mistreatment of African Americans, but the denial of free speech to evangelicals. They wish to maintain their racist, homophobic ideas, their antigay, anti-abortion, anti-science vituperative language, their unceasing demonizing of liberals, but they don't wish to be held accountable for any of it. Trump's evangelical followers want to receive their due rewards for being good Christians, who go to church, sing in the choir, write big checks, have a good time, and are true patriots. They don't want to be demeaned, criticized, and be made fun of for standing up for Jesus by rejecting persons of color.

Evangelicals, unwilling to embrace the public morality of justice for persons of color and gay marriage, have devalued those cultural goods and denied their accepted value. They insist that the public morality is actually an "abomination." With their feelings hurt, they slander the common good as if their failure to embody a new public morality represents structural oppression and thus allows them the freedom to disavow civic responsibility.

## "I'm the Least Racist Person in the World": Deny, Deny, Deny

The fabric of the cloak of invisibility is made up of denial. "I am not a racist" is intended to end all argument otherwise. It is how a woman can say that Michelle Obama is "an ape in heels" one day and the next day say, "Everyone who knows me knows I'm not a racist." She then explained that she made the statement out of frustration of being called a racist.[99] But if someone talks like a racist, acts like a racist, even if they aren't wearing a white hood, chances are she is a racist.

Two factors make the denial of racism ring false. One, 81 percent of evangelicals voted for Trump. Two, he won the presidency on the "basis of overt bigotry."[100] The Trump campaign vision makes clear that his sense of our nation is rooted in issues of identity, privilege, place, and belonging—all racial indicators. Trump offered an "excessive rhetoric of exclusion" to voters, and they swallowed it hook, line, and sinker.

Denial plays into the divisive dualism that now dominates our politics. This denial has become the defense du jour for any man accused of sexual assault from the president, to a Supreme Court nominee, to a candidate for

99. Chan, "Michelle Obama."
100. Ivie, "Trump's Unwitting Prophecy," 707.

the US Senate, to any number of famous people in other fields. To speak of the denial of sexism is relevant because of the close bond between sexism and racism. Too much of the world's history has considered the owning of women and slaves as personal property for us to escape the implications. To deny the sexual assault of a woman is to make her out to be a liar. When it's "he says, she says," what he says is considered reliable, trustworthy, truthful. What she says is denigrated, rejected, and downplayed. This tendency to intensify the goodness and honesty of the man while downplaying the goodness of the woman is a perfect defense. The denial is the same as a verdict of not guilty. What woman would expect her accusations to be believed in a world where the deck is already stacked against her? Each time Donald Trump has been accused of sexual misconduct he has vehemently denied it.

Narrative and strategy can sidetrack a wider discussion of race relations. The Trump administration put out a different narrative. One, the narrative they have constructed attacks the character of George Floyd. A key part of Trump's strategy is to downplay racism as "residual" or to redefine the act of killing Floyd as "bullying" and not racism. The Trump administration went to great lengths to produce a counter-narrative to the reality of the killing of Floyd. Political narratives, concocted after events, are revisionist attempts to put the best possible face on ugliness, violence, and, in this case, racism. The narrative and the strategy of the Trump administration follows the traditional insistence that racism is not even the issue. The defense is that the cops responsible for Floyd's death were "bad apples."

CNN's Wolf Blitzer asked Ken Cuccinelli, acting assistant secretary of Homeland Security, if he thought Floyd would still be alive if he were white, Cuccinelli said, "No, I don't think he would." In other words, the narrative from Trump headquarters is that this is not about race. "What I heard in that eight-and-a-half-minute clip was someone who was a bully, who is abusing his position of authority and power in the law," Cuccinelli said in reference to a video of Floyd's death. "And I have a funny feeling, I don't know anything about his professional history, but I have a feeling that we're going to find that he wasn't necessarily that well thought of as a role model among law enforcement through the time of his career, to say the least."[101] His comments provide a vastly different view of America than that of the thousands of protesters who demanded justice for Floyd and sought to call attention to decades of police abuse toward Black Americans as a result of what they say is institutionalized racism in law enforcement agencies. Cuccinelli, however, joined other Trump officials who claimed that systemic racism is not an issue in US law enforcement.

101. *Summarizer*, "Trump Homeland Security."

Acting Homeland Security Secretary Chad Wolf similarly dismissed the idea that racism is a problem in law enforcement, arguing instead that "some" officers "abuse their jobs." "Painting law enforcement with a broad brush of systemic racism is really a disservice to the men and women who put on the badge, the uniform every day, risk their lives every day to protect the American people," Wolf told ABC.[102] His comments echo the message of Attorney General William Barr, who said in an interview with CBS, "I think there's racism in the United States still but I don't think that the law enforcement system is systemically racist."[103]

To paraphrase the Tennessee Williams narrator in *The Glass Menagerie*: "It was the opening year of the decade of the 2020s, when the huge middle class of America's white people were matriculating in a school for the blind. Their eyes had failed them, or they had failed their eyes, and so they are having their fingers pressed forcibly down on the fiery Braille alphabet of a resurgent racism and a failing democracy."[104]

The white cloak of invisibility impedes our attempts to make progress on race. Each racist act births denial of racist intent. Conservatives swear they are not racist, and liberals are the racists. It is an odd cacophony: white people, living in glass houses, throwing huger rocks than advisable at one another, about racism. The various aspects of the cloak of invisibility demonstrate how many layers of deception exist in even sincere attempts at conversations about race. As a people who see darkly and dimly because of the white glare of the invisibility cloak there remains the ongoing efforts to bring to light our common sin of racism. The words of Coates haunt every word of this chapter:

> It has long been an axiom among certain black writers and thinkers that while whiteness endangers the bodies of black people in the immediate sense, the larger threat is to white people themselves, the shared country, and even the whole world. There is an impulse to blanch at this sort of grandiosity. When W. E. B. Du Bois claims that slavery was "singularly disastrous for modern civilization" or James Baldwin claims that whites "have brought humanity to the edge of oblivion: because they think they are white," the instinct is to cry exaggeration. But there really is no other way to read the presidency of Donald Trump. The first white president in American history is also the most dangerous president—and he is made more dangerous still by the fact that

102. Coleman, "Wolf."
103. Benner, "Barr Says."
104. Williams, *The Glass Menagerie*, 3.

those charged with analyzing him cannot name his essential nature, because they too are implicated in it.[105]

An honest attempt and admission of the existence of the invisibility cloak of whiteness and racism can be a step in healing a broken nation. The overriding disability faced by whites in reference to racism is the hiddenness of racism. In fact, racism has god-like qualities as in the biblical ideas that God is invisible, unseen, almighty. Racism possesses qualities of omnipotence and omnipresence. As Jesús Colón says in "How to Know the Puerto Ricans," "So, please excuse us if, in presenting what we have learned ourselves or added to our knowledge from the experience of others, we might sound at times a little critical, preachy or even sermonizing. The theme lends itself to committing such errors."[106] Colón is one of the many voices of persons of color doing the necessary work of insinuating himself and his people into a story that has been almost exclusively white.

Persons of color are constantly attempting to make a space for themselves in a white world. By "space" I intend a name, a home, and a place. As Darrel Wanzer Serrano points out, "When such is the case, we make do, insinuate ourselves, carve out space, but are never truly permitted to take up permanent residence (even if we hold onto the hope of some future state of emergent and transformed belonging). We move in and out, living from place to place until we lose residency in the (white) scholarly suburb."[107] They feel as if they are renters moving from place to place; vagabonds, aliens, sojourners, a people looking for a city, and white people are oblivious to the constant migrations going on under their noses. This is the horror of the invisibility cloak.

The white cloak of invisibility can be invisible even to persons of color when they are young and not yet exposed to this demon they can't see, identify, or yet call by name. Here's a snapshot of how the awakening to the cloak occurs for a young person of color. In 1915, two years before setting sail on a ship bound for New York, Jesús Colón was flipping through his newly acquired eighth-grade history textbook, *A History of the United States*. He stumbled upon a document beginning with a phrase that, in his words, "stuck with me all day like one of those musical phrases of a nameless song that keeps coming up in the sound of your whistling, again and again, sometimes for hours."[108] The document was the US Constitution, and the phrase was its famous opening "We, the people of the United States." He repeated the phrase

---

105. Coates, "The First White President."
106. Colón, "How to Know the Puerto Ricans," 197.
107. Wanzer-Serrano, "Rhetoric's rac(e/ist) problems," 466.
108. Colón, "How to Know the Puerto Ricans," 197.

over and over, reflecting on how it meant that "We [Puerto Ricans] belonged" as part of the US national imaginary. Walking home, he "accented the phrase with the pounding of [his] feet on the centuries-old cobblestones of the streets in old San Juan. We-the-people-of-the-United-States."[109]

A few days later, Colón recalls that he ran into his history teacher, a white man from Montana named Mr. Whole. The teacher, Colon says, "hailed me from the porch. He invited me to play a game of checkers. I sat in front of the checker board between us, ready to start the game. Out came somebody in authority. He informed Mr. Whole that I could not play there with him as I did not belong to the white race. Mr. Whole said not a word and the game, not yet started, ended."[110] In an essay penned many years later, Colón again reflects on "we the people," now suspecting there are "first and secondary people . . . ; gradations and classifications not only because of race but because of money and social position."[111] He identifies the ways in which Puerto Ricans and others are systematically excluded from "the people," yet clings to the premise of the Constitution's opening phrase. For Colón, "we the people" remains as a promise yet unfulfilled, underscoring its futurity, that "when," not if, "that phrase is realized in its totality, Puerto Ricans will have the right to choose the form of government they really want" and shed the racist-classist-imperialist chains of colonial oppression.[112]

As a dues-paying member of two related disciplines, homiletics and rhetoric, as a pastor, and as a seminary professor, I am aware of the thick layers of hidden racism in those disciplines. Darrel Wanzer-Serrano argues, "Rhetorical studies as a field and the *Quarterly Journal of Speech* as the journal of record for that field are racist. Racism need not imply that evildoers in pointy hoods are pulling the strings of the journal and field; indeed, the assumption that racism is rooted in the bad thoughts and deeds of intentional individuals is part of the problem and is further evidence of the field's ignorance on the subject."[113] Homiletics professor Henry H. Mitchell has observed that if "preaching were the only consideration, the Black churches would have to pray hard to keep their formally trained preachers from being called to more affluent white pulpits right now." Mitchell observes in the Introduction of his book, *Black Preaching*: "Despite the widespread acceptance of Black preaching, despite the

---

109. Colón, "How to Know the Puerto Ricans," 198.
110. Colón, "How to Know the Puerto Ricans," 198.
111. Colón, "How to Know the Puerto Ricans," 198.
112. Colón, "How to Know the Puerto Ricans," 202.
113. Wanzer-Serrano, "Rhetoric's rac(e/ist) problems," 467.

admitted strength and appeal of the best Black preaching to Black and to white congregations, it is interesting to note that very little has been done to analyze or appropriate this strength for the sterile white pulpit."[114]

The overwhelming whiteness, both embodied and intellectually, in rhetoric faculties is not new. Fernando Delgado penned an essay titled "The Dilemma of the Minority Scholar: "Finding a Legitimized Voice in an Intellectual Space" for book *Racial and Ethnic Diversity in the Twenty-First Century: A Communication Perspective*. Delgado critiques the field of twenty years ago for the same mistakes it makes today. "The field has a problem," he writes. "There are far too many symbolists and not enough materialists when it comes to dealing with diversity. The frustration of many minorities is that we become symbols whose materiality is only infrequently (and sometimes punitively) recognized."[115] There is "hierarchical model for allowing some voices and silencing others, creating certain spaces and closing off others."[116]

There are many ways that I could define racism at this point. Bonilla-Silva explains, the fact that "whites and people of color cannot agree on racial matters is because they conceive terms such as 'racism' very differently. Whereas for most whites racism is prejudice, for most people of color racism is systemic or institutionalized."[117] In the service of simplicity, I want to draw from Ibram X. Kendi's monumental *How to Be an Antiracist*, where he defines racism as "a marriage of racist policies and racist ideas that produces and normalizes racial inequities."[118] Kendi posits that "racial inequity is when two or more racial groups are not standing on approximately equal footing" and a racist policy amounts to "any measure that produces or sustains racial inequity between racial groups."[119] As a practical concern, I believe that we can accept the evangelical pleas of not being racist in individual, local, personal settings, but insist that that too is but another instance of the invisibility cloak shrouding systemic, institutional, national racism.

Until we see differently, as in identifying the white cloak of invisibility, the process of negotiating the different perspectives on racism won't be easy. As Kendi notes, "The movement from racist to antiracist is always ongoing—it requires understanding and snubbing racism based on biology, ethnicity, body, culture, behavior, color, space, and class. And

---

114. Mitchell, *Black Preaching*, 13.
115. Delgado, "The Dilemma of the Minority Scholar," 51.
116. Delgado, "The Dilemma of the Minority Scholar," 49 and 51.
117. Bonilla-Silva, *Racism Without Racists*, 8.
118. Kendi, *How to Be an Antiracist*, 18.
119. Kendi, *How to Be an Antiracist*, 18.

beyond that, it means standing ready to fight at racism's intersections with other bigotries."[120] We must fight. We must take a stand. We must have some form of hope that we can break from the modern, Western, colonial, anti-Black, racist structuration of evangelical Christianity. The alternative would be grim. As a pastor, I have been reminded, from 1978 in Jonesboro, Louisiana to 2020 in Ottawa, Kansas that the pulpit isn't the field in which to make such arguments. If not the pulpit, the place of truth, then where, I query? But what if my critics are right with the same pragmatism and Machiavellian philosophy of the evangelicals? Maybe the foundation is just fundamentally flawed and church-so-white is an unalterable fact. Maybe the wood undergirding the façade of the House of Preaching is rotted to its core. Or maybe, in one of many moves of stubborn resistance, we should grab some tools and tear this house down once and for all.

Racism occupies a mostly passive voice in our culture. Certainly, the men and women forced to live in the wake of the beating of John Lewis, the lynching of Emmett Till, the firebombing of Percy Julian's home, the assassinations of Martin Luther King, Jr., and Medgar Evers, and the choking to death of George Floyd are still marginalized and their cries of oppression mostly fall on deaf ears. The cloak of invisibility does it work daily.

Coates alludes to the reality of the cloak: "In recent times, whiteness as an overt political tactic has been restrained by a kind of cordiality that held that its overt invocation would scare off 'moderate' whites. This has proved to be only half true at best. Trump's legacy will be exposing the cloak for what it is and revealing just how much a demagogue can get away with."[121]

In his work *Under the Cover of Chaos*, Lawrence Grossberg suggests that Trump managed to pleasurize disruption. "The most obvious and pervasive feature of Trump's highly visible and almost entertaining . . . if also terrifying performance is the normalization of a frenetic chaos and hyper-activism."[122]

Trump never missed an opportunity to turn a question into a discussion of white people and their victimization. In an interview with CBS News, he was asked why police continue to shoot and kill black men. Trump, incredibly, reacted with these words: "So are white people. So are

---

120. Kendi, *How to Be an Antiracist*, 10.

121. Coates, "The First White President."

122. Grossberg, *Under the Cover of Chaos*, 3. See also Gunn, "On Political Perversion"; Ivie, "Rhetorical Aftershocks"; Ivie, "Trump's Unwitting Prophecy"; Silva, "Having the Time of Our Lives"; Levina, "Whiteness and the Joys of Cruelty"; and Richardson, "The Disgust of Donald Trump."

white people. What a terrible question to ask. So are white people. More white people, by the way," he added. "More white people."[123]

Without apology or nuance, I have argued that evangelicalism has a race problem. It is built largely upon the back of a pro-slavery segregationist (Aristotle), a second-century Christian heresy (Gnosticism). And it is overly focused on a secular, white politics of citizenship and by fact if not design has all but excluded persons of color from its places of worship. On second thought, this isn't a race problem; this is a racism problem. Actually, evangelicals don't have a race problem; they are racist. Routinely refusing this judgment, evangelicals pull the cloak tighter over their heads and keep on ignoring what calls for repentance and reparation.

What comes next? As we continue to debate the values by which the nation will live, as well as the vision that will shape our political order, how do we know what is wrong and how best to respond? I offer words of prophecy, a true prophet, a divine instrument of prophetic disclosure, a true revelation of a crisis and a way forward. There's a "sheet" in the prophecy of Isaiah: "On this mountain the Lord of hosts will make for all peoples a feast of rich food, a feast of well-aged wines, of rich food filled with marrow, of well-aged wines strained clear. And he will destroy on this mountain the *shroud* that is cast over all peoples, the *sheet* that is spread over all nations; he will swallow up death forever. Then the Lord God will wipe away the tears from all faces, and the disgrace of his people he will take away from all the earth, for the Lord has spoken."[124] The words appear again in Revelation. They are usually spiritualized to be about heaven, but they are too material, too bodily for such hermeneutical slipperiness.

This is here and now, not some illusory apocalyptic future, but a preview of God's kingdom on earth for God's people: A feast for all peoples, a shroud that is cast over all peoples and the sheet spread over all nations will be destroyed. Perhaps the work of God's kingdom always originates in a feast. The cuisines of all people are offered at the banquet table. God's kingdom comes in meals and there is a feast among enemies at the end. Imagine meals as the end of racism, rather than the video of a white policeman choking a black man to death.

God will swallow up death, especially the death done to the bodies of persons of color. God will wipe away the tears from all faces—the trillions of tears of those abused by racism. The disgrace of his people he will take away from the earth. Coates calls this sheet "the bloody heirloom."[125] Death

---

123. Montarao, "Trump Downplays."
124. Isaiah 25:6–8.
125. Coates, "The First White President."

caused by inequities of food, resources, care, and money will disappear. The ultimate answer is Jesus bringing the Jubilee—a practical, material, actual reordering of economics, not Keynesian economics or Market-God economics or "trickle down" economics, but Jesus economics: One-hour workers paid the same as all-day workers, the lifting up of all Lazaruses, the restoration of property to original owners, Good Samaritan healthcare—the images pour out of the Bible.

The way forward is an offering of rhetorics that dissent from the rhetoric of whiteness, racism exceptionalism, enemies. Such rhetorical systems will be outward and forward looking, diverse in relation to all persons, thereby disarming "the rulers and authorities and triumphing over them."[126] In addition, such a rhetoric that has for its purpose to make humans noble and to reach noble aims, will be preoccupied with a future informed by the past, non-defensive and open to Others, and non-conspiratorial. At the moment we live with knowledge that systemic bigotry is still central to our politics; the country is still susceptible to such bigotry; the evangelicals who supported the overt bigot in the White House are not that different from "those same Americans who grin back at us in lynching photos."[127]

Replacing those historic snapshots with scenes from the divine "feast of enemies," I will grin back at all others content that the psalmist has offered the best snapshot of all: "You prepare a table before me in the presence of my enemies; you anoint my head with oil; my cup overflows. Surely goodness and mercy shall follow me all the days of my life, and I shall dwell in the house of the Lord my whole life long."[128] Amen.

"There are far too many symbolists and not enough materialists when it comes to dealing with diversity. The frustration of many minorities is that we become symbols whose materiality is only infrequently (and sometimes punitively) recognized." The irony for evangelicals lies in their new commitment, not to literalism, but to symbolism—the flag, the Bible, the Ten Commandments as a stone-sculptured display, prayer in schools, "under God" in the Pledge, "In God we trust" on our money—all symbols, symbols, symbols. The flag flies in the sanctuary. The Bible is used as a photo op. Evangelicals want to give the Ten Commandments a place as a piece of artwork on federal property, but have little interest in whether or not the president of their creating actually obeys any of the commandments.

---

126. Colossians 2:15.
127. Coates, "The First White President."
128. Psalm 23:5–6.

# Bibliography

Adams, Scott. *Win Bigly: Persuasion in a World Where Facts Don't Matter*. New York: Portfolio/Penguin, 2017.
Ahmed, Sara. *The Cultural Politics of Emotion*. 2d ed. New York: Routledge, 2014.
Alberta, Tim. *American Carnage: On the Front Lines of the Republican Civil War and the Rise of President Trump*. New York: Harper Collins, 2019.
Allen, Byron. "How Jeremiah Wright became America's Religious Boogeyman." *The Grio*, October 14, 2011. https://thegrio.com/2011/10/14/how-jeremiah-wright-became-americas-religious-boogeyman/.
Allen, Ira J. "Who Owns Donald Trump's Antisemitism?" In *Faking the News: What Rhetoric Can Teach Us About Donald J. Trump*, edited by Ryan Skinnell, 53–75. Exeter: Imprint Academic, 2018.
Anderson, Benedict. *Imagined Communities: Reflections on the Origin and Spread of Nationalism*. New York: Verso, 2006.
Anderson, Carol. *White Rage: The Unspoken Truth of Our Racial Divide*. New York: Bloomsbury USA, 2017.
Andrejevic, Mark. "The Jouissance of Trump." *Television and New Media* 17 (2016) 651–55.
Arendt, Hannah. *The Origins of Totalitarianism*. New York: Houghton Mifflin, 1951.
Aristotle. *The Rhetoric and Poetics of Aristotle*. New York: Random House, 1984.
Baker, Houston A., Jr. "What Should Obama Do About Jeremiah Wright?" *Salon*, April 29, 2008. https://www.salon.com/2008/04/29/obama_wright/.
Baker, Peter. "The Profanity President: Trump's Four-Letter Vocabulary." *New York Times*, May 19, 2019. https://www.nytimes.com/2019/05/19/us/politics/trump-language.html.
Bakhtin, Mikhail. *Problems of Dostoevsky's Poetics*. Minneapolis: University of Minnesota Press, 1984.
———. *Rabelais and His World*. Bloomington, IN: Indiana University Press, 1984.
Baldwin, James. "On being white . . . and other lies." *Essence* 14, no. 12 (1984) 90–92.
Balibar, Etienne. *Race, Nation, Class: Ambiguous Identities*. 2d ed. London: Verso, 2011.
Balmer, Randall. *Evangelicalism in America*. Kindle ed. Waco, TX: Baylor University Press, 2016.
———. *Mine Eyes Have Seen the Glory: A Journey into the Evangelical Subculture in America*. Oxford: Oxford University Press, 2014.
———. "The story of Christmas makes it clear: Welcome the Refugee." *Los Angeles Times*, December 18, 2015. https://www.latimes.com/opinion/op-ed/la-oe-1220-balmer-jesus-refugee-christmas-20151220-story.html.

———. *Thy Kingdom Come: How the Religious Right Distorts Faith and Threatens America*. New York: Basic, 2007.

———. "Under Trump, America's Religious Right is rewriting its codes of ethics." *The Guardian*, February 18, 2018. https://www.theguardian.com/commentisfree/2018/feb/18/donald-trump-evangelicals-code-of-ethics.

———. "Under Trump, Evangelicals Show Their True Colors." *Los Angeles Times*, August 23, 2017. https://www.latimes.com/opinion/op-ed/la-oe-balmer-evangelical-trump-racism-2017823-story.html.

———. "What the Bible Says about Immigrants." *Des Moines Register*, August 24, 2014. https://www.desmoinesregister.com/story/opinion/columnists/2014/08/24/another-view-bible-says-immigrants.

Barrett, Ted, and Ali Zaslav. "Mitch McConnell: 'I'm not an impartial juror' ahead of Senate impeachment trial." CNN, December 17, 2019. https://www.cnn.com/2019/12/17/politics/mcconnell-impartial-juror-impeachment/index.html.

Barrett-Fox, Rebecca. *God Hates: Westboro Baptist Church, American Nationalism, and the Religious Right*. Lawrence, KS: University Press of Kansas, 2016.

Barthes, Roland. *Mythologies*. 2d ed. New York: Hill and Wang, 2013.

Bauder, Kevin, and Robert Delnay. *One in Hope and Doctrine*. Arlington Heights, IL: Regular Baptist, 2014.

Beer, Tommy. "Before Trump's Photo-Op, Police Forcibly Removed Priest From Church Grounds." *Forbes*, June 2, 2020. https://www.theguardian.com/us-news/2020/june/02/outrageous-christian-leaders-reject-trump-use-of-church-as-prop-during-george-floyd-protests.

Bender, Harold. "The Anabaptist Vision." *Church History* (March 1944) 3–24.

Benen, Steve. "Trump on his popularity within the GOP: 'I beat our Honest Abe.'" http://www.msnbc.com/rachel-maddow-show/trump-his-popularity-within-the-gop-i-beat-our-honest-abe.

Benner, Katie. "Barr Says There Is No Systemic Racism in Policing. *New York Times*, June 7, 2020. https://www.nytimes.com/2020/06/07/us/politics/justice-department-barr-racism-police.html.

Bennett, John. "White House Black Leadership Event Turns Into Mini-Trump Rally." *Roll Call*, October 26, 2018, https://www.rollcall.com/news/politics/white-house-black-leadership-event-turns-mini-trump-rally.

Berlant, Lauren. "Trump, or Political Emotions." *The New Inquiry*, August 5, 2016. https://thenewinquiry.com/trump-or-political-emotions/.

Bernasconi, Robert, and Tommy Lee Lott. *The Idea of Race*. Indianapolis: Hackett, 2000.

Berry, Jeffrey M. *The Outrage Industry: Political Opinion Media and the New Incivility*. Studies in Postwar American Political Development. New York: Oxford University Press, 2014.

Betts, Frederick William. *Billy Sunday, the Man and Method*. Boston: Murray, 1916.

Beutler, Brian. "This Single Concept Explains Trump's Many Outrages." *New Republic*, November 23, 2016. https://newrepublic.com/article/138975/single-concept-explains-trumps-many-outrages.

Beverley, James A. *God's Man in the White House: Donald Trump in Modern Christian Prophecy*. Burlington, ON: Castle Quay, 2020.

Biesecker, Barbara. "The Rhetorical Production of the Melancholic Citizen-Subject in the War on Terror." *Philosophy & Rhetoric* 40 (2007) 147–69.

Blight, David W. "Frederick Douglass's Vision for a Reborn America: In the immediate aftermath of the Civil War, he dreamed of a pluralist utopia." *The Atlantic*, December, 2019. https://www.theatlantic.com/magazine/archive/2019/12/frederick-douglass-david-blight-america/600802/.

———. *Race and Reunion: The Civil War in American Memory*. Cambridge, MA: Belknap Press of Harvard University Press, 2001.

Blumenthall, Max. "Agent of Intolerance." *The Nation*, May 16, 2007. https://www.thenation.com/article/archive/agent-intolerance/.

Bonilla-Silva, Eduardo. *Racism Without Racists: Color-Blind Racism and the Persistence of Racial Inequality in America*. 5th ed. Lanham, MD: Rowman & Littlefield, 2019.

Boone, Kathleen C. *The Bible Tells Them So: The Discourse of Protestant Fundamentalism*. Albany, NY: State University of New York Press, 1989.

Booth, Wayne C. *The Rhetoric of Fiction*. 2d ed. Chicago: University of Chicago Press, 1983.

Bostdorff, Denise M. "Obama, Trump, and Reflections on the Rhetoric of Political Change." *Rhetoric & Public Affairs* 4 (2017) 695–706.

Boston, Rob. "God Wanted Trump To Be President." *Americans United for Separation of Church and State*, March 2019. https://www.au.org/church-state/march-2019-church-state-magazine/people-events/god-wanted-trump-to-be-president-press.

Bowler, Kate. *Blessed: A History of the American Prosperity Gospel*. New York: Oxford University Press, 2013.

Boyarsky, Bill. *The Rise of Ronald Reagan*. New York: Random House, 1968.

Bradner, Eric. "Trump: Sanders 'showed such weakness' with #BlackLivesMatter Protestors." *CNN*, August 12, 2015. https://www.cnn.com/2015/08/11/politics/donald-trump-2016-index.html.

Britzky, Haley "Everything Trump Says He Knows 'More About than Anybody,'" *Axios* 2019. https://www.axios.com/everything-trump-says-he-knows-more-abut-than-anybody-b278b592-cff0-47dc-a75f-5767f42bc1e.html.

Brown, Wendy. *States of Injury: Power and Freedom in Late Modernity*. Princeton, NJ: Princeton University Press, 1995.

Browne, Stephen H. "Jefferson's First Declaration of Independence: A Summary View of the Rights of British Americans Revisited." *Quarterly Journal of Speech* 89 (2003) 235–52.

Brueggemann, Walter. *Truth Speaks to Power: The Countercultural Nature of Scripture*. Louisville, KY: Westminster John Knox, 2013.

Burke, Kenneth. *A Rhetoric of Motives*. Berkeley, CA: University of California Press, 1969.

Burkholder, Thomas A. "Kansas Populism, Woman's Suffrage, and the Agrarian Myth: A Case Study in the Limits of Transcendence." *Communication Studies* 40 (1989) 292–307.

Buttrick, David. *Homiletic: Moves and Structures*. Philadelphia: Fortress, 187.

Campbell, Will D. *Soul among Lions: Musings of a Bootleg Preacher*. Louisville, KY: Westminster John Knox, 1999.

Campbell, Will D., and Richard C. Goode, eds. *Crashing the Idols: The Vocation of Will D. Campbell*. Eugene, OR: Cascade, 2010.

Campbell, Will D., and James Y. Holloway. *Up to Our Steeples in Politics*. Eugene, OR: Wipf and Stock, 2004.

Canovan, Margaret. *Populism*. New York: Harcourt Brace Jovanovich, 1981.

Carter, J. Kameron. *Race: A Theological Account*. New York: Oxford University Press, 2008.

Cavanaugh, William T. *The Myth of Religious Violence: Secular Ideology and the Roots of Modern Conflict*. Oxford: Oxford University Press, 2009.

———. *Theopolitical Imagination: Christian Practices of Space and Time*. London: Bloomsbury T. & T. Clark, 2003.

Chakravartty, Paula. "#CommunicationSoWhite." *Journal of Communication* 68 (2018) 254–66.

Chan, Melissa. "Michelle Obama: W Virginia Official Calls Here 'Ape in Heels.'" *Time*, November 15, 2016. https://time.com/4571315/west-virginia-michelle-obama-ape-heels.

Charles, J. Brian. "Transcript of Donald Trump's Economic Policy Speech to Detroit Economic Club." *The Hill*, August 8, 2016. https://thehill.com/blogs/pundits-blog/campaign/290777-transcript-of-donald-trumps-economic-policy-speech-to-detroit.

Chideya, Farai. *The Color of Our Future*. New York: William Morrow, 2000.

Childress, Kyle. "Worship and Becoming the Body of Christ." In *Gathering Together: Baptists at Work in Worship*, edited by Rodney Wallace Kennedy and Derek C. Hatch, 1–8. Eugene, OR: Wipf and Stock, 2013.

Choi, Matthew. "Trump trade adviser: Rally comment on reducing Covid testing was just a joke." *Politico*, June 6, 2020. https://www.politco.com/news/2020/06/21/navarro-trump-coronavirus-testing-331725.

Christerson, Brad, and Richard Flory. *The Rise of Network Christianity: How Independent Leaders Are Changing the Religious Landscape*. New York: Oxford University Press, 2017.

Chung, Inyoung. "Trump Attacked and Misrepresented Democrats on Pledge of Allegiance." Businessinsider.com. https://www.businessinsider.com/trump-attacked-and-misrepresented-democrats-on-pledge-of-allegiance-2020-8.

Cillizza, Chris. "Donald Trump's Interview with '60 Minutes' Was Eye-Opening. Also, Mike Pence Was There." *Washington Post*, July 18, 2016. https://www.washingtonpost.com/news/the-fix/wp/2016/07/18/donald-trump-is-way-more-humble-than-you-could-possibly-understand/.

Cisneros, J. David, and Thomas K. Nakayama. "New Media, Old Racisms: Twitter, Miss America, and Cultural Logics of Race." *Journal of International and Intercultural Communication* 8 (2015) 108–27.

Clapp, Rodney. *Johnny Cash and the Great American Contradiction: Christianity and the Battle for the Soul of a Nation*. Louisville, KY: Westminster John Knox, 2008.

Clifford, Garry. "His Critics Speak Out and Jerry Falwell's Home Base Becomes a Flock Divided." *People*, January 10, 1983. https://people.com/archive/his-critics-speak-out-and-jerry-falwells-home-base-becomes-a-flock-divided-vol-19-no-1/.

Clinton, William Jefferson. "Statement from President Clinton on the Passing of Rev. Gardner Taylor." https://www.clintonfoundation.org/press-releases/statement-president-clinton-passing-rev-gardner-taylor.

CNN. "GOP senator claims founding fathers saw slavery as 'necessary evil.'" July 28, 2020. https://www.cnn.com/videos/politics/2020/07/28/senator-tom-cotton-slavery-necessary-evil-1619-project-ctn.sot-vpx.cnn.

Coates, Ta-Nehisi. *Between the World and Me*. New York: Spiegel & Grau, 2015.

———. "The First White President." *The Atlantic,* October 2017. https://www.theatlantic.com/magazine/archive/2017/10/the-first-white-president-ta-nehisi-coates/537909/.

Coffin, William Sloane, Jr. *The Courage to Love.* San Francisco: Harper & Row, 1982.

———. *Credo.* Louisville, KY: Westminster John Knox, 2004.

Cogan, Marin "Vladimir Putin's American Fan Club." *The Atlantic,* September 24, 2013. https://www.theatlantic.com/national/archive/2013/09/vladimir-putins-american-fan-club279943/.

Coleman, Justine. "Robert Jeffress: Trump Photo at DC Church Amid Protests 'Completely' Appropriate." *The Hill,* 2020. https://thehill.com/blogs/blog-briefing-room/news/500763-robert-jeffress-trump-photo-at-church-amid-protests-completely.

———. "Wolf: Law enforcement does not have 'systemic racism problem,' some officers 'abuse their jobs.'" MSN, June 7, 2020. https://www.msn.com/en-us/news/politics/wolf-law-enforcement-does-not-have-systemic-racism-problem-some-officers-abuse-their-jobs/ar-BB159N1p.

Colón, Jesús "How to Know the Puerto Ricans." In *A Puerto Rican in New York and Other Sketches,* 197–202. New York: International, 1982.

Condit, Celeste M. *Angry Public Rhetorics.* Ann Arbor, MI: University of Michigan Press, 2018.

———. "The Critic as Empath: Moving Away from Totalizing Theory." *Western Journal of Communication* 57 (1993) 178–90.

Cone, James H. *The Cross and the Lynching Tree.* Maryknoll, NY: Orbis, 2011.

Connelly, Thomas L. *Will Campbell and the Soul of the South.* New York: Continuum, 1982.

Conner, Claire. *Wrapped in the Flag: A Personal History of America's Radical Right.* Boston: Beacon, 2013.

Conroy, Pat. *The Lords of Discipline.* New York: Old New York Book Shop, 1991.

Cooper, Ryan. "What Donald Trump Has Said about Jews." *The Week,* April 18, 2019. https://theweek.com/articles/835714/what-donald-trump-said-about-jews.

Corn, David. "Donald Trump Is Completely Obsessed With Revenge." *Mother Jones,* October 2016. https://www.motherjones.com/politics/2016/10/donald-trup-obsessed-with-revenge/.

Croucher, Shane. "Donald Trump Mocks Mitt Romney After Utah Senator Joins Black Lives Matter March." *Newsweek,* June 6, 2020. https://www.newsweek.com/trump-tweet-romney-washington-march-protest-1509369.

Daniels, J. *White Lies: Race, Class, Gender, and Sexuality in White Supremacist Discourse.* New York: Routledge, 1997.

Davis, Ellen F. "Critical Traditioning: Seeking an Inner Biblical Hermeneutic." In *The Art of Reading Scripture,* edited by Ellen F. Davis and Richard B. Hays, 163–80. Grand Rapids: Eerdmans, 2003.

Davis, Ellen F., and Richard B. Hays, eds. *The Art of Reading Scripture.* Grand Rapids: Eerdmans, 2003.

Delgado, Fernando. "The Dilemma of the Minority Scholar: Finding a Legitimized Voice in an Intellectual Space." In *Racial and Ethnic Diversity in the 21st Century: A Communication Perspective,* edited by Sherry Morreale and Angela Arseneau Jones, 47–53. Washington, DC: Speech Communication Association, 1997.

Diamond, Jeremy, Betsy Klein, and Jake Tapper. "Trump Brags about Crowd Size during Hospital Visit in El Paso." CNN, August 8, 2019. https://www.cnn.com/2019/08/08/politics/trump-brags-crowd-size-hospital-visit-el-paso/index.html.

DiAngelo, Robin. *White Fragility: Why It's So Hard for White People to Talk about Racism.* Boston: Beacon, 2018.

Dochuk, Darren. *From Bible Belt to Sunbelt: Plain-Folk Religion, Grassroots Politics, and the Rise of Evangelical Conservatism.* New York: W. W. Norton, 2011.

Domke, David, and Kevin Coe. *The God Strategy: How Religion Became a Political Weapon in America.* New York: Oxford University Press, 2008.

Dorsett, Lyle. *Billy Sunday and the Redemption of Urban America.* Macon, GA: Mercer University Press, 2004.

Dostoevsky, Fyodor. *The Grand Inquisitor.* Eastford, CT: Martino Fine Books, 2016.

Dow, Bonnie J. "Taking Trump Seriously: Persona and Presidential Politics in 2016." *Women's Studies in Communication* 40 (2017) 136–39.

Dowd, Maureen. "Joe's Fearsome Weapon Against Trump: Simple Decency." *New York Times,* August 21, 2020. https://www.nytimes.com/2020/08/21/opinion/sunday/joe-biden-convention-donald-trump.html

Dyer Richard. "White." *Screen* 29 (1988) 44–65.

Dylan, Bob. "Slow Train Coming." https://www.azlyrics.com/lyrics/bobdylan/slowtrain.html.

Edgerton, Clyde. *Killer Diller.* Chapel Hill, NC: Algonquin, 2012.

———. *Raney.* New York: Ballantine, 1985.

Einbinder, Nicole. "White evangelicals are calling out Trump for his use of profanity." *The Insider,* August 12, 2019. https://www.insider.com/white-evangelicals-upset-president-trump-profanity-2019-8.

Eksil, Betu, and Elizabeth A. Wood. "Right-wing Populism as Gendered Performance: Janus-faced Masculinity in the Leadership of Vladimir Putin and Recep T. Erdogan." *Theory & Society* 48 (2019) 733–51.

Eldredge, John. *Wild at Heart: Discovering the Secret of a Man's Soul.* Nashville: Thomas Nelson, 2011.

Engels, Jeremy. *The Politics of Resentment: A Genealogy.* University Park, PA: The Pennsylvania State University Press, 2015.

Enns, Peter. *The Bible Tells Me So: Why Defending Scripture Has Made Us Unable to Read It.* New York: Harper Collins, 2014.

Erlich, Howard S. "Populist Rhetoric Reassessed: A Paradox." *Quarterly Journal of Speech* 63 (1977) 140–51.

Falcone, Michael. "Donald Trump's Holy War? Spokesman Defends 'Get Even' Comment at Christian University." ABC News, September 26, 2012. https://abcnews.go.com/blogs/politics/2012/09/donald-trumps-holy-war-spokesman-defends-get-even-comment-at-christian-university.

Farell, Mitch. "L. A. Officials Blast 'Callous' Bystanders Who Filmed Attack on Trans YouTube Star and Her Friends." *Washington Post,* August 21, 2020. https://www.washingtonpost.com/nation/2020/08/21/eden-doll-hate-crime/la/.

Fea, John. *Believe Me: The Evangelical Road to Donald Trump.* Grand Rapids: Eerdmans, 2018.

Feagin, J. R. *The White Racial Frame: Centuries of Racial Framing and Counter-Framing.* New York: Routledge, 2007.

Fineman, Howard. "Jerry Falwell's Political Impact." *Newsweek,* May 14, 2007. https://www.newsweek.com/fineman-jerry-falwells-political-impact-101657.
Firstenberger, William A. *In Rare Form: A Pictorial History of Baseball Evangelist Billy Sunday.* Iowa City, IA: University of Iowa Press, 2005.
Fish, Stanley. *Is There a Text in This Class?* Cambridge, MA: Harvard University Press, 1982.
Fishman, Steven M., and Lucille McCarthy. "Talk about Race: When Student Stories and Multicultural Curricula Are Not Enough." *Race, Ethnicity & Education* 8.4 (2005) 347–64.
Fitzgerald, Frances. *The Evangelicals: The Struggle to Shape America.* New York: Simon & Schuster, 2017.
Foucault, Michel. *"Society Must Be Defended": Lectures at the College de France, 1975–1976.* New York: Picador, 1997.
Fowl, Stephen E. *Engaging Scripture: A Model for Theological Interpretation.* Eugene, OR: Wipf and Stock, 2008.
Frank, David A. "The Prophetic Voice and the Face of the Other in Barack Obama's 'A More Perfect Union' Address." *Rhetoric and Public Affairs* 12 (2009) 167–94.
Frank, Doug. *A Gentler God.* Menangle, Australia: Albatross, 2010.
Frank, Douglas W. *Less Than Conquerors.* Grand Rapids: Eerdmans, 1986.
Friedman, Richard. *The Disappearance of God.* New York: Little, Brown, 1995.
Frueh, Jamie. *Political Identity and Social Change: The Remaking of the South African Social Order.* Albany, NY: State University of New York Press, 2002.
Gallagher, John. "Evangelicals finally find a reason to criticize Trump: He curses." August 18, 2019. https://www.lgbtqnation.com/2019/08/evangelicals-finally-find-reason-criticize-trump-curses/.
Gass, Nick. "With Carson on the Defense, Trump Pounces." *Politico,* November 13, 2015. https://www.politico.com/story/2015/11/ben-carson-donald-trump-feud-215829.
Gerns, Roger. "Hauerwas on President Trump's Religion and Idolatry." Episcopal Café. 2020. https://www.episcopalcafe.com/hauerwas-on-president-trumps-religion-and-American-idolatry.
Gettys, Travis. "Megachurch pastor Robert Jeffress would vote for Trump over Jesus: The Bible calls for a 'strongman.'" Raw Story, July 13, 2016. http://www.rawstory.com/2016/07/megachurch-pastor-robert-jeffress-would-vote-for-trump-over-jesus-the-bible-calls-for-a-strongman/.
Gilbert, Kenyatta R. *A Pursued Justice: Black Preaching from the Great Migration to Civil Rights.* Waco, TX: Baylor University Press, 2016.
Gittleson, Ben. "Trump says 'I don't kid' after aides argue he was joking about slowing coronavirus testing." ABC News. https://abcnews.go.com/Politics/trump-kid-aides-argue-joking-slowing-coronavirus-testing/stor?id=71404943.
Glaude, Eddie S., Jr. *Democracy in Black: How Race Still Enslaves the American Soul.* New York: Crown, 2016.
Golden, James L., Goodwin F. Berquist, and William E. Coleman. *The Rhetoric of Western Thought.* 3rd ed. Dubuque, IA: Kendall/Hunt, 1983.
Goldstein, Joelle. "Billy Graham's Preacher Son Franklin's Tour Dates Canceled Over Homophobic, Islamophobic Comments." *People,* February 6, 2020. https://people.com/human-interest/franklin-graham-tour-dates-canceled-homophobic-islamophobic-comments/.

Goodman, William R., Jr., and James J. H. Price. *Jerry Falwell: An Unauthorized Profile*. Lynchburg, VA: Paris & Associates, 1981.

Gottlieb, Jed. "All the Swear Words Fit to Print: How Newspapers Are Handling Donald Trump's Foul Mouth." *QZ*, January 11, 2018. https://qz.com/quartzy/1177146/all-the-swear-words-fit-to-print-how-newspapers-are-handling-donald-trumps-foul-mouth/.

Graham, Franklin. "Franklin Graham's Sermon President George W. Bush Inaugural Prayer Service. January 21, 2001." https://www.angelfire/com/in/HisName/inauguralsermon.html.

Greene, Allison Collis. *No Depression in Heaven: The Great Depression, the New Deal, and the Transformation of Religion in the Delta*. New York: Oxford University Press, 2016.

Gregg, Melissa, and Gregory J. Seigworth, eds. *The Affect Theory Reader*. Durham, NC: Duke University Press, 2020.

Grossberg, Lawrence. *Under the Cover of Chaos: Trump and the Battle for the American Right*. London: Pluto, 2017

*The Guardian*. "'It was all bullshit': Donald Trump delivers mocking, vitriolic speech after acquittal." February 6, 2020. https://www.theguardian.com/us-news/2020/feb/06/trump-speech-acquittal-impeachment-mocking-vitriolic.

Guillermo, Rebollo-Gil, and Amanda Moras. "Defining an 'anti' stance: key pedagogical questions about engaging anti-racism in college classrooms." *Race Ethnicity and Education* 9 (2006) 381–94,

Gunderson, Robert. "The Calamity Howlers." *Quarterly Journal of Speech* 26 (1940) 401–11.

Gunn, Joshua. "On Political Perversion." *Rhetoric Society Quarterly* 48 (2018) 161–86.

Hacker, Andrew. *Two Nations: Black and White: Separate, Hostile, Unequal*. New York: Scribners, 2003.

Hamilton, Rebecca. "Archbishop Gregory Says Trump Photo Op Misuses and Manipulates Church Facility." *Patheos*, June 2020. https://www.patheos.com/blogs/publiccatholic/2020/06/bishop-gregory-says-trump-photo-op-misuses-and-manipulates-church-facility/.

Hancock, Jeff. "Donald Trump's Ghostwriter Tells All." CNN, October 10, 2017. http://money.cnn.com'2016/10/17/technology/donald-trump-deception/.

———. "Trump's Bullsh*t: Why His Supporters Don't Care That He's Lying." CNN, October 17, 2016. http://money.cnn.com'2016/10/17/technology/donald-trump-deception/.

Hankins, Barry. *God's Rascal: J. Frank Norris and the Beginnings of Southern Fundamentalism*. Lexington, KY: University Press of Kentucky, 2010.

———. *Jesus and Gin: Evangelicalism, the Roaring Twenties and Today's Culture Wars*. New York: St. Martin's, 2010.

Harding, Susan Friend. *The Book of Jerry Falwell: Fundamentalist Language and Politics*. Princeton, NJ: Princeton University Press, 2000.

Harris, Harriet A. *Fundamentalism and Evangelicals*. New York: Oxford University Press on Demand, 1998.

Harris, John F. "Is Donald Trump a Manly Man?" *Politico*, January 2020. https://www.politico.com/news/magazine/2020/01/30/trump-what-kind-of-man-gets-impeached-109417.

Harris, Max. *Sacred Folly: A New History of the Feast of the Fools*. Ithaca, NY: Cornell University Press, 2011.
Hart, David Bentley. *The Doors of the Sea: Where Was God in the Tsunami?* Grand Rapids: Eerdmans, 2005.
Hart, Roderick P. *Modern Rhetorical Criticism*. Glenview, IL: Scott, Foresman, 1990.
———. *Trump and Us: What He Says and Why People Listen*. Cambridge: Cambridge University Press, 2020.
Hatch, Nathan O. *The Democratization of American Christianity*. New Haven, CT: Yale University Press, 1989.
Hays, Rebecca W. Poe, and Nicholas R. Werse. "Evangelicals and the Film *Fight Club*: A Cultural Comparison of Masculine Ideology Image." *Counter Currents*, May 2016. https://www.counter-currents.com/2016/05/fight-club-as-holy-writ/.
Hauerwas, Stanley. *In Good Company: The Church as Polis*. Notre Dame, IN: University of Notre Dame Press, 1995.
———. *The State of the University: Academic Knowledges and the Knowledge of God*. Malden, MA: Blackwell, 2007.
———. *Unleashing the Scripture: Freeing the Bible from Captivity to America*. Nashville: Abingdon, 1993.
———. *War and the American Difference: Theological Reflections on Violence and National Identity*. Grand Rapids: Baker Academic, 2011.
———. *Working with Words: On Learning to Speak Christian*. Eugene, OR: Cascade, 2011.
Healy, Patrick, and Maggie Haberman. "95,000 Words, Many of Them Ominous, From Donald Trump's Tongue." *New York Times*, December 5, 2015. https://www.nytimes.com/2015/12/06/us/politics/95,000-words-many-of-them-ominous-from-donald-trumps-tongue.html.
Hearn, Alison. "Trump's 'Reality' Hustle." *Television and New Media* 17 (2016) 656–59.
Hedges, Chris. "Cornel West and the Fight to Save the Black Prophetic Tradition. *Truthdig*, September 9, 2013. https://www.truthdig.com/articles/cornel-west-and-the-fight-to-save-the-black-prophetic-tradition/.
Hennigan, Elise. "All of Donald Trump's Nicknames for People, Ranked By How Inappropriate They Are." *Ranker*, April 20, 2021. https://www.ranker.com/list/donald-trump-nicknames-list/elise.
Heschel, Abraham Joshua. *The Prophets*. Vol. 2. New York: Harper & Row, 1962.
Hill, Jane H. *The Everyday Language of White Racism*. Malden, MA: Wiley-Blackwell, 2008.
Hochschild, Arlie Russell. *Strangers in Their Own Land: Anger and Mourning on the American Right*. New York: New, 2018.
Hofstadter, Richard. *Anti-Intellectualism in American Life*. New York: Random House, 1962.
———. *The Paranoid Style in American Politics*. New York: Random House, 1965.
Holcomb, Walt. *Popular Lectures of Sam P. Jones*. New York: Fleming H. Revell, 1909.
Holling, Michelle A., Dreama G. Moon, and Alexandra Jackson Nevis. "Racist Violations and Racializing Apologia in a Post-Racism Era." *Journal of International and Intercultural Communication* 7 (2014) 260–86.
Houck, Davis W. "Putting His Ass in Aspirational: Golf, Donald Trump, and the Digital Ghosts of Scotland." In *Faking the News: What Rhetoric Can Teach Us about Donald Trump*, edited by Ryan Skinnell, 142–59. Exeter: Imprint Academic, 2018.

Howe, Ben. *The Immoral Majority: Why Evangelicals Chose Political Power Over Christian Values.* New York: Broadside, 2019.

Hurston, Zora Neal. *Jonah's Gourd Vine.* New York: Amistad, 2009.

Hyber, Josh. "Barack Obama Approves David Ortiz Dropping the 'F' Bomb, Calls It 'Proud' Moment." *The Sporting News*, March 22, 2016. https://www.sportingnews.com/us/mlb/newsbarack-obama-david-ortiz-f-bomb-boston-marathon-red-sox-mlb-cuba-rays/qb9mcyhpl1oqhtgqi2wgrw8g.

Ionescu, Ghita, and Ernest Gellner, eds. *Populism: Its Meaning and National Characteristics.* New York: Macmillan, 1969.

Ivie, Robert L. "Rhetorical Aftershocks of Trump's Ascendency." *Res Rhetorica* 2 (2017) 61–80.

———. "Trump's Unwitting Prophecy." *Rhetoric and Public Affairs* 20.4 (2017) 707–18.

Ivie, Robert L., and Oscar Giner. "Hunting the Devil: Democracy's Rhetorical Impulse to War." *Presidential Studies Quarterly* 37.4 (2007) 580–98.

Jacobsen, Douglas, and William Vance Trollinger, Jr. *Re-Forming the Center: American Protestantism, 1900 to the Present.* Grand Rapids: Eerdmans, 1998.

Jackson, Alan. "Little Man." https://www.metrolyrics.com/little-man-lyrics-alan-jackson.html.

Jaffe, Greg, and Jenna Johnson. "Trump Delights in Watching the U. S. Military Display Its Strength." *Washington Post*, April 14, 2017. https://www.washingtonpost.com/politics/trump-delights-in-watching-the-us-military-display-its-strength/2017/04/14/.

Jamieson, Kathleen Hall. *Dirty Politics: Deception, Distraction , and Democracy.* New York: Oxford University Press, 1992.

Jamieson, Kathleen Hall, and Doron Taussig. "Disruption, Demonization, Deliverance, and Norm Destruction: The Rhetorical Signature of Donald J. Trump." *Political Science Quarterly* 132.4 (2017)619–51.

Jefferson, Thomas. *Notes on the State of Virginia.* New York: Penguin, 1999.

Jeffress, Robert. "America Is a Christian Nation." Sermon preached on June 17, 2017 at First Baptist Church, Dallas. https://www.oneplace.com.ministries/pathway-to-victory/listen/america/-is-a-Christian-nation-part-1-536068.html.

———. *Countdown to the Apocalypse: Why ISIS and Ebola Are Only the Beginning.* New York: FaithWords, 2015.

———. "Evangelical Pastor: Democrats Have Created An 'Imaginary God,'" HuffPost. 2020. https://www.huffpost.com/entry/robert-jeffress-imaginary-god-democrats-_n_5d1bc171e4b082e553716943.

———. "Fox News' Pastor Robert Jeffress says liberal churches 'deserve to die.'" MediaMatters, February 21, 2020. https://www.mediamatters.org/robert-jeffress/fox-news-pastor-robert-jeffress-says-liberal-churches-deserve-die.

———. Interview by David Asman. *The Lou Dobbs Show*, Fox News, May 3, 2021. https://harbingersdaily.com/dr-robert-jeffress-the-radical-democrat-party-has-become-the-the-godless-party/.

———. "Read the Sermon Donald Trump Heard Before Becoming President." *Time*, January 20, 2017. https://www.time.com/4641208/donald-trump-robert-jeffress-st-john-episcopal-inauguration/.

———. "Robert Jeffress On Mitt Romney Mormon Comments: 'I Am Not A Jeremiah Wright.'" *HuffPost*, December 8, 2011. https://www.huffpost.com/entry/robert-jeffress-mitt-romney_n_1001963.

———.*Twilight's Last Gleaming: How America's Last Days Can Be Your Best Days*. Brentwood, TN: Worthy, 2011.
Jenkins, Krista. "Trump Taints America's Views on Political Correctness." Fairleigh Dickinson University Poll, October 30, 2015. https://view2.fdu.edu/publicmind/2015/1511030.
Jennings, Willie James. *The Christian Imagination: Theology and The Origins of Race*. New Haven, CT: Yale University Press, 2010.
Jewett, Robert, and John Shelton Lawrence. *The Myth of the American Superhero*. Grand Rapids: Eerdmans. 2002.
Johnson, Paul Elliott. "The art of masculine victimhood: Donald Trump's demagoguery." *Women's Studies in Communication* 40.3 (2017) 229–50.
Joiner, Thekla Ellen. *Sin in the City: Chicago and Revivalism*. Columbia, MO: University of Missouri Press, 2007.
Jones, Robert P. *The End of White Christian America*. New York: Simon & Schuster, 2017.
———. *White Too Long: The Legacy of White Supremacy in American Christianity*. New York: Simon and Schuster, 2020.
Jordan, John W. "Profanity from the Heart as Exceptional Civic Rhetoric." *Quarterly Journal of Speech* 106 (2020) 111–32.
Joseph, Andrew. "Mike Ditka Draws Backlash for Criticism of Kneeling Athletes." *The Times*, July 27, 2020. https://www.timesonline.com/story/sports/nfl/2020/07/27/mike-ditka-to-kneeling-athletes-get-hell-out-of-country/112700490/.
Kay, Terry. *The Year the Lights Came On*. San Francisco: Untreed Reads, 2012.
Kazin, Michael. *The Populist Persuasion: An American History*. Ithaca, NY: Cornell University Press, 2017.
Kelly, Caroline, and Allie Malloy. "Trump implies that the late Rep. John Dingell is 'looking up' from hell." CNN, December 18, 2019. https://www.cnn.com/2019/12/18/politics/trump-rally-john-dingell-hell/index.html.
Kelly, Casey Ryan. "Donald J. Trump and the Rhetoric of *Ressentiment*." *Quarterly Journal of Speech* 106 (2020) 2–24.
Kendi, Ibram X. *How to Be an Antiracist*. New York: One World, 2019.
Kennedy, Randall. *Nigger: The Strange Career of a Troublesome Word*. New York: Pantheon, 2002.
Kennedy, Rodney Wallace. *The Creative Power of Metaphor: A Rhetorical Homiletics*. Lanham, MD: University Press of America, 1993.
———. "Finally, An Evangelical Defense of Donald Trump Worth Responding To (It's Still Terrible, but There It Is)." *Righting America*, December 31, 2019. https://rightingamerica.net/finally-an-evangelical-defense-of-donald-trump-worth-responding-to-its-still-terrible-but-there-it-is/.
———. "Jerry Falwell, Jr. Unzipped His Pants for the Camera . . . But It's Not About the Sex." *Righting America*, August 14, 2020. https://rightingamerica.net/jerry-falwell-jr-unzipped-his-pants-for-the-camera-but-its-not-about-sex/.
———. *Sermons from Mind and Heart: Struggling to Preach Theologically*. Eugene, OR: Wipf and Stock, 2011.
Kennedy, Rodney Wallace, and Derek Hatch. *Gathering Together: Baptists at Work in Worship*. Eugene, OR: Pickwick, 2013.
Ketchin, Susan, ed. *The Christ-Haunted Landscape: Faith and Doubt in Southern Fiction*. Oxford, MS: University Press of Mississippi, 1994.

Kierkegaard, Søren. *The Present Age: On the Death of Rebellion*. New York: Harper Perennial Modern Thought, 2010.
Killinger, John. *The Other Preacher in Lynchburg: My Life Across Town from Jerry Falwell*. New York: St Martin's, 2009.
Kimmel, Michael. *Angry White Men: American Masculinity at the End of an Era*. New York: Bold Type, 2013.
King, Andrew M. *Power and Communication*. Prospect Heights, IL: Waveland, 1987.
King, Claire Sisco. "It Cuts Both Ways: *Fight Club*, Masculinity, and Abject Hegemony." *Communication & Critical/Cultural Studies* 6 (2009) 366–85.
King, Martin Luther, Jr. "Beyond Vietnam: A Time to Break Silence." Sermon preached at Riverside Church, New York City, April 4, 1967. https://www.crmvet.org/info/mlk_viet.pdf.
Kooistra, Paul. "Criminals as Heroes: Linking Symbol to Structure." *Symbolic Interaction* 13:2, 1990. https://doi.org/10.1525/si.1990.13.2.217.
Krauthammer, Charles. "The Speech: A Brilliant Fraud." *Washington Post*, March 21, 2008.
Kruse, Kevin. *One Nation Under God: How Corporate America Invented Christian America*. Philadelphia: Basic, 2015.
Kumar, Anita, and Quint Forgey. "Unpaid bills pile up in Trump rallies' wake." *Politico*, October 8, 2019. https://www.politico.com/news/2019/10/08/trump-rallies-unpaid-bills-039631.
Kuruvilla, Carol. "Evangelical Pastor: Democrats Have Created An 'Imaginary God.'" *HuffPost*, July 2, 2019. https://www.huffpost.com/entry/robert-jeffress-imaginary-god-democrats-_n_5d1bc171e4b082e553716943.
*LA Times* Archives. "Bakker Shows No Remorse, Falwell Says: Evangelist Should 'Return Millions' to PTL, Successor Says." May 27, 1987. https://www.latimes.com/archives/la-xpm-1987-05-27-mn-1816-story.html.
Lakoff, George. *The Political Mind: A Cognitive Scientist's Guide to Your Brain and Its Politics*. New York: Viking, 2008.
Lang, Jeffery, and Patrick Trimble. "Whatever Happened to the Man of Tomorrow? An Examination of the American Monomyth and the Comic Book Superhero." *Journal of Popular Culture* 22, no. 3 (1988) 157.
Lash, Nicholas. *Theology on the Road to Emmaus*. Eugene, OR: Wipf and Stock, 2005.
Lawson, Steven F. "Introduction." In *One America in the 21st Century: The Report of President Bill Clinton's Initiative on Race*, edited by Steven F. Lawson, xv–xxxviii. New Haven, CT: Yale University Press, 2009.
Lawson, Steven F., ed. *One America in the 21st Century: The Report of President Bill Clinton's Initiative on Race*. New Haven, CT: Yale University Press, 2009.
LeBlanc, Paul. "Bishop at DC church outraged by Trump visit: 'I just can't believe what my eyes have seen.'" CNN, June 1, 2020. https://edition.cnn.com/2020/06/01/politics/cnntv-bishop-trump-photo-op/index.html.
Lee, Alicia. "Kareem Abdul-Jabbar defends protests and says racism is deadlier than Covid-19 in powerful op-ed." CNN, May 31, 2020.
Lee, Michael J. "The Populist Chameleon: The People's Party, Huey Long, and George Wallace, and the Populist Argumentative Frame." *Quarterly Journal of Speech* 92 (2004) 355–78.

Lee, Ronald. "The New Populist Campaign for Economic Democracy: A Rhetorical Exploration." *Quarterly Journal of Speech* 72.3 (1986) 274–89. DOI: 10.1080/0033563609383774.
Lee, Shayne, and Phillip Luke Sintiere. *Holy Mavericks: Evangelical Innovators and the Spiritual Marketplace*. New York: New York University Press, 2009.
Leonardo, Zeus. *Race, Whiteness, and Education*. New York: Routledge, 2009.
Levina, Marina. "Whiteness and the Joys of Cruelty." *Communication and Critical/Cultural Studies* 15 (2018) 73–78.
Lippman, Daniel. "Trump Cuts Loose with Unpredictable Characters at Mar-a-Lago." *Politico*, January 1, 2020. https://www.msn.com/en-us/news/politics/these-are-his-people-trump-cuts-loose-at-mar-a-lago/ar-BBYw2MT?ocid=spartandhp.
Lyons, Julie. "First Baptist's Robert Jeffress Says Trump is the Most Electable Republican, Not Racist." *Dallas Observer*, April 5, 2016. https://www.dallasobserver.com/news/robert-jeffress-wants-a-mean-son-of-a-gun-for-president-says-trump-isnt-a-racist-8184721.
Macon, Alex. "Why the controversial First Baptist Dallas leader is so concerned with rendering unto Caesar." *Frontburner*, August 9, 2017. https:www.dmagazine.com/frontburner/2017/08/robert-jeffress-court-evangelical/.
Maltby, Paul. *Christian Fundamentalism and the Culture of Disenchantment*. Charlottesville, VA: University of Virginia Press, 2013.
Mannoni, Octave. "I Know Well, but All the Same . . ." In *Perversion and the Social Relation*, edited by Molly Anne Rothenberg, Dennis Foster, and Slavoj Žižek, 68–92. Durham, NC: Duke University Press, 2003. https://doi.org/10.1215/9780822384724-004.
Mansfield, Stephen. *Choosing Donald Trump: God, Anger, Hope, and Why Christian Conservatives Supported Him*. Grand Rapids: Baker, 2017.
Marney, Carlyle. *Priests to Each Other*. Macon, GA: Smyth and Helwys, 2001.
———. Unpublished presentation. No date.
Marsden, George M. *Fundamentalism and American Culture: The Shaping of Twentieth-Century Evangelicalism*. Oxford: Oxford University Press, 2006.
Martin, Robert F. *Hero of the Heartland: Billy Sunday and the Transformation of American Society*. Bloomington, IN: Indiana University Press, 2002.
Maule, Will. "Stanley Hauerwas Slams Trump: 'The State Is Not Called To Be A Savior.'" *Hello Christian*, July 23, 2017. https://www.episcopalcafe.com/hauerwas-on-president-trumps-religion-and-idolatry.
May, William. *A Catalogue of Sins: A Contemporary Examination of Christian Conscience*. New York: Holt, Rinehart, and Winston, 1967.
Mayer, Jane. "Donald Trump's Ghostwriter Tells All." *New Yorker*, July 25, 2016. https://www.newyorker.com/magazine/2016/07/25/donald-trumps-ghostwriter-tells-all.
McAdams, Dan P. *The Strange Case of Donald J. Trump: A Psychological Reckoning*. New York: Oxford University Press, 2020.
McClendon, James Wm., Jr. *Ethics: Systematic Theology: Volume I*. Nashville: Abingdon, 2002.
McElvaine, Robert S. *The Great Depression: America 1929–41*. New York: Three Rivers, 1984.
McGee, Paula L. *Brand® New Theology: The Wal-Martization of T. D. Jakes and the New Black Church*. Maryknoll, NY: Orbis, 2017.

McLoughlin, William G., Jr. *Billy Sunday Was His Real Name*. Chicago: University of Chicago Press, 1955.

Mencken, H. L. *Chrestomathy*. New York: Vintage, 1982.

———. *Newspaper Days (H. L. Mencken's Autobiography)*. New York: Alfred A. Knopf, 1940.

Mercieca, Jennifer. "Afterword: Trump as Anarchist and Sun King." In *Faking the News: What Rhetoric Can Teach Us About Donald J. Trump*, edited by Ryan Skinnell, 182–187. Exeter: Imprint Academic, 2018.

———. "Dangerous Demagogues and Weaponized Communication." *Rhetoric Society Quarterly* 49.3 (2019) 264–279.

———. *Demagogue for President: The Rhetorical Genius of Donald Trump*. College Station, TX: Texas A & M University Press, 2020.

———. "A field guide to Trump's dangerous rhetoric." *Salon*, June 24, 2020. https://www.salon.com/2020/06/24/a-field-guide-to-trumps-dangerous-rhetoric_partner/.

Metha, Hemant. "Robert Jeffress, Using Bad Math, Claims Democrats Are a Godless Party." *Patheos*, August 8, 2020. https://harbingersdaily.com/dr-robert-jeffress-the-radical-democrat-party-has-become-the-godless-party.

Miciak, Jason. "Trump's Favorite Pastor Warns that Democrats Will 'Bring Out the Guillotines' If Trump Loses Reelection." *Political Flare*, June 14, 2020. https://www.politicalflare.com/2020/06/trumps-favorite-pastor-warns-that-democrats-will-bring-out-the-guillotines-if-trump-loses-reelection/.

Mikkelson, David. "Did Richard Branson Say Trump Spent a 2-Lunch Speaking of Revenge?" *Snopes*, February 11, 2020. https://www.snopes.com/fact-check/richard-branson-trump-revenge/.

Miller, Kenneth R. *Only a Theory: Evolution and the Battle for America's Soul*. New York: Viking, 2008.

Mitchell, Henry. *Black Preaching*. San Francisco: Harper & Row, 1970.

Mohr, Melissa. *Holy Sh\*t: A Brief History of Swearing*. Oxford: Oxford University Press, 2019.

Montarao, Domenico. "Trump Downplays Police Violence, Deaths of Black Americans." NPR, June 14, 2020. https://www.npr.org/sections/live-updates-protests-for-racial-justice/2020/07/14/891144579/trump-says-more-white-people-killed-by-police-violence-than-blacks.

Moon, D. G., and A. Hurst. "'Reasonable racism': The 'new' white supremacy and Hurricane Katrina." In *Through the Eyes of Katrina: Social Justice in the United States*, edited by K. A. Bates and R. Swan, 125–45. Durham, NC: Carolina Academic, 2007.

Mooney, Michael. "Trump's Apostle." *Texas Monthly*, August 2019. https://www.texasmonthly.com/articles/donald-trump-defender-dallas-pastor-robert-jeffress/.

Morrissey, Megan E., and Christy-Dale L. Sims. "Playing the Race Card: Antiracial Bordering and Rhetorical Practices of New Racism." *Review of Communication* 15 (2015) 81–101.

Moss, Otis, Jr. "A Prophetic Witness in an Anti-Prophetic Age." In *Preaching with Sacred Fire: An Anthology of African American Sermons, 1750 to the Present.*, edited by Martha Simmons and Frank A. Thomas, 777–781. New York: W. W. Norton, 2010.

Moyers, Bill. Interview with Jeremiah Wright, April 25, 2008. https://www.pbs.org/moyers/journal/04252008/transcript1.html.

Mudde, Cas. "The Populist Zeitgeist." *Government and Opposition* 39 (2004) 541–63.

Murray, Charles. "Have I Missed the Competition?" *National Review Online*, March 18, 2008. https://www.nationalreview.com/corner/have-i-missed-competition-charles-murray/.

NAACP. "Rap pioneers join NAACP in funeral for the n-word, sign on to 'stop' campaign." July 9, 2007. http://www.naacp.org/latest/the-n-word-is-laid-to-rest-by-the-naacp/.

Nakayama, Thomas K., and Robert L. Krizek. "Whiteness: A Strategic Rhetoric," *Quarterly Journal of Speech* 81 (1995) 291–309.

Nelson, Steven. "Trump Calls Nancy Pelosi a 'Sick Woman' with 'Mental Problems.'" *New York Post*, May 19, 2020. https://nypost.com/2020/05/19/trump-calls-nancy-pelosi-a-sick-woman-with-mental-problems/.

Nichols, Mike. "J. Frank Norris: One Foot in the Pulpit, One Foot in the Witness Stand." https://hometownbyhandlebar.com/.

Nietzsche, Friedrich. *On the Genealogy of Morals*. Mineola, NY: Dover, 2003.

———. *The Portable Nietzsche*. New York: Penguin, 1977.

Noll, Mark A. *America's God*. Oxford: Oxford University Press, 2005.

———. *God and Race in American Politics: A Short History*. Princeton, NJ: Princeton University Press, 2008.

Nunley, Vorris. "From the Harbor to Da Academic Hood: Hush Harbors and an African American Rhetorical Tradition." In *African American Rhetoric(s):Interdisciplinary Perspective*, edited by Elaine B. Richardson and Ronald L. Jackson, 221–42. Carbondale, IL: SIU Press, 2004.

Nussbaum, Emily. *I Like to Watch: Arguing My Way Through the TV Revolution*. New York: Random House, 2019.

Obama, Barack. "A More Perfect Union." *Politico*, March 2008. politico.com/story/2008/03/transcript-of-https://www.obama-speech-009100.

O'Connor, Flannery. *The Habit of Being: Letters of Flannery O'Connor*. New York: Farrar, Straus and Giroux, 1988.

———. *Mystery and Manners: Occasional Prose*. New York: Farrar, Straus and Giroux, 1969.

———. *The Violent Bear It Away: A Novel*. New York: HarperPerennial Classics, 2015.

———. *Wise Blood: A Novel*. New York: HarperPerennial Classics, 2015.

Octave, Mannoni. "I Know Well, but All the Same . . ." In *Perversion and the Social Relation*, edited by Molly Anne Rothenberg, Dennis A. Foster, and Slavoj Zizek, 68–92. Durham, NC: Duke University Press, 2003.

Olson, Roger. "Stanley Hauerwas, America and war (and a question about flags in churches)." *Patheos*, February 2012. https://www.patheos.com/blogs/rogereolson/2012/02/stanley-hauerwas-america-and-war-and-a-question-about-flags-in-churches/.

Ott, Brian L. "The Age of Twitter: Donald J. Trump and the Politics of Debasement." *Critical Studies in Media Communication* 34:1 (2017). https://doi.org/10.1080/15295036.2016.1266686.

Ott, Brian L., and Greg Dickinson. *The Twitter Presidency: Donald J. Trump and the Politics of White Rage*. New York: Rutledge, 2019.

Ono, K. A., and V. N. Pham. *Asian Americans in the Media*. Malden, MA: Polity, 2009.

Paletta, Damian, and Steven Mufson. "Trump federal budget 2018: Massive cuts to the arts, science, and the poor." *Washington Post*, March 3, 2015. https://www.washingtonpost.com/business/economy/trump-federal-budget-2018-massive-cuts-to-the-arts-science-and-the-poor/2017/03/15/0a0a0094-09a1-11e7-a15f-a58d4a988474_story.html.

Parry-Giles, Trevor, and Michael J. Steudeman. "Crafting Character, Moving History: John McCain's Political Identity in the 2008 Presidential Campaign." *Quarterly Journal of Speech* 103 (2017) 66–89.

Patton, Tracey Owens. "Reflections of a Black Woman Professor: Racism and Sexism in Academia." *Howard Journal of Communications* 15 (2004) 185–200.

Pavlova, M. "A real man, a leader, a person of word and deed." *Moskovskaia Pravda* 40, February 25, 2012. https://dlib-eastview-com-ezpprod1.hul.harvard.edu/browse/doc/26659347.

Payne, Charles M. *I've Got the Light of Freedom: The Organizing Tradition and the Mississippi Freedom Struggle*. With a new Preface. Berkeley, CA: University of California Press, 2007.

Payne, Peggy. *Revelation*. New York: Simon & Schuster, 1988.

Percy, Walker. *Lancelot: A Novel*. New York: Open Road, 2011.

Perelman, Chaim, and L. Olbrechts-Tyteca. *The New Rhetoric: A Treatise on Argumentation*. Notre Dame, IN: University of Notre Dame Press, 1969.

Perry, Imani. *More Beautiful and More Terrible: The Embrace and Transcendence of Racial Inequality in the United States*. New York: New York University Press, 2011.

Pierre, Robert E. "Martin Luther King Jr. made our nation uncomfortable". *Washington Post*, October 16, 2011. https://www.washingtonpost.com/blogs/therootdc/post/martin-luther-king-jr-made-our-nation-uncomfortable/2011/10/16/gIQA78NPoL_blog.html

Plato. *Gorgias*. Translated by W. R. M. Lamb. Cambridge, MA: Harvard University Press, 1967.

———. *Phaedrus*. Translated by Benjamin Jowett. Boston: Digireads.com Books, 2011.

Poniewozik, James. *Audience of One: Donald Trump, Television, and the Fracturing of America*. New York: Liveright, 2019.

———. "Trump Said, 'I Have the Best Words.' Now They're Hers." *New York Times*, May 27, 2020. https://www.nytimes.com/2020/05/27/arts/television/trump-sarah-cooper.html.

Posner, Sarah. *Unholy: Why White Evangelicals Worship at the Altar of Donald Trump*. New York: Random House, 2020.

Quinn, Melissa. "Trump Draws Criticism for Suggesting a Slowdown in Coronavirus Testing." CBS News. https://www.cbsnews.com/news/trump-tulsa-rally-coronavirus-testing-slowdown-suggsetion-criticism/.

Ramsey, G. Lee, Jr. *Preachers and Misfits, Prophets and Thieves: The Minister in Southern Fiction*. Louisville, KY: Westminster John Knox, 2008.

Ramasubramanian, Srividya, and Caitlin Miles. "White Nationalist Rhetoric, Neoliberal Multiculturalism and Colour Blind Racism: Decolonial Critique of Richard Spencer's Campus Visit." *Javnost—The Public* 25 (2018) 426–40.

Ramasubramanian, Srividya, Alexandra N. Sousa, and Vanessa Gonlin. "Facilitated Difficult Dialogues on Racism: A Goal-based Approach." *Journal of Applied Communication Research* 45 (2017) 537–56.

Rich, Marc D., and C. A. Cargile. "Beyond the Breach: Transforming White Identities in the Classroom." *Race Ethnicity and Education* 7 (2004) 351–65.

Richardson, Michael. "The Disgust of Donald Trump." *Journal of Media and Cultural Studies* 31 (2017) 747–56.

Robbins, Mary Susannah, ed. *Against the Vietnam War: Writings by Activists*. Lanham, MD: Rowman and Littlefield, 2007.

Roberts-Miller, Patricia. "Charisma Isn't Leadership, and Other Lessons We Can Learn from Trump the Businessman." In *Faking the News*, edited by Ryan Skinnell, 95–107. Exeter: Imprint Academic, 2018.

———. "Dissent as 'Aid and Comfort to the Enemy': The Rhetorical Power of Naïve Realism and Ingroup Identity." *Rhetoric and Society Quarterly* 39 (2009) 170–88.

Rosin, Hanna. "Rock of Ages, Ages of Rock." *New York Times*, November 25, 2007. https://www.nytimes.com/2007/11/25/magazine/25wwln-geologists-t.htm1.

Ryland, Alan. "Evangelist Claims Trump Was Sent by God to "Rescue" Americans from Democrats." *POLITICUSUSA*, September 9, 2020. https://www.politicususa.com/2020/09/09/evangelist-claims-trump-was-sent-by-god-to-rescue-americans-from-democrats.html.

Santucci, Jeanine. "Trump promotes claim that he is 'King of Israel' as Jewish people tweet #DisloyalToTrump." *USA Today*, August 21, 2019. https://www.usatoday.com/story/news/politics/2019/08/21/disloyaltotrump-trends-trump-tweets-quote-he-king-israel/2070585001/.

Schaefer, Donovan O. "Whiteness and civilization: shame, race, and the rhetoric of Donald Trump." *Communication and Critical/Cultural Studies* 17:1 (2020) 1–18.

Schapiro, Jeff. "Spokesman Defends Donald Trump's 'Get Even' Comment at Christian University." *Christian Post*, September 28, 2012. https://www.christianpost.com/news/spokesman-defends-donald-trumps-get-even-comment-at-christian-university.html.

Scheler, Max. *Ressentiment*. New York: Schocken, 1972.

Schepis, Michael E. *J. Frank Norris: The Fascinating, Controversial Life of a Forgotten Figure of the Twentieth Century*. Bloomington, IN: WestBow, 2012.

Schwartz, Tony. "I wrote the Art of the Deal. Donald Trump read it." Twitter, September 16, 2015. @tonyschwartz.

Scott, Eugene. "Trump threatens to sue Cruz for 'not being a natural born citizen.'" CNN, February 12, 2016. https://www.cnn.com/2016/02/12/politics/donald-trump-ted-cruz-dishonest/index.html.

Scott, James C. *Weapons of the Weak: Everyday Forms of Peasant Resistance*. New Haven, CT: Yale University Press, 1985.

Sedgwick, Eve Kosofsky. *Touching Feeling: Affect, Pedagogy, Performativity*. Durham, NC: Duke University Press, 2003.

Selk, Avi. "How Trump Took Swearing Mainstream." *Washington Post*, October 4, 2019. https://www.washingtonpost.com/lifestyle/style/if-the-president-is-doing-it----how-trump-took-swearing-mainstream/2019/10/04/f0f25096-e6a9-11e9-a6e8-8759c5c7f608_story.html.

Serwer, Adam. "The Cruelty Is the Point." *The Atlantic*, October 3, 2018. https://www.theatlantic.com/ideas/archive/2018/10/the-cruelty-is-the-point/572104.

Sharlet, Jeff. "'He's the Chosen One to Run America': Inside the Cult of Trump, His Rallies Are Church and He Is the Gospel." *Vanity Fair*, June 18, 2020. https://www.vanityfair.com/news/2020/06/inside-the-cult-of-trump-his-rallies-are-church-and-he-is-the-gospel.

Sharp, Carolyn J. *Irony and Meaning in the Hebrew Bible*. Bloomington, IN: Indiana University Press, 2009.

Silva, Kumarini. "Having the Time of Our Lives: Love-Cruelty as Patriotic Impulse." *Communication and Critical/Cultural Studies* 15 (2018) 79–84.

Sinitiere, Phillip. *Holy Mavericks: Evangelical Innovators and the Spiritual Marketplace.* New York: New York University Press, 2009.

Skinnell, Ryan, ed. *Faking the News: What Rhetoric Can Teach Us About Donald J. Trump.* Exeter: Imprint Academic, 2018.

Skinnell, Ryan. "What Passes for Truth in the Trump Era: Telling It Like It Isn't." In *Faking the News: What Rhetoric Can Teach Us About Donald J. Trump,* edited by Ryan Skinnell, 76–94. Exeter: Imprint Academic, 2018.

Smith, Christian. *The Bible Made Impossible: Why Biblicism Is Not a Truly Evangelical Reading of Scripture.* Grand Rapids: Brazos, 2011.

Smith, Craig R. "Ronald Reagan's Rhetorical Re-Invention of Conservatism." *Quarterly Journal of Speech* 103 (2016) 33–65.

Smith, David Livingstone. *Less Than Human: Why We Demean, Enslave, and Exterminate Others.* New York: St Simon's, 2012.

Stephens, Bret. "The Vertigo Presidency." *Wall Street Journal,* March 6, 2017. https://www.wsj.com/articles/the-vertigo-presidency-1488847239.

Stephens, Randall J., and Karl. W. Giberson. *The Anointed: Evangelical Truth in a Secular Age.* Cambridge, MA: Belknap Press of Harvard University Press, 2011.

Steudeman, Michael J. "Demagoguery and the Donald's Duplicitous Claims." In *Faking the News: What Rhetoric Can Teach Us about Donald J. Trump,* edited by Ryan Skinnell, 1–14. Exeter: Imprint Academic, 2018.

Stracqualursi, Veronica. "Jimmy Carter suggests Trump is an illegitimate president." CNN, June, 28, 2019. https://www.cnn.com/2019/06/28/politics/jimmy-carter-trump-russia-interference/index.html.

Strang, Stephen. *God, Trump, and the 2020 Election: Why He Must Win and What's at Stake for Christians If He Loses.* Lake Mary, FL: Charisma Media/Charisma House Book Group, 2020.

Sullivan, Sean. "The Greatest Quotes of Edwin Edwards." *Washington Post,* March 17, 2014. https://www.washingtonpost.com/news/the-fix/wp/2014/02/20/edwin-edwardss-greatest-hits-crooks-super-pacs-and-viagra/.

Sumner, Mark. "Advisers dreamed up 'the wall' as a memory aid for Trump—and now it's shutting down government." *Daily Kos,* January 5, 2019. https://www.dailykos.com/stories/2019/1/5/1823845/-The-Wall-was-created-advisers-as-a-memory-aid-to-keep-Trump-on-topic-there-was-no-plan.

Sunday, Billy. AZ Quotes. https://www.azquotes.com/author/14309-Billy_Sunday#.

———. Brainyquote. https://www.brainyquote.com/authors/billy-sunday-quotes.

———. "The Curse of the Saloon." In *Get on the Water Wagon.* N.p.: Journal Publishing, 1915. http://www.jesus-is-savior.com/Evils%20in%20America/Alcohol%20Kills/curse_of_the_saloon.htm.

———. *Hot From the Preachers Mound: The Sermons of Billy Sunday.* Compiled and edited by Daniel K. Norris. Ebook. N.p.: 2011.

Sunday, Billy, and William T. Ellis. *The Life and Death of Billy Sunday.* Ebook. www.JawboneDigital.com.

Surma, Katie, and Jen Fifield. "Meet the MAGA Diehards Who Travel the Country for Trump Rallies." *The Republic,* February 19, 2020. https://www.azcentral.com/story/news/local/phoenix/2020/02/19/phoenix-supporters-president-donald-trump-campaign-rally/4809568002/.

Showalter, Brandon. "Trump Like Samson, God's Chosen Strongman." *Christian Post*, September 28, 2018. https://www.christianpost.com/news/trump-like-samson-gods-chosen-strongman-awakening-christians-support-lance-wallnau.html.
Summarizer. "Trump Homeland Security official says he believes George Floyd would not have been spared if he were white." June 8, 2020. https://summarizer.co/article/trump-homeland-security-official-says-he-believes-george-floyd-would-not-have-been-spared-if-he-were-white#:~:text=%28CNN%29Acting%Deputy%Secretary%20of%20the%Department%20of%20Homeland,Cuccinelli%20said%20?20%22No%2C%20I%20don%27t%20think%20he%20would.
Taggart, Paul. *Populism*. Buckingham, UK: Open University, 2000.
Tannen, Deborah. *You Just Don't Understand: Women and Men in Conversation*. New York: Harper Collins E-books, 2001.
Taylor, Barbara Brown. *When God is Silent*. Lanham, MD: Rowman and Littlefield, 1998.
Taylor, Charles. *A Secular Age*. Cambridge, MA: Belknap Press of Harvard University Press, 2007.
Taylor, Gardner. "Preinaugural Sermon for William Jefferson Clinton." C-Span, January 20, 1993. https://www.c-span.org/video/?c4534389/user-clip-great-american-preacher.
Taylor, Justin. "Goodbye Mr. Chipps: The Day a Fundamentalist Pastor Shot and Killed a Catholic Layman in His Baptist Church." The Gospel Coalition, July 18, 2016. https://www.thegospelcoalition.org/blogs/evangelical-history/90-years-ago-today-when-a-pastor-in-texas-shot-and-killed-mr-chipps-in-his-baptist-church/.
Team Fix. "5th Republican Debate, Annotated." *Washington Post*, December 15, 2015. https://www.washingtonpost.com/news/the-fix/wp/2015/12/15/who-said-what-and-what-it-meant-the-fifth-gop-debated-annotated/.
Terrill, Robert E. "The Post-Racial and Post-Ethical Discourse of Donald J. Trump." *Rhetoric and Public Affairs* 20 (2017) 493–510.
Thuesen, Peter J. *In Discordance with the Scriptures: American Protestant Battles Over Translating the Bible*. Oxford: Oxford University Press, 1999.
Time. "Here's Donald Trump's Presidential Announcement Speech." June 16, 2015. https://time.com/3923128/donald-trump-announcement-speech/.
Tompkins, Jerry R., ed. *D-Days at Dayton: Reflections on the Scopes Trial*. Baton Rouge, LA: Louisiana State University Press, 1965.
Trav, S. D. *No Applause—Just Throw Money*. London: Faber & Faber, 2006.
Treat, Shaun. "How America Learned to Stop Worrying and Cynically ENJOY! The 9/11 Superhero Zeitgeist." *Communication and Critical/Cultural Studies* 6 (2009) 103–9.
Tripathi, Namrata. "Robert Jeffress, Trump's controversial pastor who thinks Islam promotes 'pedophilia' and homosexuality is filthy." https://meaww.com/robert-jeffress-trumps-controversial-pastor-islam-pedophilia-homosexuality-is-filthy-republican.
Trollinger, Susan, and William Vance Trollinger, Jr. *Righting America at the Creation Museum*. Baltimore: Johns Hopkins University Press, 2016.
Trollinger, William V., Jr. "The Church, Persecuted and Grateful." In *Conversations with Scholars: The Preacher as Scholar*, edited by Rodney Kennedy, 93–95. Eugene, OR: Wipf and Stock, 2016.
———. *God's Empire*. Madison, WI: University of Wisconsin Press, 1990.
———. "Is There a Center to American Religious History?" *Church History* 71(June 2002) 380–85.

———. "Religious Non-Affiliation: Expelled by the Right." In *Empty Churches: Non-Affiliation in America,* edited by James L. Heft and Jan Stets, 172–93. New York: Oxford University Press, 2021.

Trump, Donald J. "Full Text: Donald Trump 2016 RNC Draft Speech Transcript." *Politico,* July 21, 2016. https://www.politico.com/story/2016/07/full-transcript-donald-Trump-nomination-acceptance-speech-at-rnc-225974.

———. "Remarks by President Trump at the Conservative Political Action Conference." February 23, 2018. https://www.whitehouse.gov/briefings-statements/remarks-president-trump-conservative-political-action-conference-2/.

———. "Remarks by President Trump at South Dakota's 2020 Mount Rushmore Fireworks Celebration Keystone, South Dakota." July 4, 2020. https://www.whitehouse.gov/briefings-statements/remarks-president-trump-south-dakotas-2020-mount-rushmore-fireworks-celebration-keystone-south-dakota/.

Voltaire, F. M. "Of the Different Races of Men." In *The Idea of Race,* edited by R. Bernasconi and T. L. Lott, 5–7. Indianapolis: Hackett, 2000.

Wang, Christine. "Trump's inauguration won't be first one Rep. John Lewis will miss." CNBC, January 17, 2017. https://www.cnbc.com/2017/01/17/trumps-inauguration-wont-be-first-one-rep-john-lewis-will-miss.html.

Wanzer-Serrano, Darrel. "Rhetoric's rac(e/ist) problems." *Quarterly Journal of Speech* 105 (2019) 465–76.

Warren, John T., and Kathy Hytten. "The Faces of Whiteness: Pitfalls and the Critical Democrat." *Communication Education* 53 (2004) 321–39.

Washington, James A., ed. *A Testament of Hope: The Essential Writings of Martin Luther King.* New York: HarperCollins, 1991.

Wax, Trevin. "Lessons from a Megachurch Pastor Who Killed a Man." The Gospel Coalition. https://www.thegospelcoalition.org/blogs/treven-wax/lessons-from-the-megachurch-pastor-who-killed-a-man.

Weaver, Richard M. *The Ethics of Rhetoric.* New York: Routledge, 1985.

———. *Language Is Sermonic: Richard M. Weaver on the Nature of Rhetoric.* Edited by Richard L. Johannesen, Rennard Strickland, and Ralph T. Eubanks. Baton Rouge, LA: Louisiana State University Press, 1985.

Weisberger, Bernard A. *They Gathered at the River: The Story of the Great Revivalists and Their Impact upon Religion in America.* Boston: Little, Brown and Company, 1958.

West, Cornel. "Cornel West Says 'Neo-Fascist Gangster' Trump and Neoliberal Democrats Expose America as 'Failed Social Experiment.'" *Common Dreams,* May 30, 2020. https://www.commondreams.org/news/2020/05/30/cornel-west-says-neo-fascist-gangster-trump-and-neoliberal-democrats-expose-america.

Williams, Rowan *Tokens of Trust.* Louisville, KY: Westminster John Knox, 2010.

Williams, Tennessee. *The Glass Menagerie.* New York: New Directions, 1999.

Williams, Travis. "Demagogues and demigods: Why Kanye West could be our next president." July 14, 2017. http://www.rifuture.org/demagogues-demigods/.

Willner, Ann Ruth. *The Spellbinders: Charismatic Political Leadership.* New Haven, CT: Yale University Press, 1985.

Wilonsky, Robert. "What Robert Jeffress meant when he said removing Trump would cause 'Civil War-like fracture." *Dallas Morning News,* October 1, 2019. https://www.dallasnews.com/opinion/commentary/2019/10/01/what-robert-jeffress-meant-when-he-said-removing-trump-would-cause-civil-war-like-fracture/.

Windt, Theodore, ed. *Presidential Rhetoric (1961 to the Present)*. Dubuque, IA: Kendall/Hunt, 1983.
Windt, Theodore and Beth Ingold, eds. *Essays in Presidential Rhetoric*. Dubuque, IA: Kendall/Hunt, 1983.
Wingard, Jennifer. "Trump's Not Just One Bad Apple: He's the Product of a Spoiled Bunch." In *Faking the News: What Rhetoric Can Teach Us about Donald J. Trump*, edited by Ryan Skinnell, 33–47. Exeter: Imprint Academic, 2018.
Wittgenstein, Ludwig. *Culture and Value*. Chicago: University of Chicago Press, 1984.
———. *Philosophical Investigations*. New York: MacMillan, 1958.
Wood, Elizabeth A. "Hypermasculinity as a scenario of power: Vladimir Putin's iconic rule, 1999–2008." *International Feminist Journal of Politics* 18.3 (2016) 329–50.
Worthen, Molly. *Apostles of Reason: The Crisis of Authority in American Evangelicalism*. Oxford: Oxford University Press, 2014.
Wright, Jeremiah. "Confusing God and Government." Sermon. https://www.theatlantic.com/politics/archive/2008/04/the-full-wright-transcript/52865/.
Yen, Hope. "Trump's inaccurate boasts on China travel ban." Associated Press, March 26, 2020. https://apnews.com/article/ap-fact-check-virus-outbreak-donald-trump-politics-health-0dc271ad7f917374a5a0cfb49273783.
Yilek, Caitlin. "Jerry Falwell Jr.: Conservatives, Christians 'need to stop electing nice guys.'" *Washington Examiner*, September 29, 2018. https://www.washingtonexaminer.com/news/jerry-falwell-jr-conservatives-christians-need-to-stop-electing-nice-guys.
———. "Trump Defends 9/11 Claims: I have the world's best memory." *The Hill*, November 23, 2015. https://thehill.com/blogs/ballot-box/presidential-races/261161-trump-defends-9-11-claims-i-have-worlds-best-memory.
Yoder, John Howard. *The Original Revolution*. Scottdale, PA: Herald, 2003.
Young, Anna. "Rhetorics of Fear and Loathing: Donald Trump's Populist Style." In *Faking the News*, edited by Ryan Skinnell, 23–41. Exeter: Academic Imprint, 2018.
Young, Gayne C. "One-on-One With Vladimir Putin." *Outdoor Life*, May 17, 2011. https://www.outdoorlife.com/articles/hunting/2011/05/one-one-vladimir-putin/.
Young, Stephen. "A Guide to Robert Jeffress' Excuses for President Trump." *Dallas Observer*, August 31, 2018. https://www.dallasobserver.com/news/robert-jeffress-top-10-excuses-for-donald-trump-11085895.
Zaimov, Stoyan. "Pastor Andy Stanley calls Obama 'Pastor-in-Chief During Pre-Inauguration Sermon.'" *Christian Post*, January 23, 2013. https://www.christianpost.com/news/pastor-andy-stanley-calls-obama-pastor-in-chief-during-pre-inauguration-sermon.html.
Zauzmer, Julie. "Trump uttered what many supporters consider blasphemy. Here's why most will probably forgive him." *Washington Post*, September 13, 2019. https://www.washingtonpost.com/politics/trump-uttered-what-many-supporters-consider-blasphemy-heres-why-most-will-probably-forgive-him/2019/09/13/685c0bce-d64f-11e9-9343-40db57cf6abd_story.html.
Žižek, Slavoj. "A Permanent Economic Emergency." *New Left Review* 64 (July/August, 2010). https://newleftreview.org/issues/II64/articles/slavoj-zizek-a-permanent-economic-emergency.
———. *The Puppet and the Dwarf: The Perverse Core of Christianity*. Cambridge, MA: MIT Press, 2003.

www.ingramcontent.com/pod-product-compliance
Lightning Source LLC
Chambersburg PA
CBHW022015220426
43663CB00007B/1094